GEORGE BERKELEY
ALCIPHRON
in focus

The only available separate edition of Berkeley's text, this volume contains the four most important dialogues together with essays and commentaries from the eighteenth to the twentieth centuries.

Alciphron is Berkeley's most sustained work of philosophical theology. In it, he develops one of the last great philosophical defences of religion as well as a shrewd account of the rise and nature of deism and atheism. It contains Berkeley's final views on meaning and language, some of which (as Antony Flew argues in his essay) anticipate those of Wittgenstein. The essays and commentaries reflect the critical response to *Alciphron* from the time of its publication in 1732 to the present day, placing the work in critical context, and thus assisting readers to evaluate its theoretical and historical importance. In the introduction, David Berman shows that *Alciphron* has a closer connection with Berkeley's Immaterialist philosophy than is generally thought.

The volume will interest students of philosophy, particularly those concerned with philosophy of religion and language. It will also appeal to readers interested in religious studies and intellectual history.

David Berman is Senior Lecturer in Philosophy and Fellow of Trinity College, Dublin. His publications include *A History of Atheism: From Hobbes to Russell* (1990) and a number of works on Berkeley. He is editor of the *Berkeley Newsletter*.

ROUTLEDGE PHILOSOPHERS IN FOCUS
SERIES
General Editor: Stanley Tweyman
York University, Toronto

GÖDEL'S *THEOREM* IN FOCUS
Edited by S. G. Shanker

DAVID HUME: *DIALOGUES CONCERNING NATURAL
RELIGION* IN FOCUS
Edited by Stanley Tweyman

J. S. MILL: *ON LIBERTY* IN FOCUS
Edited by John Gray and G. W. Smith

CIVIL DISOBEDIENCE IN FOCUS
Edited by Hugo Adam Bedau

JOHN LOCKE: *A LETTER CONCERNING
TOLERATION* IN FOCUS
Edited by John Horton and Susan Mendus

WILLIAM JAMES: *PRAGMATISM* IN FOCUS
Edited by Doris Olin

GEORGE BERKELEY

ALCIPHRON, OR THE MINUTE PHILOSOPHER
in focus

Edited by David Berman

London and New York

First published 1993
by Routledge
11 New Fetter Lane, London EC4P 4EE

Simultaneously published in the USA and Canada
by Routledge
a division of Routledge, Chapman and Hall, Inc.
29 West 35th Street, New York, NY 10001

Collection as a whole © 1993 Routledge; introduction © 1993 David
Berman; articles in copyright © respective contributor

Phototypeset in 10/12pt Bembo by
Intype, London
Printed in Great Britain by
T J Press (Padstow) Ltd, Cornwall.

British Library Cataloguing in Publication Data
George Berkeley: 'Alciphron, or the Minute Philosopher' in Focus
I. Berman, David
192

Library of Congress Cataloging in Publication Data
Berkeley, George, 1685–1753
Alciphron, or the minute philosopher in focus / George Berkeley
edited by David Berman.
p. cm.
Includes bibliographical references and index.
1. Free thought—Controversial literature. 2. Apologetics—18th
century. 3. Semantics (Philosophy) I. Berman, David
II. Title. III. Title: Alciphron. IV. Title: Minute philosopher
B1316.B47B47 1993
210—dc20 92–10796
CIP

ISBN 0 415 06372 8 (hbk)
0 415 06373 6 (pbk)

CONTENTS

CONTENTS

ACKNOWLEDGEMENTS

I am grateful to Mr Vincent Denard for providing translations and references for Berkeley's Greek and Latin quotations, and to Mr Finbar Christobal for help in collating the text.

Antony Flew's 'Was Berkeley a precursor of Wittgenstein?' is reprinted from W. B. Todd (ed.), *Hume and the Enlightenment: Essays Presented to Ernest Campbell Mossner*, Edinburgh, The University Press, 1974. J. O. Urmson's 'Berkeley on Beauty' is reprinted by permission of Oxford University Press, from John Foster and Howard Robinson (eds), *Essays on George Berkeley*, Oxford, Clarendon Press, 1985. A. David Kline's 'Berkeley's Divine Language argument' is reprinted by permission of Kluwer Academic Publishers, from E. Sosa (ed.), *Essays on the Philosophy of George Berkeley*, © 1987 by D. Reidel Publishing Company, Dordrecht, Holland. D. Berman's 'Cognitive theology and emotive mysteries in Berkeley's *Alciphron*' is abridged and reprinted from *Proceedings of the Royal Irish Academy*, vol. 81, C, no. 7, 1981.

ALCIPHRON:

OR, THE

MINUTE PHILOSOPHER.

IN

SEVEN DIALOGUES.

Containing an APOLOGY *for the* Christian Religion, *against those who are called* Free-thinkers.

VOLUME *the* FIRST.

They have forsaken me the Fountain of living waters, and hewed them out cisterns, broken cisterns that can hold no water. Jerem. ii. 13.

Sin mortuus, ut quidam minuti Philosophi censent, nihil sentiam, non vereor ne hunc errorem meum mortui Philosophi irrideant.

Cicero.

LONDON:

Printed for J. TONSON in the *Strand,* 1732.

ALCIPHRON:

OR, THE

MINUTE PHILOSOPHER.

IN

SEVEN DIALOGUES.

Containing an APOLOGY *for the* Christian Religion, *against those who are called* Free-thinkers.

VOLUME *the* SECOND.

The Balances of Deceit are in his Hand. Hosea xii. 7.

Τὸ Ἐξαπατᾷν αὐτὸν ὑφ᾽ αὑτῦ, πάντων χαλεπώτατον. Plato.

LONDON:

Printed for J. TONSON in the *Strand*, 1732.

Figure 2 Title-page of the first edition of *Alciphron*, volume II. The second epigraph is from Plato's *Cratylus* 428D: 'The worst of all deceptions is self deception.'

INTRODUCTION
David Berman

BACKGROUND AND PUBLICATION

Alciphron: or, the Minute Philosopher is George Berkeley's most substantial work in philosophical theology. It was written either largely or entirely in 1729–31, during his stay in Rhode Island, where he was awaiting funds from the English Parliament for his projected college in Bermuda. The college was to educate and train missionaries, becoming, as he expressed it in his *Proposal* (1724), a 'Fountain . . . of Learning and Religion' that would purify the 'ill-manners and irreligion' of the American colonies.[1] For this purpose Berkeley had bought a farm near Newport, which was to be the college's mainland base. Some of the scenes in *Alciphron* are probably drawn from local scenery. Thus Dialogue II takes place near a beach, overlooking the ocean, in 'a hollow glade, between two rocks' – which is supposed to be the so-called 'Hanging Rocks', near Newport, where Berkeley is said to have composed much of *Alciphron*.[2] By the middle of 1731, however, Berkeley received definite word from England that the £20,000 granted by Parliament was not to be paid. Accepting the failure of his missionary project – the central cause of his career – Berkeley returned disappointed to London in late 1731. In February 1732 *Alciphron* was published, its first section alluding to the 'miscarriage' of his project: 'the affair which brought me into this remote corner of the country . . . [with] a great loss of time, pains, and expense.'[3]

Alciphron was originally issued anonymously in two volumes octavo. Its full title reads: *Alciphron: or the Minute Philosopher. In Seven Dialogues. Containing An Apology for the Christian Religion, against those who are called Free-thinkers* (London, J. Tonson). The

1

first volume contains an 'Advertisement', 'Contents', Dialogues I-V; the second volume: 'Contents', Dialogues VI-VII, and Berkeley's *Essay Towards a New Theory of Vision*, which had previously appeared in 1709. Since the *Essay of Vision* had originally carried Berkeley's name on the title-page, he could not have intended his authorship of *Alciphron* to remain completely hidden. Unlike his earlier works, *Alciphron* proved instantly successful – if success can be measured by editions published and the number of reactions it provoked. Two further editions were published in 1732: a Dublin issue and a revised London edition. Another, the so-called 'Third Edition', was published in London in 1752, again anonymously. It was Berkeley's last publication. Issued in one volume octavo, without the *Essay of Vision*, it has his final revisions. Translations had earlier appeared in Dutch (Leyden, 1733) and French (La Haye, 1734).[4] *Alciphron* continued to be relatively popular in the eighteenth century. Following Berkeley's death in 1753, posthumous editions appeared (again without the *Essay of Vision*) in 1755 (the first to carry his name), 1757, 1767, and 1777. The last separate edition to be published in English was in 1803, in New Haven, Connecticut, although *Alciphron* has been included in all the many printings of Berkeley's collected works.[5]

RECEPTION

The response to *Alciphron* was immediate and lively, although much of it was highly critical and some abusive. Berkeley seems to have taken seriously only two of his critics. The first was an anonymous letter writer in the *Daily Postboy* of September 1732, to whom Berkeley replied in a pamphlet entitled *The Theory of Vision, or Visual Language, shewing the Immediate Presence and Providence of a Deity, Vindicated and Explained*, published in January 1733. The pamphlet, although mainly concerned to vindicate the *Essay of Vision* and the theological proof in Dialogue IV which is based on it, also vindicates and deepens the historical analysis of freethinking in *Alciphron*. The second and more notable critic was Peter Browne, then Bishop of Cork and formerly Provost of Trinity College, Dublin, when Berkeley was a student and Fellow. It is generally agreed that Browne was one of Berkeley's targets in Dialogue IV.16–22, alluded to in section 17 as one of 'the most profound and speculative divines'.[6] Browne had first presented his distinctive theory of divine analogy in his *Letter* against Toland (Dublin, 1697) and then more elaborately in his *Procedure, Extent and Limits of Human Understanding* (London, 1728). He was about to publish a sequel to this work in 1732, when he was 'very accidentaly surprised with a threatening Appearance of a powerful Attack' from *Alciphron*.[7] He then added a long final chapter to the *Divine Analogy* (London, 1733) responding chiefly to Dialogue IV but also to VII. Three extracts from Browne's chapter are printed here. Berkeley responded to Browne in a vigorous letter, recently identified as by Berkeley, in which he presses Browne to accept that there is no medium between literal and metaphorical knowledge of God: God is either literally wise or (disastrously) He is not.[8]

That Berkeley took Browne's criticisms seriously is evident not only from this letter but also, very probably, from changes he made in the final, 1752 edition of *Alciphron*. Thus his three deletions of the term 'formal' or 'formally' in Dialogue IV.20 were almost certainly in response to Browne's critical observations (included here) on Berkeley's use of that term. It is also possible that it was Browne's comments (again reprinted here) on Berkeley's critique of abstract general ideas in Dialogue VII.5–7 which prompted Berkeley to omit those three sections in the 1752 edition. This is Berkeley's most considerable alteration, and a number of conjectures have been advanced to explain it. A. C. Fraser, Berkeley's nineteenth-century editor, believed that the omission meant that Berkeley had abandoned his earlier nominalism, a thesis forcefully opposed by A. A. Luce.[9] Other explanations have been offered by Ian Ramsay and T. E. Jessop.[10] According to Browne, Berkeley's critique of abstractionism was irrelevant to the issue; and one reason why Berkeley may have accepted Browne's opinion is that the two men were very much in agreement on the errors of abstractionism. Indeed, it is possible that the young Berkeley first came to see these errors under Browne's tuition. On most matters, however, the two philosophers were fundamentally opposed. Thus Browne's incredulous response to Berkeley's emotive theory of language (also included here) is of interest as it shows how innovative Berkeley's theory was.

Alciphron also came in for immediate criticism from Bernard Mandeville, whose notorious *Fable of the Bees* (fifth ed., London, 1728) Berkeley criticized particularly in Dialogue II. Mandeville replied soberly that Berkeley was attacking a straw man. His

DAVID BERMAN

pamphlet is entitled *A Letter to Dion* (London, 1732), since *Alciphron* is written as though it were a letter from Dion (to Theages), who narrates the discussion but rarely enters into it. A more insidious response came from John, Lord Hervey in his (sometimes scurrilous) *Some Remarks on the Minute Philosopher: in a Letter from a Country Clergyman to his Friend in London* (London, 1732). Pretending to be a fideistic clergyman, Hervey protests against *Alciphron*'s rationalism, claiming that it has stated the case against Christianity too forcibly.[11] Another ironic attack was *A Vindication of the Reverend D— B—y from the scandalous imputation of being the author of a late book, intitulled* Alciphron (London, 1734), in which the author, recently identified as the Revd William Wishart, defends Shaftesbury.[12] Another early defence of Shaftesbury against Berkeley appeared in the *London Journal* of 10 and 17 June, 1732. The indignant articles, signed Socrates, were probably written by Bishop Benjamin Hoadley, who certainly wrote a letter attacking *Alciphron* for bringing 'obscurity and darkness into science' and making 'nonsense essential to religion'.[13] Some of these theoretical criticisms of *Alciphron* probably conceal personal and political antagonisms. Thus both Hoadley and Hervey were close political allies of Sir Robert Walpole, the government minister largely responsible for wrecking Berkeley's Bermuda project. Hervey was also a bitter enemy of Berkeley's friend, Alexander Pope. More straightforward was a long, factual review of *Alciphron* which appeared in the *Present State of the Republic of Letters*, 1732.

Of more philosophical importance are Francis Hutcheson's criticisms (reprinted here) in the fourth edition of his *Inquiry into the Original of our Ideas of Beauty and Virtue* (London, 1738). His criticism of Berkeley's utilitarian theory of beauty in Dialogue III is interesting in its own right, but also because Hutcheson was probably one of Berkeley's targets in Dialogue III, although he is not referred to openly. Lord Shaftesbury, ridiculed as Cratylus, is the Dialogue's primary target, as is clear from the critical references to his *Characteristics* (London, 1711). However, as Peter Kivy suggests, some of Berkeley's criticisms would be closer to the mark if aimed against Hutcheson rather than Shaftesbury.[14] Hence it seems plausible that Berkeley had Hutcheson at least partly in mind – a conclusion which is supported by verbal similarities in Hutcheson's *Inquiry* and Dialogue III. This also seems to be the opinion of J. O. Urmson, whose 'Berkeley on Beauty'

4

looks critically at Berkeley's argument in Dialogue III.3–8, and reaches a conclusion in line with that of Hutcheson.

Another prominent critic of *Alciphron* was Viscount Boling-broke, a major figure in his own time, with whom Berkeley was probably acquainted through their mutual friend, Jonathan Swift. Whether Berkeley was aware of Bolingbroke's freethinking views is uncertain, since Bolingbroke's principal works were issued posthumously in 1754. It is there that Bolingbroke criticizes a key thesis in Dialogue VII, that we know no more of physical force than of divine grace. Bolingbroke had written to Swift as early as July 1732 that some of *Alciphron* was 'hard to be understood', a view which seemed to be shared by both Swift and John Gay, who found it 'too speculative'.[15] A more sympathetic notice of *Alciphron* is to be found in the *Elementa Philosophica* (Philadelphia, 1752) of Berkeley's American disciple, Samuel Johnson, whose book is dedicated to him. It is notable, however, that Johnson tries to combine Berkeley's views with those of his theological opponent, Peter Browne. Another writer who also tried to bring Berkeley and Browne together, in the interests of Christian solidarity, was Philip Skelton, an Irish writer, in his 1733 *Letter to the Authors of Divine Analogy and the Minute Philosophers* [sic]. A more creative use of *Alciphron* was made by another of Berkeley's countrymen, Edmund Burke, whose *Philosophical Enquiry into the Sublime and Beautiful* (London, 1757) applies Berkeley's emotive theory of meaning to explain poetry.[16]

Probably the most intriguing of *Alciphron*'s readers was David Hume, often regarded as Berkeley's great philosophical successor. In one of his political essays, Hume discusses an observation of 'Dr Berkeley: Minute Philosopher', from Dialogue V.27, on national character.[17] More important, however, is the suggestion made by Sir Leslie Stephen that 'Hume probably took some hints from [the] controversy' between Berkeley and Browne on divine analogy in his posthumous *Dialogues concerning Natural Religion*, on which he was working in 1751.[18] Certainly, Hume's argument in section XII (expressed by Philo) is, as John Gaskin has observed, 'strikingly similar' to that developed by Lysicles in Dialogue IV.[19] And some of Cleanthes' views on God are also similar to the position from which Berkeley opposed Browne and King. It is also, perhaps, worth mentioning that Hume's decision to call his rigidly orthodox spokesman Demea may owe something to Berkeley's brief mention of 'honest Demea', in Dialogue

VII.30, who reacted so adversely to freethinking that 'he would not suffer his own son to read Euclid, being told it might teach him to think'.

ASSESSMENTS OF *ALCIPHRON*

From this brief account, it should be clear that the initial impact of *Alciphron* was by no means inconsiderable. Probably more than his early works – the *Essay of Vision* (1709), *Principles* (1710), and *Three Dialogues* (1713) – it helped to make Berkeley's name in his lifetime. *Alciphron* also, no doubt, assisted his elevation to a bishopric in 1734. Shortly after its publication, as we learn from Lord Percival, *Alciphron* was discussed at Court and 'the Queen publicly commended it at her drawing room'.[20] Berkeley was well on his way to becoming 'the good bishop'. Nor is it surprising that the title-page of his last major work, *Siris* (1744), describes him as 'the Lord Bishop of Cloyne and the author of *The Minute Philosopher*'. Yet as Berkeley's early works, which had initially enjoyed little success, became increasingly influential in the eighteenth century, so *Alciphron*'s fortunes declined. By the late nineteenth century even admirers of Berkeley had little positive to say of it, apart from noting the elegance of its prose. Thus, according to J. S. Mill, whose judgement and that of Leslie Stephen are reprinted here, were *Alciphron* 'not the production of so eminent a man, it would have little claim to serious attention'. That this verdict is profoundly unfair will, I hope, become increasingly evident to readers of this volume. Perhaps one cause of Mill's hostility was that he identified too fully with Berkeley's targets, the freethinkers. It is certainly hard to credit his claim that: 'The opinions . . . which [Berkeley] puts into the mouths of freethinkers are mostly such as no one would now think worth refuting, for the excellent reason that nobody holds them'. Thus the agnosticism, or proto-atheism, of Lysicles in Dialogue IV was accepted in Mill's day by radical unbelievers, such as Charles Bradlaugh, and by respected believers like Henry Mansel, whose position Mill himself attacked in 1865.[21]

It is particularly Dialogues IV and VII, which contain Berkeley's most mature and sustained discussion of language, that cast the most doubt on Mill's judgement. As Antony Flew argues in his 'Was Berkeley a precursor of Wittgenstein?', reprinted here, it has not been recognized that Berkeley anticipated in Dialogue VII the advanced views on language associated with Wittgenstein. Arguing against Jonathan Bennett, Flew maintains that 'what is new in *Alciphron* is Berkeley's apparent willingness to extend indefinitely the list of significant words which do not, and perhaps cannot, stand for ideas.' Similarly, I argue, in 'Cognitive theology and emotive mysteries in Berkeley's *Alciphron*', also reprinted here, that Berkeley anticipated not only the emotive theory of meaning (usually thought to be a twentieth-century creation) but also its application to religious discourse (a development generally ascribed to the Logical Positivists). Turning to Dialogue IV, it has been forcefully maintained by Colin Murray Turbayne in his *Myth of Metaphor* (New Haven, 1962) that Berkeley's optic language theory, most fully developed there, is of major importance as a challenge and alternative to the machine model of nature put forward by Descartes and Newton. Finally, as A. David Kline tries to show in his 'Berkeley's Divine Language Argument', reprinted here, Berkeley's argument for the existence of God, in Dialogue IV.2–15, based on the optic language theory, is more formidable than is usually supposed.

ALCIPHRON AND BERKELEIANISM

The generally accepted view is that *Alciphron* is a work of Christian apologetics that has little significant connection with Berkeley's distinctive philosophy, articulated primarily in the works of 1709–13. Thus in his 1950 editor's introduction to *Alciphron*, T. E. Jessop states that there is 'no expansion of the philosophy which Berkeley published twenty years earlier . . . therefore it is idle to turn to *Alciphron* for Berkeleianism'.[22] Sir Geoffrey Warnock, too, who devotes hardly more than a page to it, has little praise for *Alciphron*, apart, as usual, from recommending its literary excellence. It was, he writes, 'a contribution to the religious controversies of the first half of the eighteenth century, an attack on the Deists . . . [it] has a disconcertingly polemical tone . . . It is on the whole not surprising that the fame of this elaborate work was short-lived.'[23] But against this prevailing view, it is important to consider the following:

(1) *Alciphron* VII advances Berkeley's discussion of language and meaning in the Introduction to the *Principles* in a number of respects, most notably on the non-cognitive, emotive theory of language and its applications. That Berkeley himself was aware

of the shortcomings of his published account of language prior to *Alciphron* is clear, I think, from his important letter to Samuel Johnson of 24 March 1730, written almost certainly while he was working on *Alciphron*. Here Berkeley advises Johnson to 'examine well what I have said about abstraction, and about the true sense and significance of words, in several parts of the things that I have published, though [he adds] much remains to be said on that subject.'[24]

(2) In *Alciphron* IV we find Berkeley making explicit, for the first time, the theological implications of the optic language theory: that visual data constitute a language in which God tells us about the tangible world. In the 1709 editions of the *Essay of Vision* this was left implicit. Similarly, *Alciphron* VII is the first publication in which Berkeley applies his emotive theory of meaning to explain religious mysteries, although he had seen the application, as is clear from the *Manuscript Introduction*, as early as 1708.[25]

(3) *Alciphron* VII.16–23 also contains Berkeley's fullest discussion of the question of free-will and determinism. On this subject *Alciphron* goes beyond anything in the writings of 1709–13. The 'reconciliation of God's foreknowledge with freedom of men' was to be one of the principal subjects in the *Principles*, as we learn from Berkeley's letter of 1 March 1709/10.[26] But it is only in *Alciphron* that we find this promised discussion.

(4) That Berkeley took *Alciphron* seriously as expressing his considered philosophical position, along with the writings of 1709–13, is shown in the alterations he made in the 1752 edition. Thus he adds a passage in VII.5, on how we have a 'notion' of terms like 'myself' and 'will', thereby bringing *Alciphron* in line with similar additions in the 1734 editions of the *Principles* and *Three Dialogues*.[27]

(5) Moreover, at least one important passage which he added in 1752 helps to explain changes he made in the 1734 edition of the *Principles*. In this addition in IV.12, Berkeley explains why the senses of smell and taste do not constitute languages, although smells and tastes are signs. Not all signs are language, he writes, since it is 'the articulation, combination, variety, copiousness, extensive and general use and easy application of signs (all of which are commonly found in vision) that constitute the nature of language'. Now in sections 66 and 108 of the *Principles* Berkeley had in the first edition (1710) described all nature (including smells and tastes) as language; but in the 1734 edition he changed 'lan-

guage' to 'signs'. In this case, it seems that Berkeley was bringing the theory of the *Principles* into line with that of *Alciphron* IV, where it is only vision that is a language.

(6) There are other ways in which a study of *Alciphron* can help us to appreciate the earlier works. Thus there are important similarities, as I have argued, between Berkeley's central attack on matter and his attack on the Browne/King theory of divine analogy in Dialogue IV. In both cases, he recognized that he was opposing sceptical, representationalist theories which also drew on a similar notion of substance.[28] Perhaps nothing shows more clearly than Dialogue IV that *Alciphron* is not mere anti-Deistic apologetics; for here we see Berkeley as a tough-minded Rationalist, battling against both religious and irreligious sceptics.

(7) Berkeley's attack on the materialists in the *Principles* and *Three Dialogues* can also be illuminated, I believe, by looking at the way he attacks the freethinkers in *Alciphron*. In both cases, he is directing his efforts against targets that shift and transform themselves and are sometimes even opposed to each other. Similarly, it is helpful to compare the way Berkeley argues against scepticism in the *Three Dialogues* with the attack on prejudice in *Alciphron*, especially in Dialogue I. Thus both works begin with the claim (which is increasingly challenged) that it is Berkeley's spokesmen who are guilty of, respectively, scepticism and prejudice.

In proposing that *Alciphron* be accorded a more privileged place in the Berkeley canon, I am not claiming that it is in the same class as the three classics of 1709–13. In general, I would suggest that *Alciphron* stands midway, both qualitatively and chronologically, between the early works and *Siris*. While less original, argumentatively forceful, and independent of authority than the former, it is a great deal more so than the latter work.

BERKELEY'S FREETHINKING ENEMIES

As its subtitle indicates, *Alciphron* is a sustained defence of Christianity in response to those 'called freethinkers', the critics of Christianity, whom Berkeley prefers to call 'minute philosophers', largely because the term 'freethinker' carries a positive emotive force. As befits the pioneer of emotivism, Berkeley was extremely sensitive to the persuasive possibilities of certain words. Here he was reacting against one of his chief targets, Anthony

Collins, who in his *Discourse of Free-thinking* (London, 1713) had cleverly sought to capture 'freethinker' as a commendatory name for the critics of Christianity. In Dialogue I Berkeley tries to block this move by renaming the critics of religion 'minute philosophers' and showing that they are only 'called freethinkers'. Really, he urges, they are extremely prejudiced. Some twenty years earlier, he had pursued a different strategy. For in the *Three Dialogues* (1713) he had tried to discredit the term 'freethinking' by characterizing it as a 'loose, rambling' form of libertinism.[29] But by 1732 he had apparently accepted that the positive emotive force of the term was too firmly established to be changed.[30] So now he tries to show that it is the critics of Christianity, like Collins, who are the bigoted, prejudiced ones, unwilling to follow impartial reason. While Berkeley argues for this in detail in the following six Dialogues, he artfully insinuates it in the first, introductory Dialogue, where Alciphron, the chief minute philosopher, delivers a long discourse on the prejudices of Christians. Although Alciphron's avowed purpose is to probe the principles of Christianity and extirpate its prejudices, he slips revealingly in section 5, when he says to Euphranor, Berkeley's spokesman, 'hold fair and stand firm, while I probe your prejudices and extirpate your principles.'[31]

Apart from Dion, mentioned above, *Alciphron* has four dramatis personae: Euphranor and Crito speak for Berkeley and Christianity. More problematic are Alciphron and Lysicles, the critics of religion, because they are spokesmen for a wide variety of freethinkers, some of whom – notably Shaftesbury and Mandeville – were largely opposed to each other. On the whole, however, Alciphron is the more sober philosopher, the defender of Shaftesbury and Collins; whereas Lysicles is the flightier figure, the man of pleasure, who defends Mandeville. Problematic, too, is the fact that Alciphron and Lysicles represent not merely the avowed, published views of freethinkers, such as Collins and Shaftesbury, but their hidden, esoteric positions. For it is Berkeley's view that the real opinions of the freethinkers were far more radical and subversive than emerges in their published writings.

Did Berkeley, as Mill and others suggest, misrepresent his opponents? This is a large and complicated issue. For, plainly, it will not be sufficient to point out that Berkeley's interpretation of Shaftesbury, say, is in conflict with Shaftesbury's explicit statements in the *Characteristics*, since Berkeley holds that Shaftesbury is there only insinuating rather than openly stating his real beliefs. Thus, although Berkeley believed that Anthony Collins was a speculative atheist, he was aware that Collins never avowed this; indeed, Collins claimed to be a sincere Christian.[32] In my view, Berkeley was right: Collins was a crypto-atheist and the free-thinkers did write in a disguised, esoteric way. The real question, I believe, is not whether they engaged in theological lying, but to what extent they did so.[33] But this can only be settled by a detailed examination of their writings, which I have elsewhere attempted, especially for Collins.

Although Berkeley does not mention Collins directly, or quote from his writings – as he does with Shaftesbury and Mandeville – there can be no doubt that he is one of Berkeley's three principal targets. This is not surprising, since it is Collins to whom Berkeley is adverting in the Advertisement and in Dialogue I.12, as having declared – privately but in Berkeley's hearing – that he 'had found out a demonstration against the being of a God'.[34] Collins looms large in the background of Dialogues I, IV and VII. In Dialogue I Berkeley's target is Collins's destructive suggestion in the *Discourse of Free-thinking* that the varieties of opinions about God and religion show that all religions are false. In Dialogue IV it is Collins's insidious exploitation of the Browne/King theory in his *Vindication of the Divine Attributes* (London, 1710).[35] In Dialogue VII it is Collins's dismissal of religion's mysteries as meaningless, in his *Essay concerning Reason* (London, 1707), which, with his *Philosophical Inquiry concerning Liberty* (London, 1717) is Berkeley's target on determinism.[36] Thus in his 1707 *Essay*, Collins issued this challenge: 'I have us'd the words certainly and necessarily for the same thing . . . because I cannot distinguish between certainly be and must be. They who object this to me must define, that I may see the difference' (p. 37). In VII.18 Euphranor seems to be taking up the challenge when he says: 'To me, certain and necessary seem very different; there being nothing in the former notion that implies constraint.'

Alciphron draws on a number of Berkeley's earlier writings. Of particular importance are his essays in the *Guardian* (London, 1713), a periodical paper in which he began his serious campaign against the freethinkers, particularly Collins. Some of Berkeley's essays, as for example no. 39, throw light on the obscurer features of *Alciphron*. In this imaginative essay of 25 April 1713 Berkeley describes how Ulysses Cosmopolita, having taken a marvellous philosophical snuff, was able to visit Collins's pineal gland. Going to Collins's understanding, Ulysses 'found the place narrower than ordinary, insomuch that there was not any room for a miracle, prophecy, or separate spirit . . . I discovered Prejudice in the figure of a woman standing in a corner, with her eyes close shut, and her fore-fingers stuck in her ears; many words in a confused order, but spoken with great emphasis, issued from her mouth.'[37]

The prejudice of the freethinkers is, as I have suggested above, a central theme in *Alciphron*. But more important, this passage helps to unravel the second of the two symbolical vignettes (see Figure 2) featured on the title-pages of the 1732 edition of *Alciphron*. So the blindfolded, open-mouthed figure on the pedestal stands for freethinking prejudice, which Berkeley believed was largely responsible for the defeat of his missionary project.[38] As he puts it in a letter of 2 March 1730/31: '. . . what [is] foolishly called freethinking seems to me the principal cause or root not only of opposition to our College but most other evils in our age.[39] The first vignette also, as I have elsewhere argued, links *Alciphron* with Berkeley's failed project: for the forsaken fountain of living waters stands for God and Christianity as well as St Paul's College, Bermuda, the 'Fountain of Learning and Religion' (see Figure 1). The quotation from Cicero under the vignette also illuminates Berkeley's use of the term 'minute philosopher'.[40]

Alciphron needs to be seen in the context of the so-called Deist debate in Britain, particularly as a reply to freethinkers such as Mandeville, Shaftesbury, and Collins, but also to Thomas Hobbes, Charles Blount, Matthew Tindal, and Thomas Woolston. Yet there was also a narrower tradition in which *Alciphron* played a central role, namely eighteenth-century Irish philosophy. I have already mentioned some of its main participants – Browne and King, Hutcheson and Burke – as well as one minor one (Skelton), but there were others, notably John Toland, whose seminal *Christianity not Mysterious* (1696) is almost certainly a principal target of *Alciphron* VII.1–4. Toland's essay on 'The Origin and Force of Prejudice' may also have been in Berkeley's mind when writing Dialogue I.[41] Another possible target here was the patron of Toland and Hutcheson, Lord Molesworth, whose castigation of prejudice and 'monk-like education' in his *Account of Denmark* (London, 1694) is similar to that in *Alciphron* I.10.[42] Another philosopher whom Berkeley is probably attacking in Dialogue VII on mysteries and also determinism is John Trenchard, a fellow graduate of Trinity College, Dublin, whose views in his influential *Cato's Letters* of 1722/3 are similar to those Berkeley outlines and tries to refute.[43] Berkeley has a more positive connection with Edward Synge, then Archbishop of Tuam, whose 1698 critique of Toland is used by him in Dialogue IV.15, I suggest, to make sense of prophecy, by comparing it with a sighted person's abilities in a nation of blind men.[44]

THE TEXT

In this edition Dialogues II, V, and VI have been omitted. The latter two, which contain Berkeley's largely traditional defence of Christian revelation, are probably the weakest of his seven Dialogues. More than any others, they justify the condescending judgements of Mill and Stephen. Dialogue II, directed against Mandeville, is also criticised by Mill and Stephen for missing the mark. Another justification (apart from space) for omitting it here is that it is the one Dialogue reprinted by T. E. Jessop in his *Berkeley: Philosophical Writings* (Edinburgh, 1952).

The text printed here is from the 1752 edition. Berkeley's capitalization and punctuation have been modernized as well as some of his spelling. His sections have also been divided into more manageable paragraphs. Significant differences between the 1752 and two earlier editions – referred to here as 1732a and 1732b – are registered in footnotes. All material within square brackets, unless otherwise indicated, is added by the editor.

NOTES

1 *The Works of George Berkeley* (Edinburgh, 1948–57), nine volumes; edited by A. A. Luce and T. E. Jessop; referred to hereafter as *Works*; see vol. vii, p. 358.
2 See A. A. Luce, *The Life of George Berkeley* (reprinted London, 1992); referred to as *Life*; see pp. 116, 133–4.
3 All quotations from Dialogues I, III, IV, and VII are from the present edition.
4 A German edition (Lemgo, 1737) is listed in Jessop's *Bibliography of George Berkeley* (second edn The Hague, 1973) and in G. Keynes's *Bibliography of George Berkeley* (Oxford, 1976); but neither Jessop nor Keynes was able to locate a copy.
5 See Jessop, *Bibliography of Berkeley*, pp. 3–5; 19–23; for an account of *Alciphron*'s first posthumous printing, see C. J. Benson, 'The Curious

Case of Berkeley's *Alciphron* printed in 1755', in the *Long Room* 28–9 (1984), pp. 17–31.

6 See A. R. Winnett, *Peter Browne: Provost, Bishop, Metaphysician* (London, 1974), chap. 11. Swift, Berkeley's friend, described Browne as 'the most speculative writer of his age' in a letter of 3 September 1735; in H. Williams (ed.), *The Correspondence of Jonathan Swift* (Oxford, 1965), vol. iv, p. 385.

7 See Browne, *Things Divine and Supernatural Conceived by Analogy with Things Natural and Human* (London, 1733) – referred to as *Divine Analogy*; see p. 374.

8 The letter, written about 1733, was first printed in the *Dublin Literary Journal*; it is reprinted and attributed to Berkeley by J.-P. Pittion, A. A. Luce and D. Berman, in 'A New Letter from Berkeley to Browne on Divine Analogy', *Mind* 311 (1969), pp. 375–92; for a useful discussion of the letter and its role in the analogy debate, see J. O'Higgins, 'Browne and King, Collins and Berkeley: Agnosticism or Anthropomorphism', *Journal of Theological Studies* 27 (1976), pp. 88–112.

9 See A. C. Fraser, *Berkeley's Complete Works* (Oxford, 1901), vol. 1, p. 219 and Luce, 'The Alleged Development of Berkeley's Philosophy', *Mind* 206 (1943), especially pp. 148–50. Fraser is followed by another editor of Berkeley, George Sampson, *Works of Berkeley* (London, 1898), vol. 2, p. 348.

10 I. T. Ramsey, 'Berkeley and the Possibility of an Empirical Metaphysics', W. Steinkraus (ed.), *New Studies in Berkeley's Philosophy* (New York, 1966), pp. 28–9; Jessop, *Works*, vol. iii, p. 291.

11 The pamphlets by Mandeville and Hervey are reprinted in D. Berman (ed.), *George Berkeley: Eighteenth-Century Responses* (New York, 1989), vol. 1.

12 See M. A. Stewart, 'William Wishart, an Early Critic of *Alciphron*', *Berkeley Newsletter* 6 (1982/3), pp. 5–9.

13 See Luce, *Life*, pp. 163–4; and *George Berkeley: Eighteenth-Century Responses*, vol. i, pp. 135–6.

14 See Peter Kivy, *The Seventh Sense: A Study of Francis Hutcheson's Aesthetics* (New York, 1976), pp. 30–33.

15 *Correspondence of Jonathan Swift* (Oxford, 1965), vol. iv, pp. 45 and 23.

16 Berman, 'The Culmination and Causation of Irish Philosophy', *Archiv für Geschichte der Philosophie* 64, 3 (1982), pp. 276–9; also see Dixon Wechter, 'Burke's Theory concerning Words, Images and Emotion', *PMLA* 55 (1940).

17 Hume, 'Of National Character', *Essays* (1742), in T. H. Green and T. H. Grose (eds), *The Philosophical Works of David Hume* (London, 1875), vol. 3, pp. 353–4.

18 Stephen, *English Thought in the Eighteenth Century* (London, 1902), vol. iii, p. 22; also see Stanley Tweyman (ed.), *David Hume, Dialogues concerning Natural Religion* (London, 1991).

19 See J. Gaskin, *Hume's Philosophy of Religion* (second edn. London, 1988), p. 126.

20 See B. Rand, *Berkeley and Percival* (Cambridge, 1914), p. 281.
21 See my *History of Atheism: from Hobbes to Russell* (London, 1990), pp. 235–41.
22 *Works*, vol. iii, pp. 12–13.
23 Warnock, *Berkeley* (London, 1953), pp. 229–30.
24 *Works*, vol. ii, p. 293.
25 See B. Belfrage (ed.), *George Berkeley's Manuscript Introduction* (Oxford, 1987), pp. 105–15.
26 The letter is to Percival; see *Works* vol. viii, p. 31.
27 See *Works*, vol. ii, pp. 53, 80, 106; and E. J. Furlong, 'Berkeley on relations, spirits and notions', *Hermathena* 106 (1968), pp. 60–6.
28 See pp. 106 and 203.
29 See *Works* vol. ii, p. 168.
30 Thus it had been used positively by Archbishop Synge in his *Free-Thinking in Matters of Religion, Stated and Recommended* (London, 1727) and Berkeley himself was to use it positively (although with some degree of irony) in a *Defence of Free-thinking in Mathematics* (London, 1735).
31 On this subject, see my 'Deliberate Parapraxes', *International Review of Psycho-Analysis* 15 (1988), pp. 381–4.
32 See my *History of Atheism*, pp. 71–8.
33 See my 'Deism, Immortality and the Art of Theological Lying', in J. A. Leo Lemay (ed.), *Deism, Masonry, and the Enlightenment* (Delaware, 1987), pp. 61–78.
34 See my *History of Atheism*, pp. 72–4.
35 See *History of Atheism*, pp. 82–7.
36 See my 'Anthony Collins: Aspects of his Work and Thought', *Hermathena* cxix (1975), pp. 53–7; for a useful discussion and edition of Collins's *Philosophical Inquiry*, see J. O'Higgins (ed.), *Determinism and Freewill* (The Hague, 1976).
37 *Works*, vol. vii, p. 188.
38 See D. and J. Berman, 'Berkeley's *Alciphron* Vignettes', *The Book Collector* 31, 1 (1985), pp. 55–62.
39 See *Works*, vol. viii, p. 212.
40 Berkeley's derivation and deployment of the term 'minute philosopher' in Dialogue I is remarkably similar to that in *The Tatler*, essay 135 (18 February 1709/10); see *The Tatler* (Oxford, 1987), edited by D. F. Bond, vol,. 2, pp. 279–82.
41 Toland's essay is in his *Letters to Serena* (London, 1704); compare *Alciphron* I.6 with *Letters*, p. 12; also *Alciphron* V.20 with *Letters*, p. 7.
42 Compare *An Account of Denmark* (fifth edn. Glasgow, 1745), pp. xxii–xxiii with *Alciphron* I.11. On the relationship between Molesworth and Berkeley, see my 'The Jacobitism of Berkeley's *Passive Obedience*', *Journal of the History of Ideas* xlvii, 2 (1986), pp. 310–12.
43 *Cato's Letters: or, Essays on Liberty, Civil and Religious* (fifth edn. London, 1748), four volumes; compare Trenchard's letters of 29 December 1722, 5 January 1722/3, 12 January 1722/3, 16 February 1722/3 with Berkeley on free-will in Dialogue VII; letter 16 March 1722/3 with the account of religious mysteries in Dialogue VII; 20.

DAVID BERMAN

July 1723 with the comments on varying notions of God in Dialogue I and negative theology in Dialogue IV. Compare, in particular, vol. 4, p. 53 with *Alciphron* VII.16.

44 See Synge's *An Appendix* to the *Gentleman's Religion* . . . (Dublin, 1698), sect. 14 and *Alciphron* IV.15.

ALCIPHRON

George Berkeley

AUTHOR'S ADVERTISEMENT

The author's design being to consider the Free-thinker in the various lights of atheist, libertine, enthusiast, scorner, critic, meta-physician, fatalist, and sceptic, it must not therefore be imagined that every one of these characters agrees with every individual Free-thinker; no more being implied than that each part agrees with some or other of the sect. There may, possibly, be a reader who shall think the character of atheist agrees with none; but though it hath been often said there is no such thing as a speculat-ive atheist, yet we must allow there are several atheists who pretend to speculation. This the author knows to be true; and is well assured that one of the most noted writers against Christian-ity in our times declared he had found out a demonstration against the being of a God. And he doubts not, whoever will be at the pains to inform himself, by a general conversation, as well as books, of the principles and tenets of our modern Free-thinkers, will see too much cause to be persuaded that nothing in the ensuing characters is beyond the life.[1]

As the author hath not confined himself to write against books alone, so he thinks it necessary to make this declaration. It must not, therefore, be thought that authors are misrepresented, if every notion of Alciphron or Lysicles is not found precisely in them. A gentleman in private conference, may be supposed to speak plainer than others write, to improve on their hints, and draw conclusions from their principles.

Whatever they pretend, it is the author's opinion that all those who write either explicitly or by insinuation, against the dignity,

[1] [The two following paragraphs appeared first in 1732b.]

17

freedom, and immortality of the human soul, may so far forth be justly said to unhinge the principles of morality, and destroy the means of making men reasonably virtuous. Much is to be apprehended from that quarter against the interests of virtue. Whether the apprehension of a certain admired writer,[2] that the cause of virtue is likely to suffer less from its witty antagonists than from its tender nurses, who are apt to overlay it, and kill it with excess of care and cherishing, and make it a mercenary thing, by talking so much of its reward – whether, I say, this apprehension be so well founded, the reader must determine.[3]

[2] [Shaftesbury] *Essay on the Freedom of Wit and Humour*, Part II, sect. 3.
[3] [In 1732a and 1732b, this paragraph was added: 'As for the Treatise concerning *Vision*, why the author annexed it to the *Minute Philosopher* will appear upon perusal of the Fourth Dialogue.']

CONTENTS

The Fourth Dialogue 84

The Seventh Dialogue 116

CONTENTS

THE FIRST DIALOGUE

1. I flattered myself, Theages, that before this time I might have been able to have sent you an agreeable account of the success of the affair which brought me into this remote corner of the country. But, instead of this, I should now give you the detail of its miscarriage, if I did not rather choose to entertain you with some amusing incidents, which have helped to make me easy under a circumstance I could neither obviate nor foresee. Events are not in our power; but it always is, to make a good use even of the worst. And, I must needs own, the course and event of this affair gave opportunity for reflexions that make me some amends for a great loss of time, pains, and expense. A life of action, which takes its issue from the counsels, passions, and views of other men, if it doth not draw a man to imitate, will at least teach him to observe. And a mind at liberty to reflect on its own observations, if it produce nothing useful to the world, seldom fails of entertainment to itself. For several months past, I have enjoyed such liberty and leisure in this distant retreat, far beyond the verge of that great whirlpool of business, faction, and pleasure, which is called *the world*. And a retreat in itself agreeable, after a long scene of trouble and disquiet, was made much more so by the conversation and good qualities of my host, Euphranor, who unites in his own person the philosopher and the farmer, two characters not so inconsistent in nature as by custom they seem to be.

Euphranor, from the time he left the university, hath lived in this small town; where he is possessed of a convenient house with a hundred acres of land adjoining to it; which, being improved by his own labour, yield him a plentiful subsistence. He hath a good collection, chiefly of old books, left him by a clergyman his

22

uncle, under whose care he was brought up. And the business of his farm doth not hinder him from making good use of it. He hath read much, and thought more; his health and strength of body enabling him the better to bear fatigue of mind. He is of opinion that he could not carry on his studies with more advantage in the closet than the field, where his mind is seldom idle while he prunes the trees, follows the plough, or looks after his flocks.

In the house of this honest friend I became acquainted with Crito, a neighbouring gentleman of distinguished merit and estate, who lives in great friendship with Euphranor. Last summer, Crito, whose parish church is in our town, dining on a Sunday at Euphranor's, I happened to inquire after his guests, whom we had seen at church with him the Sunday before. They are both well, said Crito, but, having once occasionally conformed, to see what sort of assembly our parish could afford, they had no further curiosity to gratify at church, and so chose to stay at home. How, said Euphranor, are they then dissenters? No, replied Crito, they are free-thinkers. Euphranor, who had never met with any of this species or sect of men, and but little of their writings, showed a great desire to know their principles or system. That is more, said Crito, than I will undertake to tell you. Their writers are of different opinions. Some go farther, and explain themselves more freely than others. But the current general notions of the sect are best learned from conversation with those who profess themselves of it. Your curiosity may now be satisfied, if you and Dion would spend a week at my house with these gentlemen, who seem very ready to declare and propagate their opinions. Alciphron is above forty, and no stranger either to men or books. I knew him first at the Temple, which, upon an estate's falling to him, he quitted, to travel through the polite parts of Europe. Since his return he hath lived in the amusements of the town, which, being grown stale and tasteless to his palate, have flung him into a sort of splenetic indolence. The young gentleman, Lysicles, is a near kinsman of mine, one of lively parts, and a general insight into letters; who, after having passed the forms of education, and seen a little of the world, fell into an intimacy with men of pleasure and free-thinkers, I am afraid much to the damage of his constitution and his fortune. But what I most regret is the corruption of his mind, by a set of pernicious principles, which, having been observed to survive the passions of youth, forestall even the remote hopes of amendment. They are both men of fashion, and would be agreeable enough, if they did not fancy themselves free-thinkers. But this, to speak the truth, has given them a certain air and manner, which a little too visibly declare they think themselves wiser than the rest of the world. I should therefore be not at all displeased if my guests met with their match, where they least expected it, in a country farmer.

I shall not, replied Euphranor, pretend to any more than barely to inform myself of their principles and opinions. For this end I propose tomorrow to set a week's task to my labourers, and accept your invitation, if Dion thinks good. To which I gave consent. Meanwhile, said Crito, I shall prepare my guests, and let them know that an honest neighbour hath a mind to discourse with them on the subject of their free-thinking. And, if I am not mistaken, they will please themselves with the prospect of leaving a convert behind them, even in a country-village.

Next morning Euphranor rose early, and spent the forenoon in ordering his affairs. After dinner we took our walk to Crito's, which lay through half-a-dozen pleasant fields planted round with plane trees, that are very common in this part of the country. We walked under the delicious shade of these trees for about an hour before we came to Crito's house, which stands in the middle of a small park, beautified with two fine groves of oak and walnut, and a winding stream of sweet and clear water. We met a servant at the door with a small basket of fruit, which he was carrying into a grove, where he said his master was with the two strangers. We found them all three sitting under a shade. And after the usual forms at first meeting, Euphranor and I sat down by them.

Our conversation began upon the beauty of this rural scene, the fine season of the year, and some later improvements which had been made in the adjacent country by new methods of agriculture. Whence Alciphron took occasion to observe, that the most valuable improvements came latest. I should have small temptation, said he, to live where men have neither polished manners, nor improved minds, though the face of the country were ever so well improved. But I have long observed that there is a gradual progress in human affairs. The first care of mankind is to supply the cravings of nature: in the next place they study the conveniences and comforts of life. But the subduing prejudices, and acquiring true knowledge, that Herculean labour, is the last, being what demands the most perfect abilities, and to which all other advantages are preparative. Right, said Euphranor, Alciphron hath touched our true defect. It was always my opinion that as soon as we had provided subsistence for the body our next care should be to improve the mind. But the desire of wealth steps between, and engrosseth men's thoughts.

2. *Alciphron.* Thought is that which we are told distinguisheth man from beast; and freedom of thought makes as great a difference between man and man. It is to the noble assertors of this privilege and perfection of humankind, the free-thinkers I mean, who have sprung up and multiplied of late years, that we are indebted for all those important discoveries, that ocean of light, which hath broke in and made its way, in spite of slavery and superstition.

Euphranor, who is a sincere enemy to both, testified a great esteem for those worthies who had preserved their country from being ruined by them, having spread so much light and knowledge over the land. He added, that he liked the name and character of a free-thinker: but, in his sense of the word, every honest inquirer after truth in any age or country was entitled to it. He therefore desired to know what this sect was that Alciphron had spoken of as newly sprung up? what were their tenets? what were their discoveries? and wherein they employed themselves for the benefit of mankind? Of all which, he should think himself obliged, if Alciphron would inform him.

That I shall very easily, replied Alciphron, for I profess myself one of the number, and my most intimate friends are some of the most considerable among them. And, perceiving that Euphranor heard him with respect, he proceeded very fluently. You must know, said he, that the mind of man may be fitly compared to a piece of land. What stubbing, ploughing, digging, and harrowing are to the one, that thinking, reflecting, examining is to the other. Each hath its proper culture; and, as land that is suffered to lie waste and wild for a long tract of time will be overspread with brush-wood, brambles, thorns, and such vegetables which have neither use nor beauty; even so there will not fail to sprout up in a neglected uncultivated mind a great number of prejudices and absurd opinions, which owe their origin partly to the soil itself, the passions and imperfections of the mind of

ALCIPHRON

man; and partly to those seeds which chance to be scattered in it by every wind of doctrine, which the cunning of statesmen, the singularity of pedants, the superstition of fools, or the imposture of priests shall raise. Represent to yourself the mind of man, or human nature in general, that for so many ages had lain obnoxious to the frauds of designing, and the follies of weak men; how it must be overrun with prejudices and errors; what firm and deep roots they must have taken: and consequently how difficult a task it must be to extirpate them; and yet this work, no less difficult than glorious, is the employment of the modern free-thinkers. Alciphron having said this made a pause, and looked round on the company.

Truly, said I, a very laudable undertaking!

We think, said Euphranor, that it is praiseworthy to clear and subdue the earth, to tame brute animals, to fashion the outsides of men, provide sustenance for their bodies, and cure their maladies. But what is all this in comparison of that most excellent and useful undertaking, to free mankind from their errors, and to improve and adorn their minds? For things of less merit towards the world, altars have been raised, and temples built, in ancient times.

Too many in our days, replied Alciphron, are such fools as not to know their best benefactors from their worst enemies; they have a blind respect for those who enslave them, and look upon their deliverers as a dangerous sort of men that would undermine received principles and opinions.

Euphranor. It were a great pity such worthy ingenious men should meet with any discouragement. For my part, I should think a man who spent his time in such a painful, impartial search after truth a better friend to mankind than the greatest statesman or hero; the advantage of whose labours is confined to a little part of the world and a short space of time; whereas a ray of truth may enlighten the whole world, and extend to future ages.

Alc. It will be some time, I fear, before the common herd think as you do. But the better sort, the men of parts and polite education, pay a due regard to the patrons of light and truth.

3. *Euph.* The clergy, no doubt, are on all occasions ready to forward and applaud your worthy endeavours.

Upon hearing this Lysicles could hardly refrain from laughing. And Alciphron with an air of pity told Euphranor that he per-

26

ceived he was unacquainted with the real character of those men. For, saith he, you must know that of all men living they are our greatest enemies. If it were possible, they would extinguish the very light of nature, turn the world into a dungeon, and keep mankind for ever in chains and darkness.

Euph. I never imagined anything like this of our Protestant clergy, particularly those of the Established Church, whom, if I may be allowed to judge by what I have seen of them and their writings, I should have thought lovers of learning and useful knowledge.

Alc. Take my word for it, priests of all religions are the same: wherever there are priests there will be priestcraft; and wherever there is priestcraft there will be a persecuting spirit, which they never fail to exert to the utmost of their power against all those who have the courage to think for themselves, and will not submit to be hoodwinked and manacled by their reverend leaders. Those great masters of pedantry and jargon have coined several systems, which are all equally true, and of equal importance to the world. The contending sects are each alike fond of their own, and alike prone to discharge their fury upon all who dissent from them. Cruelty and ambition being the darling vices of priests and churchmen all the world over, they endeavour in all countries to get an ascendant over the rest of mankind; and the magistrate, having a joint interest with the priest in subduing, amusing, and scaring the people, too often lends a hand to the hierarchy; who never think their authority and possessions secure, so long as those who differ from them in opinion are allowed to partake even in the common rights belonging to their birth or species. To represent the matter in a true light, figure to yourselves a monster or spectre made up of superstition and enthusiasm, the joint issue of statecraft and priestcraft, rattling chains in one hand, and with the other brandishing a flaming sword over the land, and menacing destruction to all who shall dare to follow the dictates of reason and common sense. Do but consider this, and then say if there was not danger as well as difficulty in our undertaking. Yet, such is the generous ardour that truth inspires, our free-thinkers are neither overcome by the one, nor daunted by the other. In spite of both we have already made so many proselytes among the better sort, and their numbers increase so fast, that we hope we shall be able to carry all before us, beat down the bulwarks of all tyranny, secular or ecclesiastical, break the fetters and chains of our countrymen, and restore the original inherent rights, liberties, and prerogatives of mankind.

Euphranor heard this discourse with his mouth open and his eyes fixed upon Alciphron, who, having uttered it with no small emotion, stopped to draw breath and recover himself; but, finding that nobody made answer, he resumed the thread of his discourse, and, turning to Euphranor, spoke in a lower note what follows: The more innocent and honest a man is, the more liable is he to be imposed on by the specious pretences of other men. You have probably met with certain writings of our divines that treat of grace, virtue, goodness, and such matters, fit to amuse and deceive a simple, honest mind. But, believe me when I tell you they are all at bottom (however they may gild their designs) united by one common principle in the same interest. I will not deny there may be here and there a poor half-witted man that means no mischief; but this I will be bold to say, that all the men of sense among them are true at bottom to these three pursuits of ambition, avarice, and revenge.

4. While Alciphron was speaking, a servant came to tell him and Lysicles that some men who were going to London waited to receive their orders. Whereupon they both rose and went towards the house. They were no sooner gone, but Euphranor, addressing himself to Crito, said, he believed that poor gentleman had been a great sufferer for his free-thinking; for that he seemed to express himself with the passion and resentment natural to men who have received very bad usage.

I believe no such thing, answered Crito, but have often observed those of his sect run into two faults of conversation, declaiming and bantering, just as the tragic or the comic humour prevails. Sometimes they work themselves into high passions, and are frightened at spectres of their own raising. In those fits every country curate passes for an inquisitor. At other times they affect a sly facetious manner making use of hints and allusions, expressing little, insinuating much, and upon the whole seeming to divert themselves with the subject and their adversaries. But, if you would know their opinions, you must make them speak out and keep close to the point. Persecution for free-thinking is a topic they are apt to enlarge on, though without any just cause, every one being at full liberty to think what he pleases, there being no such thing in England that I know as persecution for opinion, sentiment, or thought. But in every country, I suppose, some care is taken to restrain petulant speech; and, whatever men's inward thoughts may be, to discourage an outward contempt of what the public esteemeth sacred. Whether this care in England hath of late been so excessive as to distress the subjects of this once free and easy government; whether the free-thinkers can truly complain of any hardship upon the score of conscience or opinion; you will better be able to judge, when you hear from themselves an account of the numbers, progress, and notions of their sect; which I doubt not they will communicate fully and freely, provided nobody present seems shocked or offended. For in that case it is possible good manners may put them upon some reserve.

Oh! said Euphranor, I am never angry with any man for his opinion: whether he be Jew, Turk, or Idolator, he may speak his mind freely to me without fear of offending. I should even be glad to hear what he says, provided he saith it in an ingenuous candid manner. Whoever digs in the mine of truth, I look on as my fellow-labourer; but if, while I am taking true pains, he diverts himself with teasing me, and flinging dust in mine eyes, I shall soon be tired of him.

5. In the meantime, Alciphron and Lysicles having despatched what they went about, returned to us. Lysicles sat down where he had been before. But Alciphron stood over against us, with his arms folded across, and his head reclined on the left shoulder, in the posture of a man meditating. We sat silent not to disturb his thoughts; and after two or three minutes he uttered the words – 'Oh truth! Oh liberty!' After which he remained musing as before.

Upon this Euphranor took the freedom to interrupt him. Alciphron, said he, it is not fair to spend your time in soliloquies. The conversation of learned and knowing men is rarely to be met with in this corner, and the opportunity you have put into my hands I value too much not to make the best use of it.

Alc. Are you then in earnest a votary of truth, and is it possible you should bear the liberty of a fair inquiry?

Euph. It is what I desire of all things.

Alc. What! upon every subject? upon the notions you first sucked in with your milk, and which have been ever since nursed by parents, pastors, tutors, religious assemblies, books of devotion, and such methods of prepossessing men's minds?

Euph. I love information upon all subjects that come in my way, and especially upon those that are most important.

Alc. If then you are in earnest, hold fair and stand firm, while I probe your prejudices and extirpate your principles.

Dum veteres avias tibi de pulmone revello.[1]

Having said thus, Alciphron knit his brows and made a short pause, after which he proceeded in the following manner.

If we are at the pains to dive and penetrate into the bottom of things, and analyse opinions into their first principles, we shall find that those opinions which are thought of greatest consequence have the slightest original, being derived either from the casual customs of the country where we live, or from early instruction instilled into our tender minds, before we are able to discern between right and wrong, true and false. The vulgar (by whom I understand all those who do not make a free use of their reason) are apt to take these prejudices for things sacred and unquestionable, believing them to be imprinted on the hearts of men by God Himself, or conveyed by revelation from heaven, or to carry with them so great light and evidence as must force an assent without any inquiry or examination. Thus the shallow vulgar have their heads furnished with sundry conceits, principles, and doctrines, religious, moral, and political, all which they maintain with a zeal proportionable to their want of reason. On the other hand, those who duly employ their faculties in the search of truth, take especial care to weed out of their minds, and extirpate all such notions or prejudices as were planted in them, before they arrived at the free and entire use of reason. This difficult task hath been successfully performed by our modern free-thinkers, who have not only dissected with great sagacity the received systems, and traced every established prejudice to the fountain-head, the true and genuine motives of assent: but also, being able to embrace in one comprehensive view the several parts and ages of the world, they have observed a wonderful variety of customs and rites, of institutions religious and civil, of notions and opinions very unlike, and even contrary one to another – a certain sign they cannot all be true. And yet they are

---

[1] [That is: 'While I pluck the old grandmothers from your lungs'; Persius, V, line 92.]

all maintained by their several partisans with the same positive air and warm zeal; and, if examined, will be found to bottom on one and the same foundation, the strength of prejudice. By the help of these remarks and discoveries, they have broke through the bands of popular custom, and, having freed themselves from imposture, do now generously lend a hand to their fellow-subjects, to lead them into the same paths of light and liberty. Thus, gentlemen, I have given you a summary account of the views and endeavours of those men who are called free-thinkers. If, in the course of what I have said, or shall say hereafter, there be some things contrary to your preconceived opinions, and therefore shocking and disagreeable, you will pardon the freedom and plainness of a philosopher, and consider that, whatever displeasure I give you of that kind, I do it in strict regard to truth, and obedience to your own commands. I am very sensible that eyes long kept in the dark cannot bear a sudden view of noonday light, but must be brought to it by degrees. It is for this reason the ingenious gentlemen of our profession are accustomed to proceed gradually, beginning with those prejudices to which men have the least attachment, and thence proceeding to undermine the rest by slow and insensible degrees, till they have demolished the whole fabric of human folly and superstition. But the little time I can propose to spend here obligeth me to take a shorter course, and be more direct and plain than possibly may be thought to suit with prudence and good manners.

Upon this, we assured him, he was at full liberty to speak his mind of things, persons, and opinions, without the least reserve.

It is a liberty, replied Alciphron, that we free-thinkers are equally willing to give and take. We love to call things by their right names, and cannot endure that truth should suffer through complaisance. Let us, therefore, lay it down for a preliminary, that no offence be taken at anything whatsoever shall be said on either side. To which we all agreed.

6. In order then, said Alciphron, to find out the truth, we will suppose that I am bred up, for instance, in the Church of England. When I come to maturity of judgment, and reflect on the particular worship and opinions of this Church, I do not remember when or by what means they first took possession of my mind, but there I find them from time immemorial. Then, casting an eye on the education of children, from whence I can

make a judgment of my own, I observe they are instructed in religious matters before they can reason about them; and, consequently, that all such instruction is nothing else but filling the tender mind of a child with prejudices. I do, therefore, reject all those religious notions, which I consider as the other follies of my childhood. I am confirmed in this way of thinking when I look abroad into the world, where I observe Papists, and several sects of Dissenters, which do all agree in a general profession of belief in Christ, but differ vastly one from another in the particulars of faith and worship. I then enlarge my view so as to take in Jews and Mahometans, between whom and the Christians I perceive, indeed, some small agreement in the belief of one God; but then they have each their distinct laws and revelations, for which they express the same regard. But, extending my view still further to heathenish and idolatrous nations, I discover an endless variety, not only in particular opinions and modes of worship, but even in the very notion of a Deity, wherein they widely differ one from another, and from all the forementioned sects. Upon the whole, instead of truth simple and uniform I perceive nothing but discord, opposition and wild pretensions, all springing from the same source, to wit, the prejudice of education. From such reasonings and reflexions as these, thinking men have concluded that all religions are alike false and fabulous. One is a Christian, another a Jew, a third a Mahometan, a fourth an idolatrous Gentile, but all from one and the same reason – because they happen to be bred up each in his respective sect. In the same manner, therefore, as each of these contending parties condemns the rest, so an unprejudiced stander-by will condemn and reject them altogether, observing, that they all draw their origin from the same fallacious principle, and are carried on by the same artifice, to answer the same ends of the priest and the magistrate.

7. *Euph.* You hold then that the magistrate concurs with the priest in imposing on the people?

Alc. I do; and so must every one who considers things in a true light. For, you must know the magistrate's principal aim is to keep the people under him in awe. Now, the public eye restrains men from open offences against the laws and government. But, to prevent secret transgressions, a magistrate finds it expedient that men should believe there is an eye of Providence watching over their private actions and designs. And, to intimidate those who might otherwise be drawn into crimes by the prospect of pleasure and profit, he gives them to understand that whoever escapes punishment in this life will be sure to find it in the next; and that so heavy and lasting as infinitely to overbalance the pleasure and profit accruing from his crimes. Hence, the belief of a God, the immortality of the soul, and a future state of rewards and punishments have been esteemed useful engines of government. And, to the end that these notional airy doctrines might make a sensible impression, and be retained on the minds of men, skilful rulers have, in the several civilized nations of the earth, devised temples, sacrifices, churches, rites, ceremonies, habits, music, prayer, preaching, and the like spiritual trumpery, whereby the priest maketh temporal gains, and the magistrate findeth his account in frightening and subduing the people. This is the original of the combination between Church and State, of religion by law established, of rights, immunities, and incomes of priests all over the world: there being no government but would have you fear God, that you may honour the king or civil power. And you will ever observe that politic princes keep up a good understanding with their clergy, to the end that they in return, by inculcating religion and loyalty into the minds of the people, may render them tame, timorous, and slavish.

Crito and I heard this discourse of Alciphron with the utmost attention, though without any appearance of surprise, there being, indeed, nothing in it to us new or unexpected. But Euphranor, who had never before been present at such conversation, could not help showing some astonishment; which Lysicles observing, asked him with a lively air, how he liked Alciphron's lecture. It is, said he, the first I believe that you ever heard of the kind, and requireth a strong stomach to digest it.

Euph. I will own to you that my digestion is none of the quickest; but it hath sometimes, by degrees, been able to master things which at first appeared indigestible. At present I admire the free spirit and eloquence of Alciphron; but, to speak the truth, I am rather astonished than convinced of the truth of his opinions. How! (said he, turning to Alciphron) is it then possible you should not believe the being of a God?

Alc. To be plain with you, I do not.

8. But this is what I foresaw – a flood of light let in at once

upon the mind being apt to dazzle and disorder, rather than enlighten it. Was I not pinched in time, the regular way would be to have begun with the circumstantials of religion; next to have attacked the mysteries of Christianity; after that proceeded to the practical doctrines; and in the last place to have extirpated that which of all other religious prejudices, being the first taught and basis of the rest, hath taken the deepest root in our minds, I mean, the belief of a God. I do not wonder it sticks with you, having known several very ingenious men who found it difficult to free themselves from this prejudice.

Euph. All men have not the same alacrity and vigour in thinking; for my own part, I find it a hard matter to keep pace with you.

Alc. To help you, I will go a little way back, and resume the thread of my reasoning. First, I must acquaint you that, having applied my mind to contemplate the idea of Truth, I discovered it to be of a stable, permanent, and uniform nature; not various and changeable, like modes or fashions, and things depending on fancy. In the next place, having observed several sects and subdivisions of sects espousing very different and contrary opinions, and yet all professing Christianity, I rejected those points wherein they differed, retaining only that which was agreed to by all, and so became a *Latitudinarian.* Having afterwards, upon a more enlarged view of things, perceived that Christians, Jews, and Mahometans had each their different systems of faith, agreeing only in the belief of one God, I became a *Deist.* Lastly, extending my view to all the other various nations which inhabit this globe, and finding they agreed in no one point of faith, but differed one from another, as well as from the forementioned sects, even in the notion of a God, in which there is as great diversity as in the methods of worship, I thereupon became an *Atheist*: it being my opinion that a man of courage and sense should follow his argument wherever it leads him, and that nothing is more ridiculous than to be a free-thinker by halves. I approve the man who makes thorough work, and, not content with lopping off the branches, extirpates the very root from which they sprung.

9.   Atheism therefore, that bugbear of women and fools, is the very top and perfection of free-thinking. It is the grand *arcanum* to which a true genius naturally riseth, by a certain climax or gra-

dation of thought, and without which he can never possess his soul in absolute liberty and repose. For your thorough conviction in this main article, do but examine the notion of a God with the same freedom that you would other prejudices. Trace it to the fountain-head, and you shall not find that you had it by any of your senses, the only true means of discovering what is real and substantial in nature: you will find it lying amongst other old lumber in some obscure corner of the imagination, the proper receptacle of visions, fancies, and prejudices of all kinds; and if you are more attached to this than the rest, it is only because it is the oldest. This is all, take my word for it, and not mine only but that of many more the most ingenious men of the age, who, I can assure you, think as I do on the subject of a Deity. Though some of them hold it proper to proceed with more reserve in declaring to the world their opinion in this particular than in most others. And, it must be owned, there are still too many in England who retain a foolish prejudice against the name of atheist. But it lessens every day among the better sort; and when it is quite worn out our free-thinkers may then (and not till then) be said to have given the finishing stroke to religion; it being evident that, so long as the existence of God is believed, religion must subsist in some shape or other. But, the root being once plucked up, the scions which shoot from it will of course wither and decay. Such are all those whimsical notions of conscience, duty, principle, and the like, which fill a man's head with scruples, awe him with fears, and make him a more thorough slave than the horse he rides. A man had better a thousand times be hunted by bailiffs or messengers than haunted by these spectres, which embarrass and embitter all his pleasures, creating the most real and sore servitude upon earth. But the free-thinker, with a vigorous flight of thought, breaks through those airy springs, and asserts his original independency. Others indeed may talk, and write, and fight about liberty, and make an outward pretence to it; but the free-thinker alone is truly free.

Alciphron having ended this discourse with an air of triumph, Euphranor spoke to him in the following manner:

You make clear work. The gentlemen of your profession are, it seems, admirable weeders. You have rooted up a world of notions: I should be glad to see what fine things you have planted in their stead.

Alc. Have patience, good Euphranor. I will show you, in the first place, that whatever was sound and good we leave untouched, and encourage it to grow in the mind of man. And, secondly, I will show you what excellent things we have planted in it. You must know then that, pursuing our close and severe scrutiny, we do at last arrive at something solid and real, in which all mankind agree, to wit, the appetites, passions, and senses: these are founded in nature, are real, have real objects, and are attended with real and substantial pleasures; food, drink, sleep, and the like animal enjoyments being what all men like and love. And if we extend our view to other kinds of animals, we shall find they all agree in this, that they have certain natural appetites and senses, in the gratifying and satisfying of which they are constantly employed. Now these real natural good things, which include nothing of notion or fancy, we are so far from destroying, that we do all we can to cherish and improve them. According to us, every wise man looks upon himself, or his own bodily existence in this present world, as the centre and ultimate end of all his actions and regards. He considers his appetites as natural guides, directing to his proper good, his passions and senses as the natural true means of enjoying this good. Hence, he endeavours to keep his appetites in high relish, his passions and senses strong and lively, and to provide the greatest quantity and variety of real objects suited to them, which he studieth to enjoy by all possible means, and in the highest perfection imaginable. And the man who can do this without restraint, remorse, or fear is as happy as any other animal whatso-ever, or as his nature is capable of being. Thus I have given you a succinct view of the principles, discoveries, and tenets of the select spirits of this enlightened age.

10. Crito remarked, that Alciphron had spoken his mind with great clearness.

Yes, replied Euphranor, we are obliged to the gentleman for letting us at once into the tenets of his sect. But, if I may be allowed to speak my mind, Alciphron, though in compliance with my own request, hath given me no small uneasiness.

You need, said Alciphron, make no apology for speaking freely what you think to one who professes himself a free-thinker. I should be sorry to make one, whom I meant to oblige, uneasy. Pray let me know wherein I have offended.

I am half ashamed, replied Euphranor, to own that I, who am

no great genius, have a weakness incidental to little ones. I would say that I have favourite opinions, which you represent to be errors and prejudices. For instance, the immortality of the soul is a notion I am fond of, as what supports the mind with a very pleasing prospect. And, if it be an error, I should perhaps be of Tully's mind, who in that case professed he should be sorry to know the truth, acknowledging no sort of obligation to certain philosophers in his days, who taught that the soul of man was mortal. They were, it seems, predecessors to those who are now called free-thinkers; which name being too general and indefinite, inasmuch as it comprehends all those who think for themselves, whether they agree in opinion with these gentlemen or no – it should not seem amiss to assign them a specific appellation or peculiar name, whereby to distinguish them from other philo-sophers, at least in our present conference. For, I cannot bear to argue against free-thinking and free-thinkers.

Alc. In the eyes of a wise man words are of small moment. We do not think truth attached to a name.

Euph. If you please then, to avoid confusion, let us call your sect by the same name as Tully (who understood the force of language) bestowed upon them.

Alc. With all my heart. Pray what may that name be?

Euph. Why, he calls them *minute philosophers.*

Right, said Crito, the modern free-thinkers are the very same with those Cicero called minute philosophers, which name admir-ably suits them, they being a sort of sect which diminish all the most valuable things, the thoughts, views, and hopes of men; all the knowledge, notions, and theories of the mind they reduce to sense; human nature they contract and degrade to the narrow low standard of animal life, and assign us only a small pittance of time instead of immortality.

Alciphron very gravely remarked that the gentlemen of his sect had done no injury to man, and that, if he be a little, short-lived, contemptible animal, it was not their saying it made him so: and they were no more to blame for whatever defects they discover than a faithful glass for making the wrinkles which it only shows. As to what you observe, said he, of those we now call free-thinkers having been anciently termed *minute philosophers*, it is my opinion this appellation might be derived from their considering things minutely, and not swallowing them in the gross, as other men are used to do. Besides, we all know the best eyes are necessary to discern the minutest objects: it seems, therefore, that minute philosophers might have been so called from their distinguished perspicacity.

Euph. O Alciphron! these minute philosophers (since that is their true name) are a sort of pirates who plunder all that come in their way. I consider myself as a man left stripped and desolate on a bleak beach.

11. But who are these profound and learned men that of late years have demolished the whole fabric which lawgivers, philosophers, and divines, had been erecting for so many ages?

Lysicles, hearing these words, smiled, and said he believed Euphranor had figured to himself philosophers in square caps and long gowns: but, thanks to these happy times, the reign of pedantry was over. Our philosophers, said he, are of a very different kind from those awkward students who think to come at knowledge by poring on dead languages and old authors, or by sequestering themselves from the cares of the world to meditate in solitude and retirement. They are the best-bred men of the age, men who know the world, men of pleasure, men of fashion, and fine gentlemen.

Euph. I have some small notion of the people you mention, but should never have taken them for philosophers.

Cri. Nor would any one else till of late. The world it seems was long under a mistake about the way to knowledge, thinking it lay through a tedious course of academical education and study. But, among the discoveries of the present age, one of the principal is the finding out that such a method doth rather retard and obstruct than promote knowledge.

Alc. Academical study may be comprised in two points, reading and meditation. Their reading is chiefly employed on ancient authors in dead languages: so that a great part of their time is spent in learning words; which, when they have mastered with infinite pains, what do they get by it but old and obsolete notions, that are now quite exploded and out of use? Then, as to their meditations, what can they possibly be good for? He that wants the proper materials of thought may think and meditate forever to no purpose: those cobwebs spun by scholars out of their own brains being alike unserviceable, either for use or ornament. Proper ideas or materials are only to be got by frequenting good company. I know several gentlemen who, since their appearance in the world, have spent as much time in rubbing off the rust and pedantry of a college education as they have done before in acquiring it.

Lysicles. I'll undertake, a lad of fourteen, bred in the modern way, shall make a better figure, and be more considered in any drawing-room or assembly of polite people, than one of four and twenty, who hath lain by a long time at school and college. He shall say better things in a better manner, and be more liked by good judges.

Euph. Where doth he pick up all this improvement?

Cri. Where our grave ancestors would never have looked for it – in a drawing room, a coffee-house, a chocolate-house, at the tavern, or groom-porter's. In these and the like fashionable places of resort, it is the custom for polite persons to speak freely on all subjects, religious, moral, or political. So that a young gentleman who frequents them is in the way of hearing many instructive lectures, seasoned with wit and raillery, and uttered with spirit. Three or four sentences from a man of quality, spoke with a good air, make more impression and convey more knowledge than a dozen dissertations in a dry academical way.

Euph. There is then no method, or course of studies, in those places?

Lys. None but an easy, free conversation, which takes in everything that offers, without any rule or design.

Euph. I always thought that some order was necessary to attain any useful degree of knowledge; that haste and confusion begat a conceited ignorance; that to make our advances sure, they should be gradual, and those points first learned which might cast a light on what was to follow.

Alc. So long as learning was to be obtained only by that slow formal course of study, few of the better sort knew much of it: but, now it has grown an amusement, our young gentry and nobility imbibe it insensibly amidst their diversions, and make a considerable progress.

Euph. Hence probably the great number of minute philosophers.

Cri. It is to this that sect is owing for so many ingenious proficients of both sexes. You may now commonly see (what no former age ever saw) a young lady, or a *petit maître*, nonplus a divine, or an old-fashioned gentleman, who hath read many a

Greek and Latin author, and spent much time in hard methodical study.

Euph. It should seem then that method, exactness, and industry are a disadvantage.

Here Alciphron, turning to Lysicles, said he could make the point very clear, if Euphranor had any notion of painting.

Euph. I never saw a first-rate picture in my life, but have a tolerable collection of prints, and have seen some good drawings.

Alc. You know then the difference between the Dutch and Italian manner?

Euph. I have some notion of it.

Alc. Suppose now a drawing finished by the nice and laborious touches of a Dutch pencil, and another off-hand scratched out in the free manner of a great Italian master. The Dutch piece, which hath cost so much pains and time, will be exact indeed, but without that force, spirit, or grace which appear in the other, and are the effects of an easy, free pencil. Do but apply this, and the point will be clear.

Euph. Pray inform me, did those great Italian masters begin and proceed in their art without any choice of method or subject, and always draw with the same ease and freedom? Or did they observe some method, beginning with simple and elementary parts, an eye, a nose, a finger, which they drew with great pains and care, often drawing the same thing, in order to draw it correctly, and so proceeding with patience and industry till, after a considerable length of time, they arrived at the free, masterly manner you speak of. If this were the case, I leave you to make the application.

Alc. You may dispute the matter if you please. But a man of parts is one thing, and a pedant another. Pains and method may do for some sort of people. A man must be a long time kindling wet straw into a vile smothering flame, but spirits blaze out at once.

Euph. The minute philosophers have, it seems, better parts than other men, which qualifies them for a different education.

Alc. Tell me, Euphranor, what is it that gives one man a better mien than another; more politeness in dress, speech, and motion? Nothing but frequenting good company. By the same means men get insensibly a delicate taste, a refined judgment, a certain politeness in thinking and expressing one's self. No wonder if you countrymen are strangers to the advantage of polite conversation, which constantly keeps the mind awake and active, exercising its faculties, and calling forth all its strength and spirit, on a thousand different occasions and subjects that never came in the way of a book-worm in a college, no more than of a ploughman.

Cri. Hence those lively faculties, that quickness of apprehension, that slyness of ridicule, that egregious talent of wit and humour which distinguish the gentlemen of your profession.

Euph. It should seem then that your sect is made up of what you call fine gentlemen.

Lys. Not altogether, for we have among us some contemplative spirits of a coarser education, who, from observing the behaviour and proceedings of apprentices, watermen, porters, and assemblies of rabble in the streets, have arrived at a profound knowledge of human nature, and made great discoveries about the principles, springs, and motives of moral actions. These have demolished the received systems, and done a world of good in the city.

Alc. I tell you we have men of all sorts and professions, plodding citizens, thriving stock-jobbers, skilful men in business, polite courtiers, gallant men of the army; but our chief strength, and flower of the flock, are those promising young men who have the advantage of a modern education. These are the growing hopes of our sect, by whose credit and influence in a few years we expect to see those great things accomplished that we have in view.

Euph. I could never have imagined your sect so considerable.

Alc. There are in England many honest folk as much in the dark about these matters as yourselves.

12. To judge of the prevailing opinion among people of fashion, by what a senator saith in the house, a judge upon the bench, or a priest in the pulpit, who all speak according to law, that is, to the reverend prejudices of our forefathers, would be wrong. You should go into good company, and mind what men of parts and breeding say, those who are best heard and most admired, as well in public places of resort as in private visits. He only who hath these opportunites can know our real strength, our numbers, and the figure that we make.

Euph. By your account there must be many minute philosophers among the men of rank and fortune.

Alc. Take my word for it, not a few; and they do much contribute to the spreading our notions. For, he who knows the world must observe that fashions constantly descend. It is therefore the right way to propagate an opinion from the upper end. Not to say that the patronage of such men is an encouragement to our authors.

Euph. It seems, then, you have authors among you.

Lys. That we have, several, and those very great men, who have obliged the world with many useful and profound discoveries.

Cri. Moschon, for instance, hath proved that man and beast are really of the same nature: that consequently a man need only indulge his senses and appetites to be as happy as a brute. Gorgias hath gone further, demonstrating man to be a piece of clockwork or machine; and that thought or reason is the same thing as the impulse of one ball against another. Cimon hath made noble use of these discoveries, proving, as clearly as any proposition in mathematics, that conscience is a whim, and morality a prejudice; and that a man is no more accountable for his actions than a clock is for striking. Tryphon hath written irrefragably on the usefulness of vice. Thrasenor hath confuted the foolish prejudice men had against atheism, showing that a republic of atheists might live very happily together. Demylus hath made a jest of loyalty, and convinced the world there is nothing in it: to him and another philosopher of the same stamp this age is indebted for discovering that public spirit is an idle enthusiasm, which seizeth only on weak minds. It would be endless to recount the discoveries made by writers of this sect.

Lys. But the masterpiece and finishing stroke is a learned anecdote of our great Diagoras, containing a demonstration against the being of God: which it is conceived the public is not yet ripe for. But I am assured by some judicious friends who have seen it that it is as clear as daylight, and will do a world of good, at one blow demolishing the whole system of religion. These discoveries are published by our philosophers, sometimes in just volumes, but often in pamphlets and loose papers for their readier conveyance through the kingdom. And to them must be ascribed that absolute and independent freedom which groweth so fast to the terror of all bigots. Even the dull and ignorant begin to open their eyes, and be influenced by the example and authority of so many ingenious men.

Euph. It should seem by this account that your sect extend their discoveries beyond religion; and that loyalty to his prince and reverence for the laws are but mean things in the eye of a minute philosopher.

Lys. Very mean; we are too wise to think there is anything sacred either in king or constitution, or indeed in anything else. A man of sense may perhaps seem to pay an occasional regard to his prince; but this is no more at bottom than what he pays to God, when he kneels at the sacrament to qualify himself for an office. 'Fear God' and 'Honour the king' are a pair of slavish maxims, which had for a long time cramped human nature, and awed not only weak minds but even men of good understanding, till their eyes, as I observed before, were opened by our philosophers.

Euph. Methinks I can easily comprehend that when the fear of God is quite extinguished the mind must be very easy with respect to other duties, which become outward pretences and formalities, from the moment that they quit their hold upon the conscience, and conscience always supposeth the being of a God. But I still thought that Englishmen of all denominations (how widely soever they might differ as to some particular points) agreed in the belief of a God, and of so much at least as is called natural religion.

Alc. I have already told you my own opinion of those matters, and what I know to be the opinion of many more.

Cri. Probably, Euphranor, by the title of Deists, which is sometimes given to minute philosophers, you have been misled to imagine they believe and worship a God according to the light of nature; but, by living among them, you may soon be convinced of the contrary. They have neither time, nor place, nor form of Divine worship; they offer neither prayers nor praises to God in public; and in their private practice show a contempt or dislike even of the duties of natural religion. For instance, the saying grace before and after meals is a plain point of natural worship, and was once universally practised; but in proportion as this sect prevailed it hath been laid aside, not only by the minute philosophers themselves, who would be infinitely ashamed of such a weakness as to beg God's blessing or give God thanks for their daily food, but also by others who are afraid of being thought fools by the minute philosophers.

Euph. Is it possible that men who really believe a God should yet decline paying so easy and reasonable a duty for fear of incurring the contempt of Atheists?

Cri. I tell you there are many who, believing in their hearts the truth of religion, are yet afraid or ashamed to own it, lest they should forfeit their reputation with those who have the good luck to pass for great wits and men of genius.

Alc. O Euphranor, we must make allowance for Crito's prejudice: he is a worthy gentleman, and means well. But doth it not look like prejudice to ascribe the respect that is paid our ingenious free-thinkers rather to good luck than to merit?

Euph. I acknowledge their merit to be very wonderful, and that those authors must needs be great men who are able to prove such paradoxes: for example, that so knowing a man as a minute philosopher should be a mere machine, or at best no better than a brute.

Alc. It is a true maxim – That a man should think with the learned, and speak with the vulgar. I should be loath to place a gentleman of merit in such a light, before prejudiced or ignorant men. The tenets of our philosophy have this in common with many other truths in metaphysics, geometry, astronomy, and natural philosophy, that vulgar ears cannot bear them. All our discoveries and notions are in themselves true and certain; but they are at present known only to the better sort, and would sound strange and odd among the vulgar. But this, it is to be hoped, will wear off with time.

Euph. I do not wonder that vulgar minds should be startled at the notions of your philosophy.

Cri. Truly a very curious sort of philosophy, and much to be admired!

13. The profound thinkers of this way have taken a direct contrary course to all the great philosophers of former ages, who made it their endeavour to raise and refine humankind, and remove it as far as possible from the brute; to moderate and subdue men's appetites; to remind them of the dignity of their nature; to awaken and improve their superior faculties, and direct them to the noblest objects; to possess men's minds with a high sense of Divinity, of the Supreme Good, and the immortality of the soul. They took great pains to strengthen the obligations to virtue; and upon all those subjects have wrought out noble theories, and treated with singular force of reason. But it seems our

minute philosophers act the reverse of all other wise and thinking men; it being their end and aim to erase the principles of all that is great and good from the mind of man, to unhinge all order of civil life, to undermine the foundations of morality, and, instead of improving and ennobling our natures, to bring us down to the maxims and way of thinking of the most uneducated and barbarous nations, and even to degrade humankind to a level with the brute beasts. And all the while they would pass upon the world for men of deep knowledge. But, in effect, what is all this negative knowledge better than downright savage ignorance? That there is no Providence, no spirit, no future state, no moral duty: truly a fine system for an honest man to own, or an ingenious man to value himself upon!

Alciphron, who heard this discourse with some uneasiness, very gravely replied: – Disputes are not to be decided by the weight of authority, but by the force of reason. You may pass, indeed, general reflexions on our notions, and call them brutal and barbarous if you please: but it is such brutality and such barbarism as few could have attained to if men of the greatest genius had not broken the ice, there being nothing more difficult than to get the better of education, and conquer old prejudices. To remove and cast off a heap of rubbish that has been gathering upon the soul from our very infancy requires great courage and great strength of faculties. Our philosophers, therefore, do well deserve the name of *esprits forts, men of strong heads, free-thinkers*, and such-like appellations, betokening great force and liberty of mind. It is very possible the heroic labours of these men may be represented (for what is not capable of misrepresentation?) as a piratical plundering, and stripping the mind of its wealth and ornaments, when it is in truth divesting it only of its prejudices, and reducing it to its untainted original state of nature. Oh nature! the genuine beauty of pure nature!

Euph. You seem very much taken with the beauty of nature. Be pleased to tell me, Alciphron, what those things are which you esteem natural, or by what mark I may know them.

14. *Alc.* For a thing to be natural, for instance, to the mind of man, it must appear originally therein; it must be universally in all men; it must be invariably the same in all nations and ages. These limitations of original, universal, and invariable, exclude all those notions found in the human mind which are the effect

of custom and education. The case is the same with respect to all other species of beings. A cat, for example, hath a natural inclination to pursue a mouse, because it agrees with the forementioned marks. But, if a cat be taught to play tricks, you will not say those tricks are natural. For the same reason, if upon a plum tree, peaches and apricots are engrafted, nobody will say they are the natural growth of the plum tree.

Euph. But to return to man: it seems you allow those things alone to be natural to him which show themselves upon his first entrance into the world; to wit, the senses, and such passions and appetites as are discovered upon the first application of their respective objects.

Alc. That is my opinion.

Euph. Tell me, Alciphron, if from a young apple tree, after a certain period of time, there should shoot forth leaves, blossoms, and apples; would you deny these things to be natural, because they did not discover and display themselves in the tender bud?

Alc. I would not.

Euph. And suppose that in a man, after a certain season, the appetite of lust, or the faculty of reason shall shoot forth, open, and display themselves, as leaves and blossoms do in a tree; would you, therefore, deny them to be natural to him, because they did not appear in his original infancy?

Alc. I acknowledge I would not.

Euph. It seems, therefore, that the first mark of a thing's being natural to the mind was not warily laid down by you; to wit, that it should appear originally in it.

Alc. It seems so.

Euph. Again, inform me, Alciphron, whether you do not think it natural for an orange-plant tree to produce oranges?

Alc. I do.

Euph. But plant it in the north end of Great Britain, and it shall with care produce, perhaps, a good salad; in the southern parts of the same island, it may, with much pains and culture, thrive and produce indifferent fruit; but in Portugal or Naples it will produce much better with little or no pains. Is this true or not?

Alc. It is true.

Euph. The plant being the same in all places doth not produce the same fruit – sun, soil, and cultivation making a difference.

46

Alc. I grant it.

Euph. And, since the case is, you say, the same with respect to all species, why may we not conclude, by a parity of reason, that things may be natural to humankind, and yet neither found in all men, nor invariably the same where they are found?

Alc. Hold, Euphranor, you must explain yourself further. I shall not be over hasty in my concessions.

Lys. You are in the right, Alciphron, to stand upon your guard. I do not like these ensnaring questions.

Euph. I desire you to make no concessions in complaisance to me, but only to tell me your opinion upon each particular, that we may understand one another, know wherein we agree, and proceed jointly in finding out the truth. But (added Euphranor, turning to Crito and me) if the gentlemen are against a free and fair inquiry, I shall give them no further trouble.

Alc. Our opinions will stand the test. We fear no trial; proceed as you please.

Euph. It seems then that, from what you have granted, it should follow things may be natural to men, although they do not actually show themselves in all men, nor in equal perfection; there being a great difference of culture, and every other advantage, with respect to human nature, as is to be found with respect to the vegetable nature of plants, to use your own similitude; is it so or not?

Alc. It is.

Euph. Answer me, Alciphron, do not men in all times and places, when they arrive at a certain age, express their thoughts by speech?

Alc. They do.

Euph. Should it not seem, then, that language is natural?

Alc. It should.

Euph. And yet there is a great variety of languages?

Alc. I acknowledge there is.

Euph. From all this will it not follow a thing may be natural and yet admit of variety?

Alc. I grant it will.

Euph. Should it not seem, therefore, to follow that a thing may be natural to mankind, though it have not those marks or conditions assigned; though it be not original, universal, and invariable?

Alc. It should.

Euph. And that, consequently, religious worship and civil government may be natural to man, notwithstanding they admit of sundry forms and different degrees of perfection?

Alc. It seems so.

Euph. You have granted already that reason is natural to mankind.

Alc. I have.

Euph. Whatever, therefore, is agreeable to reason is agreeable to the nature of man.

Alc. It is.

Euph. Will it not follow from hence that truth and virtue are natural to man?

Alc. Whatever is reasonable I admit to be natural.

Euph. And, as those fruits which grow from the most generous and mature stock, in the choicest soil, and with the best culture, are most esteemed; even so ought we not to think those sublime truths, which are the fruits of mature thought, and have been rationally deduced by men of the best and most improved understandings, to be the choicest productions of the rational nature of man? And, if so, being in fact reasonable, natural, and true, they ought not to be esteemed unnatural whims, errors of education, and groundless prejudices, because they are raised and forwarded by manuring and cultivating our tender minds, because they take early root, and sprout forth betimes by the care and diligence of our instructors?

Alc. Agreed, provided still they may be rationally deduced: but to take this for granted of what men vulgarly call the truths of morality and religion, would be begging the question.

Euph. You are in the right: I do not, therefore, take for granted that they are rationally deduced. I only suppose that, if they are, they must be allowed natural to man; or, in other words, agreeable to, and growing from, the most excellent and peculiar part of human nature.

Alc. I have nothing to object to this.

Euph. What shall we think then of your former assertions – that nothing is natural to man but what may be found in all men, in all nations and ages of the world; that, to obtain a genuine view of human nature, we must extirpate all the effects of education and instruction, and regard only the senses, appetites, and passions, which are to be found originally in all mankind; that, therefore, the notion of a God can have no foundation in nature,

48

as not being originally in the mind, nor the same in all men? Be pleased to reconcile these things with your late concessions, which the force of truth seems to have extorted from you.

15. *Alc.* Tell me, Euphranor, whether truth be not one and the same, uniform, invariable thing: and, if so, whether the many different and inconsistent notions which men entertain of God and duty be not a plain proof there is no truth in them?

Euph. That truth is constant and uniform I freely own, and that consequently opinions repugnant to each other cannot be true: but I think it will not hence follow they are all alike false. If, among various opinions about the same thing, one be grounded on clear and evident reasons, that is to be thought true, and others only so far as they consist with it. Reason is the same, and rightly applied will lead to the same conclusions, in all times and places. Socrates, two thousand years ago, seems to have reasoned himself into the same notion of a God which is entertained by the philosophers of our days, if you will allow that name to any who are not of your sect.[2] And the remark of Confucius, that a man should guard in his youth against lust, in manhood against faction, and in old age against covetousness, is as current morality in Europe as in China.

Alc. But still it would be a satisfaction if all men thought the same way, difference of opinions implying uncertainty.

Euph. Tell me, Alciphron, what you take to be the cause of a lunar eclipse.

Alc. The shadow of the earth interposing between the sun and moon.

Euph. Are you sure of this?

Alc. Undoubtedly.

Euph. Are all mankind agreed in this truth?

Alc. By no means. Ignorant and barbarous people assign different ridiculous causes of this appearance.

Euph. It seems, then, there are different opinions about the nature of an eclipse.

Alc. There are.

Euph. And nevertheless one of these opinions is true.

Alc. It is.

Euph. Diversity, therefore, of opinions about a thing, doth

---

[2] [In 1732a this read 'who are not atheists.']

not hinder but that thing may be, and one of the opinions concerning it may be true.

Alc. This I acknowledge.

Euph. It should seem, therefore, that your argument against the belief of a God from the variety of opinions about his nature is not conclusive. Nor do I see how you can conclude against the truth of any moral or religious tenet, from the various opinions of men upon the same subject. Might not a man as well argue, that no historical account of a matter of fact can be true, when different relations are given of it? Or, may we not as well infer that, because the several sects of philosophy maintain different opinions, none of them can be in the right, not even the minute philosophers themselves?

During this conversation Lysicles seemed uneasy, like one that wished in his heart there was no God. Alciphron, said he, methinks you sit by very tamely, while Euphranor saps the foundation of our tenets.

Be of good courage, replied Alciphron: a skilful gamester has been known to ruin his adversary by yielding him some advantage at first. I am glad, said he, turning to Euphranor, that you are drawn in to argue, and make your appeals to reason. For my part, wherever reason leads I shall not be afraid to follow. Know then, Euphranor, that I freely give up what you now contend for. I do not value the success of a few crude notions thrown out in a loose discourse, any more than the Turks do the loss of that vile infantry which they place in the front of their armies, for no other end but to waste the powder, and blunt the swords of their enemies. Be assured I have in reserve a body of otherguess[3] arguments, which I am ready to produce. I will undertake to prove . . .

Euph. O Alciphron! I do not doubt your faculty of proving. But, before I put you to the trouble of any farther proofs, I should be glad to know whether the notions of your minute philosophy are worth proving. I mean, whether they are of use and service to mankind.

16. *Alc.* As to that, give me leave to tell you, a thing may be useful to one man's views, and not to another's: but truth is truth, whether useful or not, and must not be measured by the convenience of this or that man, or party of men.

---

[3] [That is: different, or of another kind.]

Euph. But is not the general good of mankind to be regarded as a rule or measure of moral truths, of all such truths as direct or influence the moral actions of men?

Alc. That point is not clear to me. I know, indeed, that legislators, and divines, and politicians have always alleged, that it is necessary to the well-being of mankind that they should be kept in awe by the slavish notions of religion and morality.[4] But, granting all this, how will it prove these notions to be true? Convenience is one thing, and truth is another. A genuine philosopher, therefore, will overlook all advantages, and consider only truth itself as such.

Euph. Tell me, Alciphron, is your genuine philosopher a wise man, or a fool?

Alc. Without question, the wisest of men.

Euph. Which is to be thought the wise man, he who acts with design, or he who acts at random?

Alc. He who acts with design.

Euph. Whoever acts with design, acts for some end: doth he not?

Alc. He doth.

Euph. And a wise man for a good end?

Alc. True.

Euph. And he showeth his wisdom in making choice of fit means to obtain his end?

Alc. I acknowledge it.

Euph. By how much, therefore, the end proposed is more excellent, and by how much fitter the means employed are to obtain it, so much the wiser is the agent to be esteemed?

Alc. This seems to be true.

Euph. Can a rational agent propose a more excellent end than happiness?

Alc. He cannot.

Euph. Of good things, the greater good is most excellent?

Alc. Doubtless.

Euph. Is not the general happiness of mankind a greater good than the private happiness of one man, or of some certain men?

Alc. It is.

Euph. Is it not therefore the most excellent end?

Alc. It seems so.

[4] The moral virtues are the political offspring which flattery begot upon pride. *Fable of the Bees*, Part I, p. 37. [Note added to 1752 edition.]

Euph. Are not then those who pursue this end, by the properest methods, to be thought the wisest men?

Alc. I grant they are.

Euph. Which is a wise man governed by, wise or foolish notions?

Alc. By wise, doubtless.

Euph. It seems then to follow, that he who promotes the general well-being of mankind, by the proper necessary means, it truly wise, and acts upon wise grounds.

Alc. It should seem so.

Euph. And is not folly of an opposite nature to wisdom?

Alc. It is.

Euph. Might it not therefore be inferred, that those men are foolish who go about to unhinge such principles as have a necessary connexion with the general good of mankind?

Alc. Perhaps this might be granted: but at the same time I must observe that it is in my power to deny it.

Euph. How! you will not surely deny the conclusion, when you admit the premises?

Alc. I would fain know upon what terms we argue; whether in this progress of question and answer, if a man makes a slip, it be utterly irretrievable? For, if you are on the catch to lay hold of every advantage, without allowing for surprise or inattention, I must tell you this is not the way to convince my judgment.

Euph. O Alciphron! I aim not at triumph, but at truth. You are therefore at full liberty to unravel all that hath been said, and to recover or correct any slip you have made. But then you must distinctly point it out: otherwise it will be impossible ever to arrive at any conclusion.

Alc. I agree with you upon these terms jointly to proceed in search of truth, for to that I am sincerely devoted. In the progress of our present inquiry, I was, it seems, guilty of an oversight, in acknowledging the general happiness of mankind to be a greater good than the particular happiness of one man. For in fact the individual happiness of every man alone constitutes his own entire good. The happiness of other men, making no part of mine, is not with respect to me a good: I mean a true natural good. It cannot therefore be a reasonable end to be proposed by me, in truth and nature (for I do not speak of political pretences), since no wise man will pursue an end which doth not concern

52

him. This is the voice of nature. O nature! thou art the fountain, original, and pattern of all that is good and wise.

Euph. You would like then to follow nature, and propose her as a guide and pattern for your imitation?

Alc. Of all things.

Euph. Whence do you gather this respect for nature?

Alc. From the excellency of her productions.

Euph. In a vegetable, for instance, you say there is use and excellency; because the several parts of it are so connected and fitted to each other as to protect and nourish the whole, make the individual grow, and propagate the kind; and because in its fruits or qualities it is adapted to please the sense, or contribute to the benefit of man.

Alc. Even so.

Euph. In like manner, do you not infer the excellency of animal bodies from observing the frame and fitness of their several parts, by which they mutually conspire to the well-being of each other as well as of the whole? Do you not also observe a natural union and consent between animals of the same kind; and that even different kinds of animals have certain qualities and instincts whereby they contribute to the exercise, nourishment, and delight of each other? Even the inanimate unorganized elements seem to have an excellence relative to each other. Where was the excellency of water, if it did not cause herbs and vegetables to spring from the earth, and put forth flowers and fruits? And what would become of the beauty of the earth, if it was not warmed by the sun, moistened by water, and fanned by air? Throughout the whole system of the visible and natural world, do you not perceive a mutual connexion and correspondence of parts? And is it not from hence that you frame an idea of the perfection, and order, and beauty of nature?

Alc. All this I grant.

Euph. And have not the Stoics heretofore said (who were no more bigots than you are), and did you not yourself say, this pattern of order was worthy the imitation of rational agents?

Alc. I do not deny this to be true.

Euph. Ought we not, therefore, to infer the same union, order, and regularity in the moral world that we perceive to be in the natural?

Alc. We ought.

Euph. Should it not therefore seem to follow, that reasonable creatures were, as the philosophical Emperor[5] observes, made one for another; and, consequently, that *man* ought not to consider himself as an independent individual, whose happiness is not connected with that of other men; but rather as the part of a whole, to the common good of which he ought to conspire, and order his ways and actions suitably, if he would live according to nature?

Alc. Supposing this to be true, what then?

Euph. Will it not follow that a wise man should consider and pursue his private good, with regard to, and in conjunction with that of other men? In granting of which, you thought yourself guilty of an oversight. Though, indeed, the sympathy of pain and pleasure, and the mutual affections by which mankind are knit together have been always allowed a plain proof of this point: and though it was the constant doctrine of those who were esteemed the wisest and most thinking men among the ancients, as the Platonists, Peripatetics, and Stoics; to say nothing of Christians, whom you pronounce to be an unthinking, prejudiced sort of people.

Alc. I shall not dispute this point with you.

Euph. Since, therefore, we are so far agreed, should it not seem to follow from the premises – that the belief of a God, of a future state, and or moral duties are the only wise, right, and genuine principles of human conduct, in case they have a necessary connexion with the well-being of mankind? This conclusion you have been led to by your own concessions, and by the analogy of nature.

Alc. I have been drawn into it step by step through several preliminaries, which I cannot well call to mind; but one thing I observe, that you build on the necessary connexion those principles have with the well-being of mankind, which is a point neither proved nor granted.

Lys. This I take to be a grand fundamental prejudice, as I doubt not, if I had time, I could make appear. But it is now late, and we will, if you think fit, defer this subject till tomorrow.

Upon which motion of Lysicles, we put an end to our conversation for that evening.

---

[5] M. Antonin. lib. iv. [3.]

THE THIRD DIALOGUE

1. The following day, as we sat round the tea-table, in a summer parlour which looks into the garden, Alciphron after the first dish turned down his cup, and, reclining back on his chair, proceeded as follows. Above all the sects upon earth, it is the peculiar privilege of ours, not to be tied down by any principles. While other philosophers profess a servile adherence to certain tenets, ours assert a noble freedom, differing not only one from another, but very often the same man from himself. Which method of proceeding, beside other advantages, hath this annexed to it, that we are of all men the hardest to confute. You may, perhaps, confute a particular tenet, but then this affects only him who maintains it, and so long only as he maintains it. Some of our sect dogmatize more than others, and in some more than other points. The doctrine of the usefulness of vice is a point wherein we are not all agreed. Some of us are great admirers of virtue. With others the points of vice and virtue are problematical. For my part, though I think the doctrine maintained yesterday by Lysicles an ingenious speculation; yet upon the whole, there are divers reasons which incline me to depart from it, and rather to espouse the virtuous side of the question; with the smallest, per-haps, but the most contemplative and laudable part of our sect. It seemeth, I say, after a nice inquiry and balancing on both sides, that we ought to prefer virtue to vice; and that such preference would contribute both to the public weal, and the reputation of our philosophers.

You are to know then, we have among us several that, without one grain of religion, are men of the nicest honour, and therefore men of virtue because men of honour. Honour is a noble unpol-luted source of virtue, without the least mixture of fear, interest, or superstition. It hath all the advantages without the evils which attend religion. It is the mark of a great and fine soul, and is to be found among persons of rank and breeding. It affects the court, the senate, and the camp, and in general every rendezvous of people of fashion.

Euph. You say then that honour is the source of virtue?

Alc. I do.

Euph. Can a thing be the source of itself?

Alc. It cannot.

Euph. The source, therefore, is distinguished from that of which it is the source?

Alc. Doubtless.

Euph. Honour then is one thing, and virtue another?

Alc. I grant it. Virtuous actions are the effect, and honour is the source or cause of that effect.

Euph. Tell me. Is honour the will producing those actions, or the final cause for which they are produced; or right reason which is their rule and limit, or the object about which they are conversant? Or do you by the word *honour* understand a faculty or appetite? all which are supposed, in one sense or other, to be the source of human actions.

Alc. Nothing of all this.

Euph. Be pleased then to give me some notion or definition of it.

Alciphron, having mused a while, answered, that he defined honour to be a principle of virtuous actions. To which Euphranor replied: If I understand it rightly, the word principle is variously taken. Sometimes by principles we mean the parts of which a whole is composed, and into which it may be resolved. Thus the elements are said to be principles of compound bodies. And thus words, syllables, and letters are the principles of speech. Sometimes by principle we mean a small particular seed, the growth or gradual unfolding of which doth produce an organized body, animal or vegetable, in its proper size and shape. Principles at other times are supposed to be certain fundamental theorems in arts and sciences, in religion and politics. Let me know in which of these senses, or whether it be in some other sense, that you understand this word, when you say, honour is a principle of virtue.

To this Alciphron replied, that for his part he meant it in none of those senses, but defined honour to be a certain ardour of enthusiasm that glowed in the breast of a gallant man.

Upon this, Euphranor observed, it was always admitted to put the definition in place of the thing defined. Is this allowed, said he, or not?

Alc. It is.

Euph. May we not therefore say, that a man of honour is a warm man, or an enthusiast?

Alciphron, hearing this, declared that such exactness was to no purpose; that pedants, indeed, may dispute and define, but could never reach that high sense of honour which distinguished the fine gentleman, and was a thing rather to be felt than explained.

2. Crito, perceiving that Alciphron could not bear being pressed any further on that article, and willing to give some satisfaction to Euphranor, said that of himself indeed he should not undertake to explain so nice a point, but he would retail to them part of a conversation he once heard between *Nicander* a minute philosopher and *Menecles* a Christian, upon the same subject, which was for substance as follows.

M. From what principle are you gentlemen virtuous?

N. From honour. We are men of honour.

M. May not a man of honour debauch another's wife, or get drunk, or sell a vote, or refuse to pay his debts, without lessening or tainting his honour?

N. He may have the vices and faults of a gentleman: but is obliged to pay debts of honour, that is, all such as are contracted by play.

M. Is not your man of honour always ready to resent affronts and engage in duels?

N. He is ready to demand and give gentleman's satisfaction upon all proper occasions.

M. It should seem, by this account, that to ruin tradesmen, break faith to one's own wife, corrupt another man's, take bribes, cheat the public, cut a man's throat for a word, are all points consistent with your principle of honour.

N. It cannot be denied that we are men of gallantry, men of fire, men who know the world, and all that.

M. It seems therefore that honour among infidels is like honesty among pirates; something confined to themselves, and which the fraternity perhaps may find their account in, but everyone else should be constantly on his guard against.

By this dialogue, continued Crito, a man who lives out of the *grand monde* may be enabled to form some notion of what the world calls honour and men of honour.

Euph. I must entreat you not to put me off with Nicander's opinion, whom I know nothing of, but rather give me your own judgment, drawn from your own observation upon men of honour.

Cri. If I must pronounce, I can very sincerely assure you that, by all I have heard or seen, I could never find that honour, considered as a principle distinct from conscience, religion, reason, and virtue, was more than an empty name. And I do verily believe that those who build upon that notion have less virtue than other men; and that what they have, or seem to have, is owing to fashion (being of the reputable kind), if not to a conscience early imbued with religious principles, and afterwards retaining a tincture from them without knowing it. These two principles seem to account for all that looks like virtue in those gentlemen. Your men of fashion, in whom animal life abounds, a sort of bullies in morality, who disdain to have it thought they are afraid of conscience; these descant much upon honour, and affect to be called men of honour, rather than conscientious or honest men. But, by all that I could ever observe, this specious character, where there is nothing of conscience or religion underneath, to give it life and substance, is no better than a meteor or painted cloud.

Euph. I had a confused notion that honour was something nearly connected with truth; and that men of honour were the greatest enemies to all hypocrisy, fallacy, and disguise.

Cri. So far from that, an infidel, who sets up for the nicest honour, shall, without the least grain of faith or religion, pretend himself a Christian, take any test, join in any act of worship, kneel, pray, receive the sacrament, to serve an interest. The same person, without any impeachment of his honour, shall most solemnly declare and promise, in the face of God and the world, that he will love his wife, and forsaking all others keep only to her, when at the same time it is certain he intends never to perform one tittle of his vow; and convinceth the whole world of this as soon as he gets her in his power, and her fortune, for the sake of which this man of untainted honour makes no scruple to cheat and lie.

Euph.   We had a notion here in the country that it was of all things most odious, and a matter of much risk and peril, to give the lie to a man of honour.

Cri.   It is very true. He abhors to take the lie, but not to tell it.

3.   Alciphron, having heard all this with great composure of mind and countenance, spake as follows:- The word free-thinker, as it comprehends men of very different sorts and sentiments, cannot, in a strict sense, be said to constitute one particular sect, holding a certain system of positive and distinct opinions. Though it must be owned we do all agree in certain points of unbelief, or negative principles, which agreement, in some sense, unites us under the common idea of one sect. But then, those negative principles, as they happen to take root in men of different age, temper, and education, do produce various tendencies, opinions, and characters, widely differing one from another.[1] You are not to think that our greatest strength lies in our greatest number – libertines, and mere men of honour. No: we have among us philosophers of a very different character, men of curious contemplation, not governed by such gross things as sense and custom, but of an abstracted virtue and sublime morals: and the less religious the more virtuous. For virtue of the high and disinterested kind no man is so well qualified as an infidel; it being a mean and selfish thing to be virtuous through fear or hope. The notion of a Providence, and future state of rewards and punishments, may indeed tempt or scare men of abject spirit into practices contrary to the natural bent of their souls, but will never produce a true and genuine virtue. To go to the bottom of things, to analyse virtue into its first principles, and fix a scheme of duty on its true basis, you must understand that there is an idea of beauty natural to the mind of man. This all men desire, this they are pleased and delighted with for its own sake, purely from an instinct of nature. A man needs no arguments to make him discern and approve what is beautiful; it strikes at first sight, and attracts without a reason. And as this beauty is found in the shape and form of corporeal things; so also is there analogous to it a beauty of another kind, an order, a symmetry, and comeliness,

[1] [Alciphron's speech from its beginning to this point was added in 1752.]

in the moral world. And as the eye perceiveth the one, so the mind doth, by a certain interior sense, perceive the other; which sense, talent, or faculty is ever quickest and purest in the noblest minds. Thus, as by sight I discern the beauty of a plant or an animal, even so the mind apprehends the moral excellence, the beauty, and decorum of justice and temperance. And as we readily pronounce a dress becoming, or an attitude graceful, we can, with the same free untutored judgment, at once declare whether this or that conduct or action be comely and beautiful. To relish this kind of beauty there must be a delicate and fine taste; but, where there is this natural taste, nothing further is wanting, either as a principle to convince, or as a motive to induce men to the love of virtue. And more or less there is of this taste or sense in every creature that hath reason. All rational beings are by nature social. They are drawn one towards another by natural affections. They unite and incorporate into families, clubs, parties, and commonwealths by mutual sympathy. As, by means of the sensitive soul, our several distinct parts and members do consent towards the animal functions, and are connected in one whole; even so, the several parts of these rational systems or bodies politic, by virtue of this moral or interior sense, are held together, have a fellow feeling, do succour and protect each other, and jointly co-operate towards the same end. Hence that joy in society, that propension towards doing good to our kind, that gratulation and delight in beholding the virtuous deeds of other men, or in reflecting on our own. By contemplation of the fitness and order of the parts of a moral system, regularly operating, and knit together by benevolent affections, the mind of man attaineth to the highest notion of beauty, excellence, and perfection. Seized and rapt with this sublime idea, our philosophers do infinitely despise and pity whoever shall propose or accept any other motive to virtue. Interest is a mean ungenerous thing, destroying the merit of virtue; and falsehood of every kind is inconsistent with the genuine spirit of philosophy.

Cri. The love therefore that you bear to moral beauty, and your passion for abstracted truth, will not suffer you to think with patience of those fraudulent impositions upon mankind, providence, the immortality of the soul, and a future retribution of rewards and punishments; which, under the notion of promoting, do, it seems, destroy all true virtue, and at the same time contradict and disparage your noble theories, manifestly tending to the perturbation and disquiet of men's minds, and filling them with fruitless hopes and vain terrors.

Alc. Men's first thoughts and natural notions are the best in moral matters. And there is no need that mankind should be preached, or reasoned, or frightened into virtue, a thing so natural and congenial to every human soul. Now, if this be the case, as it certainly is, it follows that all the ends of society are secured without religion, and that an infidel bids fair to be the most virtuous man, in a true, sublime, and heroic sense.

4. *Euph.* O Alciphron, while you talk, I feel an affection in my soul like the trembling of one lute upon striking the unison strings of another. Doubtless there is a beauty of the mind, a charm in virtue, a symmetry and proportion in the moral world. This moral beauty was known to the ancients by the name of *honestum*, or τὸ καλὸν. And, in order to know its force and influence, it may not be amiss to inquire what it was understood to be, and what light it was placed in, by those who first considered it, and gave it a name. Τὸ καλὸν, according to Aristotle, is the ἐπαινετὸν or laudable; according to Plato, it is the ἡδὺ or ὠφέλιμον, pleasant or profitable, which is meant with respect to a reasonable mind and its true interest.[2] Now, I would fain know whether a mind which considers an action as laudable be not carried beyond the bare action itself, to regard the opinion of others concerning it?

Alc. It is.

Euph. And whether this be a sufficient ground or principle of virtue, for a man to act upon, when he thinks himself removed from the eye and observation of every other intelligent being?

Alc. It seems not.

Euph. Again: I ask whether a man who doth a thing pleasant or profitable, as such, must not be supposed to forbear doing it, or even to do the contrary, upon the prospect of greater pleasure or profit?

Alc. He must.

Euph. Doth it not follow from hence that the beauty of virtue, or τὸ καλὸν, in either Aristotle's or Plato's sense, is not a sufficient principle or ground to engage sensual and worldly minded men in the practice of it?

---

[2] [Aristotle, *Nicomachean Ethics*, 1109a, 29; 1144a, 26; 1169a, 30–1. Plato, *Protagoras*, 358b.]

Alc. What then?

Euph. Why then it will follow that hope of reward and fear of punishment are highly expedient to cast the balance of pleasant and profitable on the side of virtue, and thereby very much conduce to the benefit of human society.

Alciphron upon this appealed:- Gentlemen, said he, you are witnesses of this unfair proceeding of Euphranor, who argues against us from explications given by Plato and Aristotle of the beauty of virtue, which are things we have nothing to say to; the philosophers of our sect abstracting from all praise, pleasure, and interest, when they are enamoured and transported with that sublime idea.

I beg pardon, replied Euphranor, for supposing the minute philosophers of our days think like those ancient sages. But you must tell me, Alciphron, since you do not think fit to adopt the sense of Plato or Aristotle, what sense it is in which you understand the beauty of virtue. Define it, explain it, make me to understand your meaning, that so we may argue about the same thing, without which we can never come to a conclusion.

5. *Alc.* Some things are better understood by definitions and descriptions; but I have always observed that those who would define, explain, and dispute about this point make the least of it. Moral beauty is of so peculiar and abstracted a nature, something so subtle, fine, and fugacious, that it will not bear being handled and inspected, like every gross and common subject. You will, therefore, pardon me if I stand upon my philosophic liberty; and choose rather to intrench myself within the general and indefinite sense, rather than, by entering into a precise and particular explication of this beauty, perchance lose sight of it; or give you some hold whereon to cavil, and infer, and raise doubts, queries, and difficulties about a point as clear as the sun, when nobody reasons upon it.

Euph. How say you, Alciphron, is that notion clearest when it is not considered?

Alc. I say it is rather to be felt than understood – a certain *je ne sais quoi*. An object, not of the discursive faculty, but of a peculiar sense, which is properly called the *moral sense*, being adapted to the perception of moral beauty, as the eye to colours, or the ear to sounds.

Euph. That men have certain instinctive sensations or passions from nature, which make them amiable and useful to each other, I am clearly convinced. Such are a fellow-feeling with the distressed, a tenderness for our offspring, an affection towards our friends, our neighbours, and our country, an indignation against things base, cruel, or unjust. These passions are implanted in the human soul, with several other fears and appetites, aversions and desires, some of which are strongest and uppermost in one mind, others in another. Should it not therefore seem a very uncertain guide in morals, for a man to follow his passion or inward feeling; and would not this rule infallibly lead different men different ways, according to the prevalency of this or that appetite or passion?

Alc. I do not deny it.

Euph. And will it not follow from hence that duty and virtue are in a fairer way of being practised, if men are led by reason and judgment, balancing low and sensual pleasures with those of a higher kind, comparing present losses with future gains, and the uneasiness and disgust of every vice with the delightful practice of the opposite virtue, and the pleasing reflexions and hopes which attend it? Or can there be a stronger motive to virtue than the showing that, considered in all lights, it is every man's true interest?

6. *Alc.* I tell you, Euphranor, we condemn the virtue of that man who computes and deliberates, and must have a reason for being virtuous. The refined moralists of our sect are ravished and transported with the abstract beauty of virtue. They disdain all forensic motives to it; and love virtue only for virtue's sake. Oh rapture! oh enthusiasm! oh the quintessence of beauty! methinks I could dwell for ever on this contemplation: but, rather than entertain myself, I must endeavour to convince you. Make an experiment on the first man you meet. Propose a villainous or unjust action. Take his first sense of the matter, and you shall find he detests it. He may, indeed, be afterwards misled by arguments, or overpowered by temptation; but his original, unpremeditated, and genuine thoughts are just and orthodox. How can we account for this but by a moral sense, which, left to itself, hath as quick and true a perception of the beauty and deformity of human actions as the eye hath of colours?

Euph. May not this be sufficiently accounted for by conscience, affection, passion, education, reason, custom, religion;

which principles and habits, for aught I know, may be what you metaphorically call a moral sense?

Alc. What I call a moral sense is strictly, properly, and truly such, and in kind different from all those things you enumerate. It is what all men have, though all may not observe it.

Upon this Euphranor smiled and said, Alciphron has made discoveries where I least expected it. For, said he, in regard to every other point I should hope to learn from him; but for the knowledge of myself, or the faculties and powers of my own mind, I should have looked at home. And there I might have looked long enough without finding this new talent, which even now, after being tutored, I cannot comprehend. For Alciphron, I must needs say, is too sublime and enigmatical upon a point which of all others ought to be most clearly understood. I have often heard that your deepest adepts and oldest professors in science are the obscurest. Lysicles is young, and speaks plain. Would he but favour us with his sense of this point, it might perhaps prove more upon a level with my apprehension.

7. Lysicles shook his head, and in a grave and earnest manner addressed the company. Gentlemen, said he, Alciphron stands upon his own legs. I have no part in these refined notions he is at present engaged to defend. If I must subdue my passions, abstract, contemplate, be enamoured of virtue; in a word, if I must be an enthusiast, I owe so much deference to the laws of my country as to choose being an enthusiast in their way. Besides, it is better being so for some end than for none. This doctrine hath all the solid inconveniences, without the amusing hopes and prospects, of the Christian.

Alc. I never counted on Lysicles for my second in this point; which after all doth not need his assistance or explication. All subjects ought not to be treated in the same manner. The way of definition and division is dry and pedantic. Besides, the subject is sometimes too obscure, sometimes too simple for this method. One while we know too little of a point, another too much, to make it plainer by discourse.

Cri. To hear Alciphron talk puts me in mind of that ingenious Greek who, having wrapped a man's brother up in a cloak, asked him whether he knew that person; being ready, either by keeping on or pulling off the cloak, to confute his answer, whatever it should be. For my part, I believe, if matters were fairly stated, that rational satisfaction, that peace of mind, that inward comfort, and conscientious joy, which a good Christian finds in good actions, would not be found to fall short of all the ecstasy, rapture, and enthusiasm supposed to be the effect of that high and undescribed principle. In earnest, can any ecstasy be higher, any rapture more affecting, than that which springs from the love of God and man, from a conscience void of offence, and an inward discharge of duty, with the secret delight, trust, and hope that attend it?

Alc. O Euphranor, we votaries of truth do not envy but pity the groundless joys and mistaken hopes of a Christian. And, as for conscience and rational pleasure, how can we allow a conscience without allowing a vindictive Providence? Or how can we suppose the charm of virtue consists in any pleasure or benefit attending virtuous actions,[3] without giving great advantages to the Christian religion, which, it seems, excites its believers to virtue by the highest interests and pleasures in reversion. Alas! should we grant this, there would be a door opened to all those rusty declaimers upon the necessity and usefulness of the great points of faith, the immortality of the soul, a future state, rewards and punishments, and the like exploded conceits; which, according to our system and principles, may perhaps produce a low, popular, interested kind of virtue, but must absolutely destroy and extinguish it in the sublime and heroic sense.

8. *Euph.* What you now say is very intelligible: I wish I understood your main principle as well.

Alc. And are you then in earnest at a loss? Is it possible you should have no notion of beauty, or that having it you should not know it to be amiable – amiable, I say, in itself and for itself?

Euph. Pray tell me, Alciphron, are all mankind agreed in the notion of a beauteous face?

Alc. Beauty in humankind seems to be of a mixed and various nature; forasmuch as the passions, sentiments, and qualities of the soul, being seen through and blending with the features, work differently on different minds, as the sympathy is more or less. But with regard to other things is there no steady principle of

---

[3] There can never be less self-enjoyment than in these supposed wise characters, these selfish computers of happiness and private good. *Characteristics*, vol. III, p. 301. [Note added to 1752.]

beauty? Is there upon earth a human mind without the idea of order, harmony, and proportion?

Euph. O Alciphron, it is my weakness that I am apt to be lost in abstractions and generalities, but a particular thing is better suited to my faculties. I find it easy to consider and keep in view the objects of sense: let us therefore try to discover what their beauty is, or wherein it consists; and so, by the help of these sensible things, as a scale or ladder, ascend to moral and intellectual beauty. Be pleased then to inform me, what is it we call beauty in the objects of sense?

Alc. Everyone knows beauty is that which pleases.

Euph. There is then beauty in the smell of a rose, or the taste of an apple?

Alc. By no means. Beauty is, to speak properly, perceived only by the eye.

Euph. It cannot therefore be defined in general that which pleaseth?

Alc. I grant it cannot.

Euph. How then shall we limit or define it?

Alciphron, after a short pause, said that beauty consisted in a certain symmetry or proportion pleasing to the eye.

Euph. Is this proportion one and the same in all things, or is it different in different kinds of things?

Alc. Different, doubtless. The proportions of an ox would not be beautiful in a horse. And we may observe also in things inanimate, that the beauty of a table, a chair, a door, consists in different proportions.

Euph. Doth not this proportion imply the relation of one thing to another?

Alc. It doth.

Euph. And are not these relations founded in size and shape?

Alc. They are.

Euph. And, to make the proportions just, must not those mutual relations of size and shape in the parts be such as shall make the whole complete and perfect in its kind?

Alc. I grant they must.

Euph. Is not a thing said to be perfect in its kind when it answers the end for which it was made?

Alc. It is.

Euph. The parts, therefore, in true proportions must be so related, and adjusted to one another, as that they may best conspire to the use and operation of the whole?

Alc. It seems so.

Euph. But the comparing parts one with another, the considering them as belonging to one whole, and the referring this whole to its use or end, should seem the work of reason: should it not?

Alc. It should.

Euph. Proportions, therefore, are not, strictly speaking, perceived by the sense of sight, but only by reason through the means of sight.

Alc. This I grant.

Euph. Consequently, beauty, in your sense of it, is an object, not of the eye, but of the mind.

Alc. It is.

Euph. The eye, therefore, alone cannot see that a chair is handsome, or a door well proportioned.

Alc. It seems to follow; but I am not clear as to this point.

Euph. Let us see if there be any difficulty in it. Could the chair you sit on, think you, be reckoned well proportioned or handsome, if it had not such a height, breadth, wideness, and was not so far reclined as to afford a convenient seat?

Alc. It could not.

Euph. The beauty, therefore, or symmetry of a chair cannot be apprehended but by knowing its use, and comparing its figure with that use; which cannot be done by the eye alone, but is the effect of judgment. It is, therefore, one thing to see an object, and another to discern its beauty.

Alc. I admit this to be true.

9. *Euph.* The architects judge a door to be of a beautiful proportion, when its height is double of the breadth. But if you should invert a well-proportioned door, making its breadth become the height, and its height the breadth, the figure would still be the same, but without that beauty in one situation which it had in another. What can be the cause of this, but that, in the forementioned supposition, the door would not yield convenient entrances to creatures of a human figure? But, if in any other part of the universe there should be supposed rational animals of an inverted stature, they must be supposed to invert the rule for

proportion of doors; and to them that would appear beautiful which to us was disagreeable.

Alc. Against this I have no objection.

Euph. Tell me, Alciphron, is there not something truly decent and beautiful in dress?

Alc. Doubtless, there is.

Euph. Are any likelier to give us an idea of this beauty in dress than painters and sculptors, whose proper business and study it is to aim at graceful representations?

Alc. I believe not.

Euph. Let us then examine the draperies of the great masters in these arts: how, for instance, they use to clothe a matron, or a man of rank. Cast an eye on those figures (said he, pointing to some prints after Raphael and Guido, that hung upon the wall): what appearance do you think an English courtier or magistrate, with his Gothic, succinct, plaited garment, and his full-bottomed wig; or one of our ladies in her unnatural dress, pinched and stiffened and enlarged, with hoops and whale-bone and buckram, must make, among those figures so decently clad in draperies that fall into such a variety of natural, easy, and ample folds, that cover the body without encumbering it, and adorn without altering the shape?

Alc. Truly I think they must make a very ridiculous appearance.

Euph. And what do you think this proceeds from? Whence is it that the eastern nations, the Greeks, and the Romans, naturally ran into the most becoming dresses; while our Gothic gentry, after so many centuries racking their inventions, mending, and altering, and improving, and whirling about in a perpetual rotation of fashions, have never yet had the luck to stumble on any that was not absurd and ridiculous? Is it not from hence that, instead of consulting use, reason, and convenience, they abandon themselves to irregular fancy, the unnatural parent of monsters? Whereas the ancients, considering the use and end of dress, made it subservient to the freedom, ease, and convenience of the body; and, having no notion of mending or changing the natural shape, they aimed only at showing it with decency and advantage. And, if this be so, are we not to conclude that the beauty of dress depends on its subserviency to certain ends and uses?

Alc. This appears to be true.

Euph. This subordinate relative nature of beauty, perhaps, will be yet plainer, if we examine the respective beauties of a horse and a pillar. Virgil's description of the former is –

Illi ardua cervix,
Argutumque caput, brevis alvus, obesaque terga,
Luxuriatque toris animosum pectus.[4]

Now, I would fain know whether the perfections and uses of a horse may not be reduced to these three points: courage, strength, and speed; and whether each of the beauties enumerated doth not occasion or betoken one of these perfections? After the same manner, if we inquire into the parts and proportions of a beautiful pillar, we shall perhaps find them answer to the same idea. Those who have considered the theory of architecture tell us,[5] the proportions of the three Grecian orders were taken from the human body, as the most beautiful and perfect production of nature. Hence were derived those graceful ideas of columns, which had a character of strength without clumsiness, or of delicacy without weakness. Those beautiful proportions were, I say, taken originally from nature, which, in her creatures, as hath been already observed, referreth them to some end, use, or design. The *gonfiezza* also, or swelling, and the diminution of a pillar, is it not in such proportion as to make it appear strong and light at the same time? In the same manner, must not the whole entablature, with its projections, be so proportioned, as to seem great but not heavy, light but not little; inasmuch as a deviation into either extreme would thwart that reason and use of things wherein their beauty is founded, and to which it is subordinate? The entablature, and all its parts and ornaments, architrave, frieze, cornice, triglyphs, metopes, modiglions, and the rest, have each a use or appearance of use, in giving firmness and union to the building, in protecting it from the weather and casting off the rain, in representing the ends of beams with their intervals, the production of rafters, and so forth. And if we consider the graceful angles in frontispieces, the spaces between the columns, or the ornaments of their capitals, shall we not find, that their beauty riseth from the appearance of use, or the imitation of natural things, whose beauty is originally founded on the same principle?

[4] [That is: 'He has a proud neck, a finely chiselled head, a short belly, well-rounded flanks, and his fiery chest ripples with muscles' (Virgil, *Georgics*, III, line 79ff.)]
[5] See the learned Patriarch of Aquileia's *Commentary on Vitruvius*, lib. iv, cap. I.

which is, indeed, the grand distinction between Grecian and Gothic architecture; the latter being fantastical, and for the most part founded neither in nature nor in reason, in necessity nor use, the appearance of which accounts for all the beauty, grace, and ornament of the other.

Cri. What Euphranor hath said confirms the opinion I always entertained, that the rules of architecture were founded, as all other arts which flourished among the Greeks, in truth, and nature, and good sense. But the ancients, who, from a thorough consideration of the grounds and principles of art, formed their idea of beauty, did not always confine themselves strictly to the same rules and proportions; but, whenever the particular distance, position, elevation, or dimension of the fabric or its parts seemed to require it, made no scruple to depart from them, without deserting the original principles of beauty, which governed whatever deviations they made. This latitude or licence might not, perhaps, be safely trusted with most modern architects, who in their bold sallies seem to act without aim or design; and to be governed by no idea, no reason, or principle of art, but pure caprice, joined with a thorough contempt of that noble simplicity of the ancients, without which there can be no unity, gracefulness, or grandeur in their works; which of consequence must serve only to disfigure and dishonour the nation, being so many monuments to future ages of the opulence and ill taste of the present; which, it is to be feared, would succeed as wretchedly, and make as mad work in other affairs, were men to follow, instead of rules, precepts, and morals, their own taste and first thoughts of beauty.

Alc. I should now, methinks, be glad to see a little more distinctly the use and tendency of this digression upon architecture.

Euph. Was not beauty the very thing we inquired after?

Alc. It was.

Euph. What think you, Alciphron, can the appearance of a thing please at this time, and in this place, which pleased two thousand years ago, and two thousand miles off, without some real principle of beauty?

Alc. It cannot.

Euph. And is not this the case with respect to a just piece of architecture?

Alc. Nobody denies it.

Euph. Architecture, the noble offspring of judgment and fancy, was gradually formed in the most polite and knowing countries of Asia, Egypt, Greece, and Italy. It was cherished and esteemed by the most flourishing states and most renowned princes, who with vast expense improved and brought it to perfection. It seems, above all other arts, peculiarly conversant about order, proportion, and symmetry. May it not therefore be supposed, on all accounts, most likely to help us to some rational notion of the *je ne sais quoi* in beauty? And, in effect, have we not learned from this digression that, as there is no beauty without proportion, so proportions are to be esteemed just and true, only as they are relative to some certain use or end, their aptitude and subordination to which end is, at bottom, that which makes them please and charm?

Alc. I admit all this to be true.

10. *Euph.* According to this doctrine, I would fain know what beauty can be found in a moral system, formed, connected, and governed by chance, fate, or any other blind unthinking principle? Forasmuch as without thought there can be no end or design; and without an end there can be no use; and without use there is no aptitude or fitness of proportion, from whence beauty springs.

Alc. May we not suppose a certain vital principle of beauty, order, and harmony, diffused throughout the world, without supposing a Providence inspecting, punishing, and rewarding the moral actions of men; without supposing the immortality of the soul, or a life to come; in a word, without admitting any part of what is commonly called faith, worship, and religion?

Cri. Either you suppose this principle intelligent, or not intelligent: if the latter, it is all one with chance or fate, which was just now argued against: if the former, let me entreat Alciphron to explain to me wherein consists the beauty of a moral system, with a supreme Intelligence at the head of it which neither protects the innocent, punishes the wicked, nor rewards the virtuous. To suppose indeed a society of rational agents, acting under the eye of Providence, concurring in one design to promote the common benefit of the whole, and conforming their actions to the established laws and order of the Divine paternal wisdom: wherein each particular agent shall not consider himself apart, but as the member of a great city, whose author and founder is God: in which the civil laws are no other than the rules of virtue and the duties of religion: and where everyone's true interest is combined with his duty: to suppose this would be delightful: on this supposition a man need be no Stoic or knight-errant, to account for his virtue. In such a system, vice is madness, cunning is folly, wisdom and virtue are the same thing; where, notwithstanding all the crooked paths and by-roads, the wayward appetites and inclinations of men, sovereign reason is sure to reform whatever seems amiss, to reduce that which is devious, make straight that which is crooked, and, in the last act, wind up the whole plot according to the exactest rules of wisdom and justice. In such a system or society, governed by the wisest precepts, enforced by the highest rewards and discouragements, it is delightful to consider how the regulation of laws, the distribution of good and evil, the aim of moral agents, do all conspire in due subordination to promote the noblest end, to wit, the complete happiness or well-being of the whole. In contemplating the beauty of such a moral system, we may cry out with the Psalmist, 'Very excellent things are spoken of thee, thou City of God.'

11. In a system of spirits, subordinate to the will, and under the direction of the Father of spirits, governing them by laws, and conducting them by methods suitable to wise and good ends, there will be great beauty. But in an incoherent fortuitous system, governed by chance, or in a blind system, governed by fate, or in any system where Providence doth not preside, how can beauty be, which cannot be without order, which cannot be without design? When a man is conscious that his will is inwardly conformed to the Divine will, producing order and harmony in the universe, and conducting the whole by the justest methods to the best end: this gives a beautiful idea. But, on the other hand, a consciousness of virtue overlooked, neglected, distressed by men, and not regarded or rewarded by God, ill-used in this world, without hope or prospect of being better used in another, I would fain know where is the pleasure of this reflexion, where is the beauty of this scene? Or, how could any man in his senses think the spreading such notions the way to spread or propagate virtue in the world? Is it not, I beseech you, an ugly system in which you can suppose no law and prove no duty, wherein men thrive by wickedness and suffer by virtue? Would it not be a disagreeable sight to see an honest man peeled by sharpers, to see virtuous

men injured and despised while vice triumphed? An enthusiast may entertain himself with visions and fine talk about such a system; but when it comes to be considered by men of cool heads and close reason, I believe they will find no beauty nor perfection in it; nor will it appear that such a moral system can possibly come from the same hand, or be of a piece with the natural, throughout which there shines so much order, harmony, and proportion.

Alc.   Your discourse serves to confirm me in my opinion. You may remember, I declared that touching this beauty of morality in the high sense, a man's first thoughts are the best; and that, if we pretend to examine, inspect, and reason, we are in danger to lose sight of it.[6] That in fact there is such a thing cannot be doubted, when we consider that in these days some of our philosophers have a high sense of virtue, without the least notion of religion, a clear proof of the usefulness and efficacy of our principles?

12. *Cri.*   Not to dispute the virtue of minute philosophers, we may venture to call its cause in question, and make a doubt whether it be an inexplicable enthusiastic notion of moral beauty, or rather, as to me it seems, what was already assigned by Euphranor, complexion, custom, and religious education? But, allowing what beauty you please to virtue in an irreligious system, it cannot be less in a religious, unless you will suppose that her charms diminish as her dowry increaseth. The truth is, a believer hath all the motives from the beauty of virtue in any sense whatsoever that an unbeliever can possibly have, besides other motives which an unbeliever hath not. Hence, it is plain those of your sect who have moral virtue owe it not to their peculiar tenets, which serve only to lessen the motives to virtue. Those, therefore, who are good are less good, and those who are bad are more bad, than they would have been were they believers.

Euph.   To me it seems those heroic infidel inamoratos of abstracted beauty are much to be pitied, and much to be admired.

Lysicles hearing this, said with some impatience:- Gentlemen, you shall have my whole thoughts upon this point plain and frank. All that is said about a moral sense, or moral beauty, in

---

[6] Men's first thoughts on moral matters are generally better than their second: their natural notions better than those refined by study. *Characteristics*, vol. I, p. 13. [Note added to 1752.]

ALCIPHRON

any signification, either of Alciphron, or Euphranor, or any other, I take to be at bottom mere bubble and pretence. The καλὸν and the πρέπον, the beautiful and decent, are things outward, relative, and superficial, which have no effect in the dark, but are specious topics to discourse and expatiate upon, as some formal pretenders of our sect, though in other points very orthodox, are used to do. But should one of them get into power, you would find him no such fool as Euphranor imagines. He would soon show he had found out that the love of one's country is a prejudice: that mankind are rogues and hypocrites, and that it were folly to sacrifice one's-self for the sake of such: that all regards centre in this life, and that, as this life is to every man his own life, it clearly follows that charity begins at home. Benevolence to mankind is perhaps pretended, but benevolence to himself is practised by the wise. The livelier sort of our philosophers do not scruple to own these maxims; and as for the graver, if they are true to their principles, one may guess what they must think at bottom.

Cri. Whatever may be the effect of pure theory upon certain select spirits, of a peculiar make, or in some other parts of the world, I do verily think that in this country of ours, reason, religion, and law are all together little enough to subdue the outward to the inner man; and that it must argue a wrong head and weak judgment to suppose that without them men will be enamoured of the golden mean. To which my countrymen perhaps are less inclined than others, there being in the make of an English mind a certain gloom and eagerness, which carries to the sad extreme: religion to fanaticism; free-thinking to atheism; liberty to rebellion: nor should we venture to be governed by taste, even in matters of less consequence. The beautiful in dress, furniture, and building is, as Euphranor hath observed, something real and well grounded: and yet our English do not find it out of themselves. What wretched work do they and other northern people make when they follow their own taste of beauty in any of these particulars, instead of acquiring the true, which is to be got from ancient models and the principles of art, as in the case of virtue from great models and meditation, so far as natural means can go? But in no case is it to be hoped that τὸ καλὸν will be the leading idea of the many, who have quick senses, strong passions, and gross intellects.

13. *Alc.* The fewer they are the more ought we to esteem

74

and admire such philosophers, whose souls are touched and transported with this sublime idea.

Cri. But then one might expect from such philosophers so much good sense and philanthropy as to keep their tenets to themselves, and consider their weak brethren, who are more strongly affected by certain senses and notions of another kind than that of the beauty of pure disinterested virtue. Cratylus, a man prejudiced against the Christian religion, of a crazy constitution, of a rank above most men's ambition, and a fortune equal to his rank, had little capacity for sensual vices, or temptation to dishonest ones. Cratylus, having talked himself, or imagined that he had talked himself, into a stoical enthusiasm about the beauty of virtue, did, under the pretence of making men heroically virtuous, endeavour to destroy the means of making them reasonably and humanly so: a clear instance that neither birth, nor books, nor conversation can introduce a knowledge of the world into a conceited mind, which will ever be its own object, and contemplate mankind in its own mirror!

Alc. Cratylus was a lover of liberty, and of his country, and had a mind to make men incorrupt and virtuous upon the purest and most disinterested principles.

Cri. It is true the main scope of all his writings (as he himself tells us) was to assert the reality of a beauty and charm in moral as well as in natural subjects; to demonstrate a taste which he thinks more effectual than principle; to recommend morals on the same foot with manners; and so to advance philosophy on the very foundation of what is called agreeable and polite. As for religious qualms – the belief of a future state of rewards and punishments, and such matters, this great man sticks not to declare that the liberal, polished, and refined part of mankind must needs consider them only as children's tales and amusements of the vulgar. For the sake therefore of the better sort, he hath, in great goodness and wisdom, thought of something else, to wit, a taste or relish: this, he assures us, is at least what will influence; since, according to him, whoever has any impression of gentility (as he calls it) or politeness, is so acquainted with the decorum and grace of things as to be readily transported with the contemplation thereof.[7] His conduct seems just as wise as if a monarch should give out that there was neither jail nor

[7] See *Characteristics*, vol. III; *Miscel.* V, cap. 3; and *Miscel.* III, cap. 2. [The note and Crito's speech up to this point were both added in the errata of 1732b.]

executioner in his kingdom to enforce the laws, but that it would be beautiful to observe them, and that in so doing men would taste the pure delight which results from order and decorum.

Alc. After all, is it not true that certain ancient philosophers, of great note, held the same opinion with Cratylus, declaring that he did not come up to the character, or deserve the title of a good man, who practised virtue for the sake of anything but its own beauty?

Cri. I believe, indeed, that some of the ancients said such things as gave occasion for this opinion. Aristotle[8] distinguisheth between two characters of a good man; the one he calleth ἀγαθὸς, or simply good: the other καλὸς κἀγαθὸς, from whence the compound term καλοκαγαθία, which cannot, perhaps, be rendered by any word in our language. But his sense is plainly this: ἀγαθὸς he defineth to be, that man to whom the good things of nature are good: for, according to him, those things which are vulgarly esteemed the greatest goods, as riches, honours, power, and bodily perfections, are indeed good by nature, but they happen nevertheless to be hurtful and bad to some persons, upon the account of evil habits; inasmuch as neither a fool, nor an unjust man, nor an intemperate, can be at all the better for the use of them, any more than a sick man for using the nourishment proper for those who are in health. But καλὸς κἀγαθὸς is that man in whom are to be found all things worthy and decent and laudable, purely as such and for their own sake, and who practiseth virtue from no other motive than the sole love of her own innate beauty. That philosopher observes likewise that there is a certain political habit, such as the Spartans and others had, who thought virtue was to be valued and practised on account of the natural advantages that attend it. For which reason, he adds, they are indeed good men, but they have not the καλοκαγαθία, or supreme consummate virtue. From hence it is plain that, according to Aristotle, a man may be a good man without believing virtue its own reward, or being only moved to virtue by the sense of moral beauty. It is also plain that he distinguisheth the political virtues of nations, which the public is everywhere concerned to maintain, from this sublime and speculative kind.

It might also be observed that his exalted idea did consist with

---

[8] *Ethic. ad Eudemum*, lib. vii, cap. ult.

supposing a Providence which inspects and rewards the virtues of the best men. For, saith he, in another place[9]– If the gods have any care of human affairs, as it appears they have, it should seem reasonable to suppose they are most delighted with the most excellent nature, and most approaching their own, which is the mind, and that they will reward those who chiefly love and cultivate what is most dear to them. The same philosopher observes,[10] that the bulk of mankind are not naturally disposed to be awed by shame, but by fear; nor to abstain from vicious practices on account of their deformity, but only of the punishment which attends them. And again,[11] he tells us that youth, being of itself averse from abstinence and sobriety, should be under the restraint of laws regulating their education and employment, and that the same discipline should be continued even after they became men. For which, saith he, we want laws, and, in one word, for the whole ordering of life; inasmuch as the generality of mankind obey rather force than reason, and are influenced rather by penalties than the beauty of virtue; ζημίαις ἢ τῷ καλῷ.

From all which, it is very plain what Aristotle would have thought of those who should go about to lessen or destroy the hopes and fears of mankind, in order to make them virtuous on this sole principle of the beauty of virtue.

14. *Alc.* But, whatever the Stagirite and his Peripatetics might think, is it not certain that the Stoics maintained this doctrine in its highest sense, asserting the beauty of virtue to be all-sufficient, that virtue was her own reward, that this alone could make a man happy, in spite of all those things which are vulgarly esteemed the greatest woes and miseries of human life? And all this they held at the same time that they believed the soul of man to be of a corporeal nature, and in death dissipated like a flame or vapour.

Cri. It must be owned the Stoics sometimes talk as if they believed the mortality of the soul. Seneca, in a letter of his to Lucilius, speaks much like a minute philosopher in this particular. But, in several other places, he declares himself of a clear contrary opinion, affirming that the souls of men after death mount aloft into the heavens, look down upon earth, entertain themselves with the theory of celestial bodies, the course of nature, and the

[9] *Ad Nicom.*, lib. x, cap. 8.
[10] Ibid., lib. x, cap. 10.
[11] Ibid., lib. x, cap. 9.

conversation of wise and excellent men, who, having lived in distant ages and countries upon earth, make one society in the other world.

It must also be acknowledged that Marcus Antoninus sometimes speaks of the soul as perishing, or dissolving into its elementary parts. But it is to be noted that he distinguisheth three principles in the composition of human nature, the σῶμα, ψυχὴ, νοῦς,[12] – body, soul, mind; or, as he otherwise expresseth himself, σαρκία, πνευμάτιον, and ἡγεμονικὸν – flesh, spirit, and governing principle. What he calls the ψυχὴ, or soul, containing the brutal part of our nature, is indeed represented as a compound dissoluble, and actually dissolved by death; but the νοῦς, or τὸ ἡγεμονικὸν – the mind, or ruling principle – he held to be of a pure celestial nature, θεοῦ ἀπόσπασμα, a particle of God, which he sends back entire to the stars and the Divinity. Besides, among all his magnificent lessons and splendid sentiments upon the force and beauty of virtue, he is positive as to the being of God; and that not merely as a plastic nature, or soul of the world, but in the strict sense of a Providence inspecting and taking care of human affairs.[13]

The Stoics, therefore, though their style was high, and often above truth and nature, yet it cannot be said that they so resolved every motive to a virtuous life into the sole beauty of virtue as to endeavour to destroy the belief of the immortality of the soul and a distributive Providence. After all, allowing the disinterested Stoics (therein not unlike our modern Quietists) to have made virtue its own sole reward, in the most rigid and absolute sense, yet what is this to those who are no Stoics? If we adopt the whole principles of that sect, admitting their notions of good and evil, their celebrated apathy, and, in one word, setting up for complete Stoics, we may possibly maintain this doctrine with a better grace; at least it will be of a piece, and consistent with the whole. But he who shall borrow this splendid patch from the Stoics, and hope to make a figure by inserting it into a piece of modern composition, seasoned with the wit and notions of these times, will indeed make a figure, but perhaps it may not be in the eyes of a wise man the figure he intended.

15.   Though it must be owned the present age is very indul-

---

[12] Marc. Antonin., lib. iii, cap. 16.
[13] Marc. Antonin., lib. ii, cap. 11.

gent to everything that aims at profane raillery; which is alone sufficient to recommend any fantastical composition to the public. You may behold the tinsel of a modern author pass upon this knowing and learned age for good writing; affected strains for wit; pedantry for politeness; obscurities for depths; ramblings for flights; the most awkward imitation for original humour; and all this upon the sole merit of a little artful profaneness.

Alc. Everyone is not alike pleased with writings of humour, nor alike capable of them. It is the fine irony of an author of quality, 'that certain reverend authors, who can condescend to lay-wit, are nicely qualified to hit the air of breeding and gentility, and that they will in time, no doubt, refine their manner to the edification of the polite world; who have been so long seduced by the way of raillery and wit.'[14] The truth is, the various tastes of readers requireth various kinds of writers. Our sect hath provided for this with great judgment. To proselyte the graver sort, we have certain profound men at reason and argument. For the coffee-houses and populace, we have declaimers of a copious vein. Of such a writer it is no reproach to say, *fluit lutulentus*; he is the fitter for his readers. Then, for men of rank and politeness, we have the finest and wittiest *railleurs* in the world, whose ridicule is the surest test of truth.

Euph. Tell me, Alciphron, are those ingenious *railleurs* men of knowledge?

Alc. Very knowing.

Euph. Do they know, for instance, the Copernican system, or the circulation of the blood?

Alc. One would think you judged of our sect by your country neighbours: there is nobody in town but knows all those points.

Euph. You believe then antipodes, mountains in the moon, and the motion of the earth?

Alc. We do.

Euph. Suppose, five or six centuries ago, a man had maintained these notions among the *beaux esprits* of an English court; how do you think they would have been received?

Alc. With great ridicule.

Euph. And now it would be ridiculous to ridicule them?

Alc. It would.

Euph. But truth was the same then and now?

[14] [See *Characteristics*, vol. III, p. 291.]

Alc. It was.

Euph. It should seem, therefore, that ridicule is no such sovereign touchstone and test of truth as you gentlemen imagine.

Alc. One thing we know: our raillery and sarcasms gall the black tribe, and that is our comfort.

Cri. There is another thing it may be worth your while to know: that men in a laughing fit may applaud a ridicule which shall appear contemptible when they come to themselves. Witness the ridicule of Socrates by the comic poet, the humour and reception it met with no more proving that than the same will yours to be just, when calmly considered by men of sense.

Alc. After all, thus much is certain, our ingenious men make converts by deriding the principles of religion. And, take my word, it is the most successful and pleasing method of conviction. These authors laugh men out of their religion as Horace did out of their vices: *Admissi circum praecordia ludunt.*[15] But a bigot cannot relish or find out their wit.

16. *Cri.* Wit without wisdom, if there be such a thing, is hardly worth finding. And as for the wisdom of these men, it is of a kind so peculiar one may well suspect it. Cicero was a man of sense, and no bigot; nevertheless, he makes Scipio own himself much more vigilant and vigorous in the race of virtue, from supposing heaven the prize.[16] And he introduceth Cato declaring he would never have undergone those virtuous toils for the service of the public, if he had thought his being was to end with this life.[17]

Alc. I acknowledge Cato, Scipio, and Cicero were very well for their times; but you must pardon me if I do not think they arrived at the high, consummate virtue of our modern freethinkers.

Euph. It should seem then that virtue flourisheth more than ever among us?

Alc. It should.

Euph. And this abundant virtue is owing to the method taken by your profound writers to recommend it.

Alc. This I grant.

Euph. But you have acknowledged that the enthusiastic lovers

---

[15] [Persius I, line 117. That is: 'Admitted to the heart, they play.']
[16] *Somn. Scipionis.*
[17] *De Senectute.*

of virtue are not the many of your sect, but only a few select spirits.

To which Alciphron making no answer, Crito addressed himself to Euphranor: To make, said he, a true estimate of the worth and growth of modern virtue, you are not to count the virtuous men, but rather to consider the quality of their virtue. Now, you must know the virtue of these refined theorists is something so pure and genuine that a very little goes far, and is in truth invaluable. To which that reasonable interested virtue of the old English or Spartan kind can bear no proportion.

Euph. Tell me, Alciphron, are there not diseases of the soul as well as of the body?

Alc. Without doubt.

Euph. And are not those diseases vicious habits?

Alc. They are.

Euph. And, as bodily distempers are cured by physic, those of the mind are cured by philosophy: are they not?

Alc. I acknowledge it.

Euph. It seems, therefore, that philosophy is a medicine for the soul of man.

Alc. It is.

Euph. How shall we be able to judge of medicines, or know which to prefer? Is it not from the effects wrought by them?

Alc. Doubtless.

Euph. Where an epidemical distemper rages, suppose a new physician should condemn the known established practice, and recommend another method of cure, would you not, in proportion as the bills of mortality increased, be tempted to suspect this new method, notwithstanding all the plausible discourse of its abettors?

Alc. This serves only to amuse and lead us from the question.

Cri. It puts me in mind of my friend Lamprocles, who needed but one argument against infidels. I observed, said he, that as infidelity grew, there grew corruption of every kind, and new vices. This simple observation on matter of fact was sufficient to make him, notwithstanding the remonstrance of several ingenious men, imbue and season the minds of his children betimes with the principles of religion. The new theories, which our acute moderns have endeavoured to substitute in place of religion, have had their full course in the present age, and produced their effect on the minds and manners of men. That men are men, is a sure maxim: but it is as sure that Englishmen are not the same men they were; whether better or worse, more or less virtuous, I need not say. Every one may see and judge. Though, indeed, after Aristides had been banished, and Socrates put to death at Athens, a man, without being a conjuror, might guess what the Beauty of Virtue could do in England. But there is now neither room nor occasion for guessing. We have our own experience to open our eyes; which yet, if we continue to keep shut till the remains of religious education are quite worn off from the minds of men, it is to be feared we shall then open them wide, not to avoid, but to behold and lament our ruin.

Alc. Be the consequences what they will, I can never bring myself to be of a mind with those who measure truth by convenience. Truth is the only divinity that I adore. Wherever truth leads, I shall follow.

Euph. You have then a passion for truth?

Alc. Undoubtedly.

Euph. For all truths?

Alc. For all.

Euph. To know, or to publish them?

Alc. Both.

Euph. What! would you undeceive a child that was taking physic? Would you officiously set an enemy right that was making a wrong attack? Would you help an enraged man to his sword?

Alc. In such cases, common sense directs one how to behave.

Euph. Common sense, it seems then, must be consulted whether a truth be salutary or hurtful, fit to be declared or concealed.

Alc. How? you would have me conceal and stifle the truth, and keep it to myself. Is this what you aim at?

Euph. I only make a plain inference from what you grant. As for myself, I do not believe your opinions true. And, although you do, you should not therefore, if you would appear consistent with yourself, think it necessary or wise to publish hurtful truths. What service can it do mankind to lessen the motives to virtue, or what damage to increase them?

Alc. None in the world. But, I must needs say I cannot reconcile the received notions of a God and Providence to my understanding, and my nature abhors the baseness of conniving at a falsehood.

Euph. Shall we therefore appeal to truth, and examine the reasons by which you are withheld from believing these points?

Alc. With all my heart; but enough for the present. We will make this the subject of our next conference.

THE FOURTH DIALOGUE

1.   Early the next morning, as I looked out of my window, I saw Alciphron walking in the garden with all the signs of a man in deep thought. Upon which I went down to him.

Alciphron, said I, this early and profound meditation puts me in no small fright. How so? Because I should be sorry to be convinced there was no God. The thought of anarchy in nature is to me more shocking than in civil life: inasmuch as natural concerns are more important than civil, and the basis of all others.

I grant, replied Alciphron, that some inconvenience may possibly follow from disproving a God: but as to what you say of fright and shocking, all that is nothing but prejudice, mere prejudice. Men frame an idea or chimera in their own minds, and then fall down and worship it. Notions govern mankind: but of all notions that of God's governing the world hath taken the deepest root and spread the farthest: it is therefore in philosophy an heroical achievement to dispossess this imaginary monarch of his government, and banish all those fears and spectres which the light of reason alone can dispel:

Non radii solis, non lucida tela diei
Discutiunt, sed naturae species ratioque.[1]

My part, said I, shall be to stand by, as I have hitherto done, and take notes of all that passeth during this memorable event; while a minute philosopher, not six feet high, attempts to dethrone the monarch of the universe.

Alas! replied Alciphron, arguments are not to be measured by feet and inches. One man may see more than a million; and a

[1] Lucretius [vi, 40. That is: 'Neither the rays of the sun, nor the bright shafts of day dispel it, but the form and principle of Nature.']

short argument, managed by a free-thinker, may be sufficient to overthrow the most gigantic chimera.

As we were engaged in this discourse, Crito and Euphranor joined us.

I find you have been beforehand with us today, said Crito to Alciphron, and taken the advantage of solitude and early hours, while Euphranor and I were asleep in our beds. We may, therefore, expect to see atheism placed in the best light, and supported by the strongest arguments.

2. *Alc.* The being of a God is a subject upon which there has been a world of commonplace, which it is needless to repeat. Give me leave therefore to lay down certain rules and limitations, in order to shorten our present conference. For, as the end of debating is to persuade, all those things which are foreign to this end should be left out of our debate.

First then, let me tell you I am not to be persuaded by metaphysical arguments; such, for instance, as are drawn from the idea of an all-perfect being, or the absurdity of an infinite progression of causes. This sort of arguments I have always found dry and jejune; and, as they are not suited to my way of thinking, they may perhaps puzzle, but never will convince me. Secondly, I am not to be persuaded by the authority either of past or present ages, of mankind in general, or of particular wise men, all which passeth for little or nothing with a man of sound argument and free thought. Thirdly, all proofs drawn from utility or convenience are foreign to the purpose. They may prove indeed the usefulness of the notion, but not the existence of the thing. Whatever legislators or statesmen may think, truth and convenience are very different things to the rigorous eyes of a philosopher.

And now, that I may not seem partial, I will limit myself also not to object, in the first place, from anything that may seem irregular or unaccountable in the works of nature, against a cause of infinite power and wisdom; because I already know the answer you would make, to wit, that no one can judge of the symmetry and use of the parts of an infinite machine, which are all relative to each other, and to the whole, without being able to comprehend the entire machine, or the whole universe. And, in the second place, I shall engage myself not to object against the justice and providence of a supreme Being from the evil that befalls good men, and the prosperity which is often the portion of wicked men in this life; because I know that, instead of admitting this to be an objection against a Deity, you would make it an argument for a future state, in which there shall be such a retribution of rewards and punishments as may vindicate the Divine attributes, and set all things right in the end. Now, these answers, though they should be admitted for good ones, are in truth no proofs of the being of God, but only solutions of certain difficulties which might be objected, supposing it already proved by proper arguments. Thus much I thought fit to premise, in order to save time and trouble both to you and myself.

Cri. I think that as the proper end of our conference ought to be supposed the discovery and defence of truth, so truth may be justified, not only by persuading its adversaries, but, where that cannot be done, by showing them to be unreasonable. Arguments, therefore, which carry light have their effect, even against an opponent who shuts his eyes, because they show him to be obstinate and prejudiced. Besides, this distinction between arguments that puzzle and that convince, is least of all observed by minute philosophers, and need not therefore be observed by others in their favour. But, perhaps, Euphranor may be willing to encounter you on your own terms, in which case I have nothing further to say.

3. *Euph.* Alciphron acts like a skilful general, who is bent upon gaining the advantage of the ground, and alluring the enemy out of their trenches. We who believe a God are intrenched within tradition, custom, authority, and law. And, nevertheless, instead of attempting to force us, he proposes that we should voluntarily abandon these intrenchments, and make the attack; when we may act on the defensive with much security and ease, leaving him the trouble to dispossess us of what we need not resign. Those reasons (continued he, addressing himself to Alciphron) which you have mustered up in this morning's meditation, if they do not weaken, must establish our belief of a God; for the utmost is to be expected from so great a master in his profession, when he sets his strength to a point.

Alc. I hold the confused notion of a Deity, or some invisible power, to be of all prejudices the most unconquerable. When half-a-dozen ingenious men are got together over a glass of wine, by a cheerful fire, in a room well lighted, we banish with ease all the spectres of fancy or education, and are very clear in our decisions. But, as I was taking a solitary walk before it was broad daylight in yonder grove, methought the point was not quite so clear; nor could I readily recollect the force of those arguments which used to appear so conclusive at other times. I had I know not what awe upon my mind, and seemed haunted by a sort of panic, which I cannot otherwise account for than by supposing it the effect of prejudice: for, you must know that I, like the rest of the world, was once upon a time catechized and tutored into the belief of a God or Spirit. There is no surer mark of prejudice than the believing a thing without reason. What necessity then can there be that I should set myself the difficult task of proving a negative when it is sufficient to observe that there is no proof of the affirmative, and that the admitting it without proof is unreasonable? Prove therefore your opinion; or, if you cannot, you may indeed remain in possession of it, but you will only be possessed of a prejudice.

Euph. O Alciphron, to content you we must prove, it seems, and we must prove upon your own terms. But, in the first place, let us see what sort of proof you expect.

Alc. Perhaps I may not expect it, but I will tell you what sort of proof I would have: and that is, in short, such proof as every man of sense requires of a matter of fact, or the existence of any other particular thing. For instance, should a man ask why I believe there is a king of Great Britain? I might answer – Because I had seen him. Or a king of Spain? Because I had seen those who saw him. But as for this King of kings, I neither saw Him myself, nor anyone else that ever did see Him. Surely, if there be such a thing as God, it is very strange that He should leave Himself without a witness; that men should still dispute His being; and that there should be no one evident, sensible, plain proof of it, without recourse to philosophy or metaphysics. A matter of fact is not to be proved by notions, but by facts. This is clear and full to the point. You see what I would be at. Upon these principles I defy superstition.

Euph. You believe then as far as you can see?

Alc. That is my rule of faith.

Euph. How! will you not believe the existence of things which you hear, unless you also see them?

Alc. I will not say so neither. When I insisted on seeing, I would be understood to mean perceiving in general. Outward objects make very different impressions upon the animal spirits, all which are comprised under the common name of sense. And whatever we can perceive by any sense we may be sure of.

4. *Euph.* What! do you believe then that there are such things as animal spirits?

Alc. Doubtless.

Euph. By what sense do you perceive them?

Alc. I do not perceive them immediately by any of my senses. I am nevertheless persuaded of their existence, because I can collect it from their effects and operations. They are the messengers which, running to and fro in the nerves, preserve a communication between the soul and outward objects.

Euph. You admit then the being of a soul?

Alc. Provided I do not admit an immaterial substance, I see no inconvenience in admitting there may be such a thing as a soul. And this may be no more than a thin fine texture of subtile parts or spirits residing in the brain.

Euph. I do not ask about its nature. I only ask whether you admit that there is a principle of thought and action, and whether it be perceivable by sense.

Alc. I grant that there is such a principle, and that it is not the object of sense itself, but inferred from appearances which are perceived by sense.

Euph. If I understand you rightly, from animal functions and motions you infer the existence of animal spirits, and from reasonable acts you infer the existence of a reasonable soul. Is it not so?

Alc. It is.

Euph. It should seem, therefore, that the being of things imperceptible to sense may be collected from effects and signs, or sensible tokens.

Alc. It may.

Euph. Tell me, Alciphron, is not the soul that which makes the principal distinction between a real person and a shadow, a living man and a carcass?

Alc. I grant it is.

Euph. I cannot, therefore, know that you for instance, are a distinct thinking individual, or a living real man, by surer or other signs than those from which it can be inferred that you have a soul?

Alc. You cannot.

Euph. Pray tell me, are not all acts immediately and properly perceived by sense reducible to motion?

Alc. They are.

Euph. From motions, therefore, you infer a mover or cause; and from reasonable motions (or such as appear calculated for a reasonable end) a rational cause, soul or spirit?

Alc. Even so.

5. *Euph.* The soul of man actuates but a small body, an insignificant particle, in respect of the great masses of nature, the elements and heavenly bodies, and system of the world. And the wisdom that appears in those motions which are the effect of human reason is incomparably less than that which discovers itself in the structure and use of organized natural bodies, animal or vegetable. A man with his hand can make no machine so admirable as the hand itself; nor can any of those motions by which we trace out human reason approach the skill and contrivance of those wonderful motions of the heart, and brain, and other vital parts, which do not depend on the will of man.

Alc. All this is true.

Euph. Doth it not follow, then, that from natural motions, independent of man's will, may be inferred both power and wisdom incomparably greater than that of the human soul?

Alc. It should seem so.

Euph. Further, is there not in natural productions and effects a visible unity of counsel and design? Are not the rules fixed and immoveable? Do not the same laws of motion obtain throughout? The same in China and here, the same two thousand years ago and at this day?

Alc. All this I do not deny.

Euph. Is there not also a connexion or relation between animals and vegetables, between both and the elements, between the elements and heavenly bodies; so that, from their mutual respects, influences, subordinations, and uses, they may be collected to be parts of one whole, conspiring to one and the same end, and fulfilling the same design?

Alc. Supposing all this to be true.

Euph. Will it not then follow that this vastly great, or infinite power and wisdom must be supposed in one and the same Agent, Spirit, or Mind; and that we have at least as clear, full, and immediate certainty of the being of this infinitely wise and powerful Spirit, as of any one human soul whatsoever besides our own?

Alc. Let me consider: I suspect we proceed too hastily. What! Do you pretend you can have the same assurance of the being of a God that you can have of mine, whom you actually see stand before you and talk to you?

Euph. The very same, if not greater.

Alc. How do you make this appear?

Euph. By the person Alciphron is meant an individual thinking thing, and not the hair, skin, or visible surface, or any part of the outward form, colour, or shape, of Alciphron.

Alc. This I grant.

Euph. And, in granting this, you grant that, in a strict sense, I do not see Alciphron, *i.e.* that individual thinking thing, but only such visible signs and tokens as suggest and infer the being of that invisible thinking principle or soul. Even so, in the selfsame manner, it seems to me that, though I cannot with eyes of flesh behold the invisible God, yet I do in the strictest sense behold and perceive by all my senses such signs and tokens, such effects and operations, as suggest, indicate, and demonstrate an invisible God, as certainly, and with the same evidence, at least, as any other signs, perceived by sense, do suggest to me the existence of your soul, spirit, or thinking principle; which I am convinced of only by a few signs or effects, and the motions of one small organized body: whereas I do at all times and in all places perceive sensible signs which evince the being of God. The point, therefore, doubted or denied by you at the beginning, now seems manifestly to follow from the premises. Throughout this whole inquiry, have we not considered every step with care, and made not the least advance without clear evidence? You and I examined and assented singly to each foregoing proposition: what shall we do then with the conclusion? For my part, if you do not help me out, I find myself under an absolute necessity of admitting it for true. You must therefore be content henceforward to bear the blame, if I live and die in the belief of a God.

6. *Alc.* It must be confessed, I do not readily find an answer. There seems to be some foundation for what you say. But, on the other hand, if the point was so clear as you pretend, I cannot conceive how so many sagacious men of our sect should be so much in the dark as not to know or believe one syllable of it.

Euph. O Alciphron, it is not our present business to account for the oversights, or vindicate the honour, of those great men the free-thinkers, when their very existence is in danger of being called in question.

Alc. How so?

Euph. Be pleased to recollect the concessions you have made, and then show me, if the arguments for a Deity be not conclusive, by what better arguments you can prove the existence of that thinking thing which in strictness constitutes the free-thinker.

As soon as Euphranor had uttered these words, Alciphron stopped short, and stood in a posture of meditation, while the rest of us continued our walk and took two or three turns, after which he joined us again with a smiling countenance, like one who had made some discovery.

I have found, said he, what may clear up the point in dispute, and give Euphranor entire satisfaction; I would say an argument which will prove the existence of a free-thinker, the like whereof cannot be applied to prove the existence of God. You must know then that your notion of our perceiving the existence of God, as certainly and immediately as we do that of a human person, I could by no means digest, though I must own it puzzled me, till I had considered the matter. At first methought a particular structure, shape, or motion was the most certain proof of a thinking reasonable soul. But a little attention satisfied me that these things have no necessary connexion with reason, knowledge, and wisdom; and that, allowing them to be certain proofs of a living soul, they cannot be so of a thinking and reasonable one. Upon second thoughts, therefore, and a minute examination of this point, I have found that nothing so much convinces me of the existence of another person as his speaking to me. It is my hearing you talk that, in strict and philosophical truth, is to me the best argument for your being. And this is a peculiar argument, inapplicable to your purpose; for, you will not, I suppose, pretend that God speaks to man in the same clear and sensible manner as one man doth to another?

7. *Euph.* How! is then the impression of sound so much more evident than that of other senses? Or, if it be, is the voice of man louder than that of thunder?

Alc. Alas! you mistake the point. What I mean is not the sound of speech merely as such, but the arbitrary use of sensible signs, which have no similitude or necessary connexion with the things signified; so as by the apposite management of them to suggest and exhibit to my mind an endless variety of things, differing in nature, time, and place; thereby informing me, entertaining me, and directing me how to act, not only with regard to things near and present, but also with regard to things distant and future. No matter whether these signs are pronounced or written; whether they enter by the eye or ear: they have the same use, and are equally proofs of an intelligent, thinking, designing cause.

Euph. But what if it should appear that God really speaks to man; should this content you?

Alc. I am for admitting no inward speech, no holy instincts, or suggestions of light or spirit. All that, you must know, passeth with men of sense for nothing. If you do not make it plain to me that God speaks to men by outward sensible signs, of such sort and in such manner as I have defined, you do nothing.

Euph. But if it shall appear plainly that God speaks to men by the intervention and use of arbitrary, outward, sensible signs, having no resemblance or necessary connexion with the things they stand for and suggest: if it shall appear that, by innumerable combinations of these signs, an endless variety of things is discovered and made known to us; and that we are thereby instructed or informed in their different natures; that we are taught and admonished what to shun, and what to pursue; and are directed how to regulate our motions, and how to act with respect to things distant from us, as well in time as place, will this content you?

Alc. It is the very thing I would have you make out; for therein consists the force, and use, and nature of language.

8. *Euph.* Look, Alciphron, do you not see the castle upon yonder hill?

Alc. I do.

Euph. Is it not at a great distance from you?

Alc. It is.

Euph. Tell me, Alciphron, is not distance a line turned endwise to the eye?

Alc. Doubtless.

Euph. And can a line, in that situation, project more than one single point on the bottom of the eye?

Alc. It cannot.

Euph. Therefore the appearance of a long and of a short distance is of the same magnitude, or rather of no magnitude at all, being in all cases one single point.

Alc. It seems so.

Euph. Should it not follow from hence that distance is not immediately perceived by the eye?

Alc. It should.

Euph. Must it not then be perceived by the mediation of some other thing?

Alc. It must.

Euph. To discover what this is, let us examine what alteration there may be in the appearance of the same object, placed at different distances from the eye. Now, I find by experience that when an object is removed still farther and farther off in a direct line from the eye, its visible appearance still grows lesser and fainter; and this change of appearance being proportional and universal, seems to me to be that by which we apprehend the various degrees of distance.

Alc. I have nothing to object to this.

Euph. But littleness or faintness, in their own nature, seem to have no necessary connexion with greater length of distance?

Alc. I admit this to be true.

Euph. Will it not follow then that they could never suggest it but from experience?

Alc. It will.

Euph. That is to say, we perceive distance, not immediately, but by mediation of a sign, which hath no likeness to it, or necessary connexion with it, but only suggests it from repeated experience, as words do things.

Alc. Hold, Euphranor: now I think of it, the writers in optics tell us of an angle made by the two optic axes, where they meet in the visible point or object; which angle, the obtuser it is the nearer it shows the object to be, and by how much the acuter, by so much the farther off; and this from a necessary demonstrable connexion.

Euph. The mind then finds out the distance of things by geometry?

Alc. It doth.

Euph. Should it not follow, therefore, that nobody could see but those who had learned geometry, and knew something of lines and angles?

Alc. There is a sort of natural geometry which is got without learning.

Euph. Pray inform me, Alciphron, in order to frame a proof of any kind, or deduce one point from another, is it not necessary that I perceive the connexion of the terms in the premises, and the connexion of the premises with the conclusion; and, in general, to know one thing by means of another, must I not first know that other thing? When I perceive your meaning by your words, must I not first perceive the words themselves? and must I not know the premises before I infer the conclusion?

Alc. All this is true.

Euph. Whoever, therefore, collects a nearer distance from a wider angle, or a farther distance from an acuter angle, must first perceive the angles themselves. And he who doth not perceive those angles can infer nothing from them. Is it so or not?

Alc. It is as you say.

Euph. Ask now the first man you meet whether he perceives or knows anything of those optic angles? or whether he ever thinks about them, or makes any inferences from them, either by natural or artificial geometry? What answer do you think he would make?

Alc. To speak the truth, I believe his answer would be, that he knew nothing of those matters.

Euph. It cannot therefore be that men judge of distance by angles: nor, consequently, can there be any force in the argument you drew from thence, to prove that distance is perceived by means of something which hath a necessary connexion with it.

Alc. I agree with you.

9. *Euph.* To me it seems that a man may know whether he perceives a thing or no; and, if he perceives it, whether it be immediately or mediately: and, if mediately, whether by means of something like or unlike, necessarily or arbitrarily connected with it.

Alc. It seems so.

Euph. And is it not certain that distance is perceived only by experience, if it be neither perceived immediately by itself, nor by means of any image, nor of any lines and angles which are like it, or have a necessary connexion with it?

Alc. It is.

Euph. Doth it not seem to follow, from what hath been said and allowed by you, that before all experience a man would not imagine the things he saw were at any distance from him?

Alc. How! let me see.

Euph. The littleness or faintness of appearance, or any other idea or sensation not necessarily connected with or resembling distance, can no more suggest different degrees of distance, or any distance at all, to the mind which hath not experienced a connexion of the things signifying and signified, than words can suggest notions before a man hath learned the language.

Alc. I allow this to be true.

Euph. Will it not thence follow that a man born blind, and made to see, would, upon first receiving his sight, take the things he saw not to be at any distance from him, but in his eyes, or rather in his mind?

Alc. I must own it seems so. And yet, on the other hand, I can hardly persuade myself that, if I were in such a state, I should think those objects which I now see at so great distance to be at no distance at all.

Euph. It seems, then, that you now think the objects of sight are at a distance from you?

Alc. Doubtless I do. Can any one question but yonder castle is at a great distance?

Euph. Tell me, Alciphron, can you discern the doors, windows, and battlements of that same castle?

Alc. I cannot. At this distance it seems only a small round tower.

Euph. But I, who have been at it, know that it is no small round tower, but a large square building with battlements and turrets, which it seems you do not see.

Alc. What will you infer from thence?

Euph. I would infer that the very object which you strictly and properly perceive by sight is not that thing which is several miles distant.

Alc. Why so?

Euph. Because a little round object is one thing, and a great square object is another. Is it not?

Alc. I cannot deny it.

Euph. Tell me, is not the visible appearance alone the proper object of sight?

95

Alc. It is.

What think you now (said Euphranor, pointing towards the heavens) of the visible appearance of yonder planet? Is it not a round luminous flat, no bigger than a sixpence?

Alc. What then?

Euph. Tell me then, what you think of the planet itself. Do you not conceive it to be a vast opaque globe, with several unequal risings and valleys?

Alc. I do.

Euph. How can you therefore conclude that the proper object of your sight exists at a distance?

Alc. I confess I know not.

Euph. For your farther conviction, do but consider that crimson cloud. Think you that, if you were in the very place where it is, you would perceive anything like what you now see?

Alc. By no means. I should perceive only a dark mist.

Euph. Is it not plain, therefore, that neither the castle, the planet, nor the cloud, which you see here, are those real ones which you suppose exist at a distance?

10. *Alc.* What am I to think then? Do we see anything at all, or is it altogether fancy and illusion?

Euph. Upon the whole, it seems the proper objects of sight are light and colours, with their several shades and degrees; all which, being infinitely diversified and combined, do form a language wonderfully adapted to suggest and exhibit to us the distances, figures, situations, dimensions, and various qualities of tangible objects: not by similitude, nor yet by inference of necessary connexion, but by the arbitrary imposition of Providence, just as words suggest the things signified by them.

Alc. How! Do we not, strictly speaking, perceive by sight such things as trees, houses, men, rivers, and the like?

Euph. We do, indeed, perceive or apprehend those things by the faculty of sight. But, will it follow from thence that they are the proper and immediate objects of sight, any more than that all those things are the proper and immediate objects of hearing which are signified by the help of words or sounds?

Alc. You would have us think, then, that light, shades, and colours, variously combined, answer to the several articulations of sound in language; and that, by means thereof, all sorts of objects are suggested to the mind through the eye, in the same manner as they are suggested by words or sounds through the ear: that is, neither from necessary deduction to the judgment, nor from similitude to the fancy, but purely and solely from experience, custom, and habit.

Euph. I would not have you think anything more than the nature of things obligeth you to think, nor submit in the least to my judgment, but only to the force of truth: which is an imposition that I suppose the freest thinkers will not pretend to be exempt from.

Alc. You have led me, it seems, step by step, till I am got I know not where. But I shall try to get out again, if not by the way I came, yet by some other of my own finding.

Here Alciphron, having made a short pause, proceeded as follows.

11. Answer me, Euphranor, should it not follow from these principles that a man born blind, and made to see, would, at first sight, not only not perceive their distance, but also not so much as know the very things themselves which he saw, for instance, men or trees? which surely to suppose must be absurd.

Euph. I grant, in consequence of those principles, which both you and I have admitted, that such a one would never think of men, trees, or any other objects that he had been accustomed to perceive by touch, upon having his mind filled with new sensations of light and colours, whose various combinations he doth not yet understand, or know the meaning of; no more than a Chinese, upon first hearing the words *man* and *tree* would think of the things signified by them. In both cases, there must be time and experience, by repeated acts, to acquire a habit of knowing the connexion between the signs and things signified; that is to say, of understanding the language, whether of the eyes or of the ears. And I conceive no absurdity in all this.

Alc. I see, therefore, in strict philosophical truth, that rock only in the same sense that I may be said to hear it, when the word *rock* is pronounced.

Euph. In the very same.

Alc. How comes it to pass then that everyone shall say he sees, for instance, a rock or a house, when those things are before his eyes; but nobody will say he hears a rock or a house, but only the words or sounds themselves by which those things are said to be signified or suggested but not heard? Besides, if vision be only a language speaking to the eyes, it may be asked, when did men learn this language? To acquire the knowledge of so many signs as go to the making up a language is a work of some difficulty. But, will any man say he hath spent time, or been at pains, to learn this language of vision?

Euph. No wonder, we cannot assign a time beyond our remotest memory. If we have been all practising this language, ever since our first entrance into the world: if the Author of Nature constantly speaks to the eyes of all mankind, even in their earliest infancy, whenever the eyes are open in the light, whether alone or in company: it doth not seem to me at all strange that men should not be aware they had ever learned a language begun so early, and practised so constantly, as this of vision. And, if we also consider that it is the same throughout the whole world, and not, like other languages, differing in different places, it will not seem unaccountable that men should mistake the connexion between the proper objects of sight and the things signified by them to be founded in necessary relation or likeness; or, that they should even take them for the same things. Hence it seems easy to conceive why men who do not think should confound in this language of vision the signs with the things signified, otherwise than they are wont to do in the various particular languages formed by the several nations of men.

12. It may be also worth while to observe that signs, being little considered in themselves, or for their own sake, but only in their relative capacity, and for the sake of those things whereof they are signs, it comes to pass that the mind overlooks them, so as to carry its attention immediately on to the things signified. Thus, for example, in reading we run over the characters with the slightest regard, and pass on to the meaning. Hence it is frequent for men to say, they see words, and notions, and things in reading of a book; whereas in strictness they see only the characters which suggest words, notions, and things. And, by parity of reason, may we not suppose that men, not resting in, but overlooking the immediate and proper objects of sight, as in their own nature of small moment, carry their attention onward to the very things signified, and talk as if they saw the secondary objects? which, in truth and strictness, are not seen, but only suggested and apprehended by means of the proper objects of sight, which alone are seen.

Alc. To speak my mind freely, this dissertation grows tedious, and runs into points too dry and minute for a gentleman's attention.

I thought, said Crito, we had been told that minute philosophers loved to consider things closely and minutely.

Alc. That is true, but in so polite an age who would be a mere philosopher? There is a certain scholastic accuracy which ill suits the freedom and ease of a well-bred man. But, to cut short this chicane, I propound it fairly to your own conscience, whether you really think that God Himself speaks every day and in every place to the eyes of all men.

Euph. That is really and in truth my opinion; and it should be yours too, if you are consistent with yourself, and abide by your own definition of language. Since you cannot deny that the great Mover and Author of nature constantly explaineth Himself to the eyes of men by the sensible intervention of arbitrary signs, which have no similitude or connexion with the things signified; so as, by compounding and disposing them, to suggest and exhibit an endless variety of objects, differing in nature, time, and place; thereby informing and directing men how to act with respect to things distant and future, as well as near and present. In consequence, I say, of your own sentiments and concessions, you have as much reason to think the Universal Agent or God speaks to your eyes, as you can have for thinking any particular person speaks to your ears.

Alc. I cannot help thinking that some fallacy runs through this whole ratiocination, though perhaps I may not readily point it out. It seems to me that every other sense may as well be deemed a language as that of vision. Smells and tastes, for instance, are signs that inform us of other qualities to which they have neither likeness or necessary connexion.

Euph. That they are signs is certain, as also that language and all other signs agree in the general nature of sign, or so far forth as signs. But it is as certain that all signs are not language; not even all significant sounds: such as the natural cries of animals, or the inarticulate sounds and interjections of men. It is the articulation, combination, variety, copiousness, extensive and general use and easy application of signs (all which are commonly found in vision) that constitute the true nature of language. Other senses may indeed furnish signs; and yet those signs have no more right than inarticulate sounds to be thought a language.

Alc. Hold! let me see. In language the signs are arbitrary, are they not?[2]

Euph. They are.

Alc. And, consequently, they do not always suggest real matters of fact. Whereas this natural language, as you call it, or these visible signs, do always suggest things in the same uniform way, and have the same constant regular connexion with matters of fact: whence it should seem the connexion was necessary; and, therefore, according to the definition premised, it can be no language. How do you solve this objection?

Euph. You may solve it yourself by the help of a picture or looking-glass.

Alc. You are in the right. I see there is nothing in it. I know not what else to say to this opinion, more than that it is so odd and contrary to my way of thinking that I shall never assent to it.

13. *Euph.* Be pleased to recollect your own lectures upon prejudice, and apply them in the present case. Perhaps they may help you to follow where reason leads, and to suspect notions which are strongly rivetted, without having been ever examined.

Alc. I disdain the suspicion of prejudice. And I do not speak only for myself. I know a club of most ingenious men, the freest from prejudice of any men alive, who abhor the notion of a God, and I doubt not would be very able to untie this knot.

Upon which words of Alciphron, I, who had acted the part of an indifferent stander-by, observed to him: That it misbecame his character and repeated professions, to own an attachment to the judgment, or build upon the presumed abilities of other men, how ingenious soever; and that this proceeding might encourage his adversaries to have recourse to authority, in which perhaps they would find their account more than he.

Oh! said Crito, I have often observed the conduct of minute philosophers. When one of them has got a ring of disciples round him, his method is to exclaim against prejudice, and recommend thinking and reasoning, giving to understand that himself is a man of deep researches and close argument, one who examines

[2] [In 1732a and 1732b, instead of the previous three speeches, there was the following:
'*Alc.* I cannot help thinking that some fallacy runs throughout this whole ratiocination, though perhaps I may not readily point it out. Hold! let me see. In language the signs are arbitrary, are they not?']

impartially, and concludes warily. The same man, in other company, if he chance to be pressed with reason, shall laugh at logic, and assume the lazy supine airs of a fine gentleman, a wit, a *railleur*, to avoid the dryness of a regular and exact inquiry. This double face of the minute philosopher is of no small use to propagate and maintain his notions. Though to me it seems a plain case that if a fine gentleman will shake off authority, and appeal from religion to reason, unto reason he must go: and, if he cannot go without leading-strings, surely he had better be led by the authority of the public than by that of any knot of minute philosophers.

Alc. Gentlemen, this discourse is very irksome, and needless. For my part, I am a friend to inquiry. I am willing reason should have its full and free scope. I build on no man's authority. For my part, I have no interest in denying a God. Any man may believe or not believe a God, as he pleases, for me. But, after all, Euphranor must allow me to stare a little at his conclusions.

Euph. The conclusions are yours as much as mine, for you were led to them by your own concessions.

14. You, it seems, stare to find that God is not far from every one of us; and that in Him we live, and move, and have our being. You, who, in the beginning of this morning's conference, thought it strange that God should leave Himself without a witness do now think it strange the witness should be so full and clear.

Alc. I must own I do. I was aware, indeed, of a certain metaphysical hypothesis of our seeing all things in God by the union of the human soul with the intelligible substance of the Deity, which neither I, nor anyone else could make sense of. But I never imagined it could be pretended that we saw God with our fleshly eyes as plain as we see any human person whatsoever, and that He daily speaks to our senses in a manifest and clear dialect.

Cri.[3] As for that metaphysical hypothesis, I can make no more of it than you. But I think it plain this optic language hath a necessary connexion with knowledge, wisdom, and goodness. It is equivalent to a constant creation, betokening an immediate act of power and providence. It cannot be accounted for by mechanical

---

[3] [In 1732a this speech began thus: 'This language hath a necessary connexion . . .']

principles, by atoms, attractions, or effluvia. The instantaneous production and reproduction of so many signs, combined, dissolved, transposed, diversified, and adapted to such an endless variety of purposes, ever shifting with the occasions and suited to them, being utterly inexplicable and unaccountable by the laws of motion, by chance, by fate, or the like blind principles, doth set forth and testify the immediate operation of a spirit or thinking being; and not merely of a spirit, which every motion or gravitation may possibly infer, but of one wise, good, and provident Spirit, which directs and rules and governs the world. Some philosophers, being convinced of the wisdom and power of the Creator, from the make and contrivance of organized bodies and orderly system of the world, did nevertheless imagine that he left this system with all its parts and contents well adjusted and put in motion, as an artist leaves a clock, to go thenceforward of itself for a certain period. But this visual language proves, not a Creator merely, but a provident Governor, actually and intimately present, and attentive to all our interests and motions, who watches over our conduct, and takes care of our minutest actions and designs throughout the whole course of our lives, informing, admonishing, and directing incessantly, in a most evident and sensible manner. This is truly wonderful.

Euph. And is it not so, that men should be encompassed by such a wonder, without reflecting on it?

15. Something there is of divine and admirable in this language, addressed to our eyes, that may well awaken the mind, and deserve its utmost attention: it is learned with so little pains: it expresseth the differences of things so clearly and aptly: it instructs with such facility and despatch, by one glance of the eye conveying a greater variety of advices, and a more distinct knowledge of things, than could be got by a discourse of several hours. And, while it informs, it amuses and entertains the mind with such singular pleasure and delight. It is of such excellent use in giving a stability and permanency to human discourse, in recording sounds and bestowing life on dead languages, enabling us to converse with men of remote ages and countries. And it answers so apposite to the uses and necessities of mankind, informing us more distinctly of those objects whose nearness and magnitude qualify them to be of greatest detriment or benefit to

our bodies, and less exactly in proportion as their littleness or distance makes them of less concern to us.

Alc. And yet these strange things affect men but little.

Euph. But they are not strange, they are familiar; and that makes them be overlooked. Things which rarely happen strike; whereas frequency lessens the admiration of things, though in themselves ever so admirable. Hence, a common man, who is not used to think and make reflexions, would probably be more convinced of the being of a God by one single sentence heard once in his life from the sky than by all the experience he has had of this visual language, contrived with such exquisite skill, so constantly addressed to his eyes, and so plainly declaring the nearness, wisdom, and providence of Him with whom we have to do.

Alc. After all, I cannot satisfy myself how men should be so little surprised or amazed about this visive faculty, if it was really of a nature so surprising and amazing.

Euph. But let us suppose a nation of men blind from their infancy, among whom a stranger arrives, the only man who can see in all the country; let us suppose this stranger travelling with some of the natives, and that one while he foretells to them that, in case they walk straight forward, in half an hour they shall meet men or cattle, or come to a house; that, if they turn to the right and proceed, they shall in a few minutes be in danger of falling down a precipice; that, shaping their course to the left, they will in such a time arrive at a river, a wood, or a mountain. What think you? Must they not be infinitely surprised that one who had never been in their country before should know it so much better than themselves? And would not those predictions seem to them as unaccountable and incredible as prophecy to a minute philosopher?

Alc. I cannot deny it.

Euph. But it seems to require intense thought to be able to unravel a prejudice that has been so long forming; to get over the vulgar error of ideas common to both senses; and so to distinguish between the objects of sight and touch,[4] which have grown (if I may so say), blended together in our fancy, as to be

---

[4] [The *Essay of Vision* was appended to the 1732 editions of *Alciphron*, and at this point, this note occurred: 'See the annexed Treatise, wherein this point and the whole theory of vision are more fully explained: the paradoxes of which theory, though at first received with great ridicule by those who think ridicule the test of truth, were many years after surprisingly confirmed, by a case of a person made to see who had been blind from his birth. See *Philos. Transact.*, No. 402.']

able to suppose ourselves exactly in the state that one of those men would be in, if he were made to see. And yet this I believe is possible, and might seem worth the pains of a little thinking, especially to those men whose proper employment and profession it is to think and unravel prejudices, and confute mistakes.

Alc. I frankly own I cannot find my way out of this maze, and should gladly be set right by those who see better than myself.

Cri. The pursuing this subject in their own thoughts would possibly open a new scene to those speculative gentlemen of the minute philosophy. It puts me in mind of a passage in the Psalmist, where he represents God to be covered with light as with a garment, and would methinks be no ill comment on that ancient notion of some eastern sages – that God had light for His body, and truth for His soul.

This conversation lasted till a servant came to tell us the tea was ready: upon which we walked in, and found Lysicles at the tea-table.

16. As soon as we sat down, I am glad, said Alciphron, that I have here found my second, a fresh man to maintain our common cause, which, I doubt, Lysicles will think hath suffered by his absence.

Lys. Why so?

Alc. I have been drawn into some concessions you won't like.

Lys. Let me know what they are.

Alc. Why, that there is such a thing as a God, and that His existence is very certain.

Lys. Bless me! How came you to entertain so wild a notion?

Alc. You know we profess to follow reason wherever it leads. And in short I have been reasoned into it.

Lys. Reasoned! You should say, amused with words, bewildered with sophistry.

Euph. Have you a mind to hear the same reasoning that led Alciphron and me step by step, that we may examine whether it be sophistry or no?

Lys. As to that I am very easy. I guess all that can be said on that head. It shall be my business to help my friend out, whatever arguments drew him in.

Euph. Will you admit the premises and deny the conclusions?

Lys. What if I admit the conclusion?

Euph. How! will you grant there is a God?

Lys. Perhaps I may.

Euph. Then we are agreed.

Lys. Perhaps not.

Euph. O Lysicles, you are a subtile adversary. I know not what you would be at.

Lys. You must know then that at bottom the being of God is a point in itself of small consequence, and a man may make this concession without yielding much. The great point is what sense the word God is to be taken in. The very Epicureans allowed the being of gods; but then they were indolent gods, unconcerned with human affairs. Hobbes allowed a corporeal God: and Spinosa held the universe to be God. And yet nobody doubts they were staunch free-thinkers. I could wish indeed the word God were quite omitted; because in most minds it is coupled with a sort of superstitious awe, the very root of all religion. I shall not, nevertheless, be much disturbed, though the name be retained, and the being of God allowed in any sense but in that of a Mind, which knows all things, and beholds human actions, like some judge or magistrate, with infinite observation and intelligence. The belief of a God in this sense fills a man's mind with scruples, lays him under constraints, and embitters his very being: but in another sense it may be attended with no great ill consequence. This I know was the opinion of our great Diagoras, who told me he would never have been at the pains to find out a demonstration that there was no God, if the received notion of God had been the same with that of some Fathers and Schoolmen.

Euph. Pray what was that?

17. *Lys.* You must know, Diagoras, a man of much reading and inquiry, had discovered that once upon a time the most profound and speculative divines, finding it impossible to reconcile the attributes of God, taken in the common sense, or in any known sense, with human reason, and the appearances of things, taught that the words knowledge, wisdom, goodness, and such like, when spoken of the Deity, must be understood in a quite different sense from what they signify in the vulgar acceptation, or from anything that we can form a notion of or conceive. Hence, whatever objections might be made against the attributes of God they easily solved, by denying those attributes belonged to God, in this, or that, or any known particular sense or notion;

which was the same thing as to deny they belonged to Him at all. And thus denying the attributes of God, they in effect denied His being, though perhaps they were not aware of it.

Suppose, for instance, a man should object that future contingencies were inconsistent with the foreknowledge of God, because it is repugnant that certain knowledge should be of an uncertain thing: it was a ready and an easy answer to say that this may be true with respect to knowledge taken in the common sense, or in any sense that we can possibly form any notion of; but that there would not appear the same inconsistency between the contingent nature of things and Divine foreknowledge, taken to signify somewhat that we know nothing of, which in God supplies the place of what we understand by knowledge; from which it differs not in quantity or degree of perfection, but altogether, and in kind, as light doth from sound; and even more, since these agree in that they are both sensations; whereas knowledge in God hath no sort of resemblance or agreement with any notion that man can frame of knowledge. The like may be said of all the other attributes, which indeed may by this means be equally reconciled with everything or with nothing. But all men who think must needs see this is cutting knots and not untying them. For, how are things reconciled with the Divine attributes when these attributes themselves are in every intelligible sense denied; and, consequently, the very notion of God taken away, and nothing left but the name without any meaning annexed to it? In short, the belief that there is an unknown subject of attributes absolutely unknown is a very innocent doctrine; which the acute Diagoras well saw, and was therefore wonderfully delighted with this system.

18. For, said he, if this could once make its way and obtain in the world, there would be an end of all natural or rational religion, which is the basis both of the Jewish and the Christian: for he who comes to God, or enters himself in the church of God, must first believe that there is a God in some intelligible sense; and not only that there is something in general, without any proper notion, though never so inadequate, of any of its qualities or attributes: for this may be fate, or chaos, or plastic nature, or anything else as well as God. Nor will it avail to say there is something in this unknown being analogous to knowledge and goodness; that is to say, which produceth those effects

which we could not conceive to be produced by men, in any degree, without knowledge and goodness. For, this is in fact to give up the point in dispute between theists and atheists, the question having always been, not whether there was a principle (which point was allowed by all philosophers, as well before as since Anaxagoras), but whether this principle was a νοῦς, a thinking intelligent being: that is to say, whether that order, and beauty, and use, visible in natural effects, could be produced by anything but a Mind or Intelligence, in the proper sense of the word? And whether there must not be true, real, and proper knowledge, in the First Cause? We will, therefore, acknowledge that all those natural effects which are vulgarly ascribed to knowledge and wisdom, proceed from a being in which there is, properly speaking, no knowledge or wisdom at all, but only something else, which in reality is the cause of those things which men, for want of knowing better, ascribe to what they call knowledge and wisdom and understanding. You wonder perhaps to hear a man of pleasure, who diverts himself as I do, philosophize at this rate. But you should consider that much is to be got by conversing with ingenious men, which is a short way to knowledge, that saves a man the drudgery of reading and thinking.

And, now we have granted to you that there is a God in this indefinite sense, I would fain see what use you can make of this concession. You cannot argue from unknown attributes, or, which is the same thing, from attributes in an unknown sense. You cannot prove that God is to be loved for His goodness, or feared for His justice, or respected for His knowledge: all which consequences, we own, would follow from those attributes admitted in an intelligible sense. But we deny that those or any other consequences can be drawn from attributes admitted in no particular sense, or in a sense which none of us understand. Since, therefore, nothing can be inferred from such an account of God, about conscience, or worship, or religion, you may even make the best of it. And, not to be singular, we will use the name too, and so at once there is an end of atheism.

Euph. This account of a Deity is new to me. I do not like it, and therefore shall leave it to be maintained by those who do.

19. *Cri.* It is not new to me. I remember not long since to have heard a minute philosopher triumph upon this very point; which put me on inquiring what foundation there was for it in

the Fathers or Schoolmen. And, for aught that I can find, it owes its original to those writings which have been published under the name of Dionysius the Areopagite. The author of which, it must be owned, hath written upon the Divine attributes in a very singular style. In his treatise of the Celestial Hierarchy,[5] he saith that God is something above all essence and life, ὑπὲρ πᾶσαν οὐσίαν καὶ ζωὴν; and again, in his treatise of the Divine Names,[6] that He is above all wisdom and understanding, ὑπὲρ πᾶσαν σοφίαν καὶ σύνεσιν, ineffable and innominable, ἄῤῥητος καὶ ἀνώνυμος; the wisdom of God he terms an unreasonable, unintelligent, and foolish wisdom; τὴν ἄλογον, καὶ ἄνουν, καὶ μωρὰν σοφίαν. But then the reason he gives for expressing himself in this strange manner is, that the Divine wisdom is the cause of all reason, wisdom, and understanding, and therein are contained the treasures of all wisdom and knowledge. He calls God ὑπέρσοφος and ὑπέρζως; as if wisdom and life were words not worthy to express the Divine perfections: and he adds that the attributes unintelligent and unperceiving must be ascribed to the Divinity, not κατ᾽ ἔλλειψιν, by way of defect, but καθ᾽ ὑπεροχὴν, by way of eminency; which he explains by our giving the name of darkness to light inaccessible. And, notwithstanding the harshness of his expressions in some places, he affirms over and over in others, that God knows all things; not that He is beholden to the creatures for His knowledge, but by knowing Himself, from whom they all derive their being, and in whom they are contained as in their cause. It was late before these writings appear to have been known in the world; and, although they obtained credit during the age of the Schoolmen, yet, since critical learning hath been cultivated, they have lost that credit, and are at this day given up for spurious, as containing several evident marks of a much later date than the age of Dionysius. Upon the whole, although this method of growing in expression and dwindling in notion, of clearing up doubts by nonsense, and avoiding difficulties by running into affected contradictions, may perhaps proceed from a well-meant zeal, yet it appears not to be according to knowledge; and, instead of reconciling atheists to the truth, hath, I doubt, a tendency to confirm them in their own persuasion. It should seem, therefore, very weak and rash in a Christian to adopt this harsh language of an apocryphal writer preferable to that of the Holy Scriptures.

[5] *De Hierarch. Cælest.*, cap. 2.
[6] *De Nom. Div.*, cap. 7.

I remember, indeed, to have read of a certain philosopher, who lived some centuries ago, that used to say, if these supposed works of Dionysius had been known to the primitive Fathers, they would have furnished them admirable weapons against the heretics, and would have saved a world of pains. But the event since their discovery hath by no means confirmed his opinion.

It must be owned, the celebrated Picus of Mirandula, among his nine hundred conclusions (which that prince, being very young, proposed to maintain by public disputation at Rome), hath this for one – to wit, that it is more improper to say of God, He is an intellect or intelligent Being, than to say of a reasonable soul that it is an angel: which doctrine it seems was not relished. And Picus, when he comes to defend it, supports himself altogether by the example and authority of Dionysius, and in effect explains it away into a mere verbal difference, affirming that neither Dionysius nor himself ever meant to deprive God of knowledge, or to deny that He knows all things; but that, as reason is of kind peculiar to man, so by intellection he understands a kind or manner of knowing peculiar to angels; and that the knowledge which is in God is more above the intellection of angels than angel is above man. He adds that, as his tenet consists with admitting the most perfect knowledge in God, so he would by no means be understood to exclude from the Deity intellection itself, taken in the common or general sense, but only that peculiar sort of intellection proper to angels, which he thinks ought not to be attributed to God any more than human reason. Picus,[7] therefore, though he speaks as the apocryphal Dionysius, yet, when he explains himself, it is evident he speaks like other men. And, although the forementioned books of the Celestial Hierarchy and of the Divine Names, being attributed to a saint and martyr of the apostolical age, were respected by the Schoolmen, yet it is certain they rejected or softened his harsh expressions, and explained away or reduced his doctrine to the received notions taken from Holy Scripture and the light of nature.

20.   Thomas Aquinas expresseth his sense of this point in the following manner. All perfections, saith he, derived from God to the creatures are in a certain higher sense, or (as the Schoolmen term it) eminently in God. Whenever, therefore, a name borrowed from any perfection in the creature is attributed to God,

---

[7] Pic. Mirand., *in Apolog.*, p. 155, ed. Bas.

we must exclude from its signification everything that belongs to the imperfect manner wherein that attribute is found in the creature. Whence he concludes that knowledge in God is not a habit but a pure act.[8] And again, the same Doctor observes that our intellect gets its notions of all sorts of perfections from the creatures, and that as it apprehends those perfections so it signifies them by names. Therefore, saith he, in attributing these names to God we are to consider two things: first the perfections themselves, as goodness, life, and the like, which are properly in God; and secondly, the manner which is peculiar to the creature, and cannot, strictly and properly speaking, be said to agree to the Creator.[9]

And although Suarez, with other Schoolmen, teacheth that the mind of man conceiveth knowledge and will to be in God as faculties or operations, by analogy only to created beings, yet he gives it plainly as his opinion that when knowledge is said not to be properly in God it must be understood in a sense including imperfection, such as discursive knowledge, or the like imperfect kind found in the creatures: and that, none of those imperfections in the knowledge of men or angels belonging to[10] knowledge as such, it will not thence follow that knowledge, in its proper sense,[11] may not be attributed to God. And of knowledge taken in general for the clear evident understanding of all truth, he expressly affirms that it is in God, and that this was never denied by any philosopher who believed a God.[12] It was, indeed, a current opinion in the schools that even Being itself should be attributed analogically to God and the creatures. That is, they held that God, the supreme, independent, self-originate cause and source of all beings, must not be supposed to exist in the same sense with created beings; not that He exists less truly, or properly than they, but only because He exists in a more eminent and perfect manner.

21.   But, to prevent any man's being led, by mistaking the scholastic use of the terms *analogy* and *analogical*, into an opinion that we cannot frame in any degree a true and proper notion of

[8]   *Sum. Theolog.*, p. i, quest. xiv, art. 1.
[9]   Ibid., quest. xiii, art. 3.
[10]   [Here 1732a and 1732b read 'the formal notion of knowledge or to knowledge as such'.]
[11]   ['Proper formal sense' in 1732a and 1732b.]
[12]   Suarez, *Dis. Metaph.*, tom. II, disp. xxx, sec. 15.

attributes applied by analogy, or, in the school phrase, predicated analogically, it may not be amiss to inquire into the true sense and meaning of those words. Everyone knows that analogy is a Greek word used by mathematicians to signify a similitude of proportions. For instance, when we observe that two is to six as three is to nine, this similitude or equality of proportion is termed analogy. And, although proportion strictly signifies the habitude or relation of one quantity to another, yet, in a looser and translated sense, it hath been applied to signify every other habitude; and consequently, the term analogy comes to signify all similitude of relations or habitudes whatsoever. Hence the Schoolmen tell us there is analogy between intellect and sight; forasmuch as intellect is to the mind what sight is to the body, and that he who governs the state is analogous to him who steers a ship. Hence a prince is analogically styled a pilot, being to the state as a pilot is to his vessel.[13]

For the further clearing of this point, it is to be observed that a twofold analogy is distinguished by the Schoolmen – metaphorical and proper. Of the first kind there are frequent instances in Holy Scripture, attributing human parts and passions to God. When He is represented as having a finger, an eye, or an ear; when He is said to repent, to be angry, or grieved; everyone sees that analogy is merely metaphorical. Because those parts and passions, taken in the proper signification, must in every degree necessarily, and from the formal nature of the thing, include imperfection. When, therefore, it is said the finger of God appears in this or that event, men of common sense mean no more but that it is as truly ascribed to God as the works wrought by human fingers are to man: and so of the rest. But the case is different when wisdom and knowledge are attributed to God. Passions and senses, as such, imply defect; but in knowledge simply, or as such, there is no defect. Knowledge, therefore, in the proper formal meaning of the word, may be attributed to God proportionably, that is, preserving a proportion to the infinite nature of God. We may say, therefore, that as God is infinitely above man, so is the knowledge of God infinitely above the knowledge of man, and this is what Cajetan calls *analogia proprie facta*. And after this same analogy we must understand all those attributes to belong to the Deity which in themselves simply, and as such,

---

[13] *Vide* Cajetan, *de Nom. Analog.*, cap. 3.

denote perfection. We may, therefore, consistently with what hath been premised, affirm that all sorts of perfection which we can conceive in a finite spirit are in God, but without any of that allay which is found in the creatures. This doctrine, therefore, of analogical perfections in God, or our knowing God by analogy, seems very much misunderstood and misapplied by those who would infer from thence that we cannot frame any direct or proper notion, though never so inadequate, of knowledge or wisdom, as they are in the Deity; or understand any more of them than one born blind can of light and colours.

22. And now, gentlemen, it may be expected I should ask your pardon for having dwelt so long on a point of metaphysics, and introduced such unpolished and unfashionable writers as the Schoolmen into good company: but, as Lysicles gave the occasion, I leave him to answer for it.

Lys. I never dreamed of this dry dissertation. But, if I have been the occasion of discussing these scholastic points, by my unlucky mentioning the Schoolmen, it was my first fault of the kind, and I promise it shall be the last. The meddling with crabbed authors of any sort is none of my taste. I grant one meets now and then with a good notion in what we call dry writers, such a one for example as this I was speaking of, which I must own struck my fancy. But then, for these we have such as Prodicus or Diagoras, who look into obsolete books, and save the rest of us that trouble.

Cri. So you pin your faith upon them?

Lys. It is only for some odd opinions, and matters of fact, and critical points. Besides, we know the men to whom we give credit: they are judicious and honest, and have no end to serve but truth. And I am confident some author or other has maintained the forementioned notion in the same sense as Diagoras related it.

Cri. That may be. But it never was a received notion, and never will, so long as men believe a God: the same arguments that prove a first cause proving an intelligent cause; intelligent, I say, in the proper sense; wise and good in the true and formal acceptation of the words. Otherwise, it is evident that every syllogism brought to prove those attributes, or, which is the same thing, to prove the being of a God, will be found to consist of four terms, and consequently can conclude nothing. But for your part, Alciphron, you have been fully convinced that God is a thinking intelligent being, in the same sense with other spirits; though not in the same imperfect manner or degree.

23. *Alc.* And yet I am not without my scruples: for, with knowledge you infer wisdom, and with wisdom goodness. Though I cannot see that it is either wise or good to enact such laws as can never be obeyed.

Cri. Doth any one find fault with the exactness of geometrical rules, because no one in practice can attain to it? The perfection of a rule is useful, even though it is not reached. Many approach what all may fall short of.[14]

Alc. But how is it possible to conceive God so good and man so wicked? It may, perhaps, with some colour be alleged that a little soft shadowing of evil sets off the bright and luminous parts of the creation, and so contributes to the beauty of the whole piece; but for blots so large and so black it is impossible to account by that principle. That there should be so much vice, and so little virtue upon earth, and that the laws of God's kingdom should be so ill observed by His subjects, is what can never be reconciled with that surpassing wisdom and goodness of the supreme Monarch.

Euph. Tell me, Alciphron, would you argue that a state was ill administered, or judge of the manners of its citizens, by the disorders committed in the jail or dungeon?

Alc. I would not.

Euph. And, for aught we know, this spot, with the few sinners on it, bears no greater proportion to the universe of intelligences than a dungeon doth to a kingdom. It seems we are led not only by revelation, but by common sense, observing and inferring from the analogy of visible things, to conclude there are innumerable orders of intelligent beings more happy and more perfect than man; whose life is but a span, and whose place, this earthly globe, is but a point, in respect of the whole system of God's creation. We are dazzled, indeed, with the glory and grandeur of things here below, because we know no better. But, I am apt to think, if we knew what it was to be an angel for one hour, we should return to this world, though it were to sit on the brightest throne in it, with vastly more loathing and reluctance

---

[14] [The previous four sentences, beginning, 'Though I cannot . . .', were added in 1732b.]

than we would now descend into a loathsome dungeon or sepulchre.

24. *Cri.* To me it seems natural that such a weak, passionate, and short-sighted creature as man should be ever liable to scruples of one kind or other. But, as this same creature is apt to be over-positive in judging, and over-hasty in concluding, it falls out that these difficulties and scruples about God's conduct are made objections to His being. And so men come to argue from their own defects against the Divine perfections. And, as the views and humours of men are different and often opposite, you may sometimes see them deduce the same atheistical conclusions from contrary premises. I knew an instance of this in two minute philosophers of my acquaintance, who used to argue each from his own temper against a Providence. One of them, a man of a choleric and vindictive spirit, said he could not believe a Providence, because London was not swallowed up or consumed by fire from heaven; the streets being, as he said, full of people who show no other belief or worship of God but perpetually praying that He would damn, rot, sink, and confound them. The other, being of an indolent easy temper, concluded there could be no such thing as Providence; for that a being of consummate wisdom must needs employ himself better than in minding the prayers and actions and little interests of mankind.

Alc. After all, if God have no passions, how can it be true that vengeance is His? Or how can He be said to be jealous of His glory?

Cri. We believe that God executes vengeance without revenge, and is jealous without weakness, just as the mind of man sees without eyes, and apprehends without hands.

25. *Alc.* To put a period to this discourse, we will grant there is a God in this dispassionate sense: but what then? What hath this to do with religion or divine worship? To what purpose are all these prayers, and praises, and thanksgivings, and singing of psalms, which the foolish vulgar call serving God? What sense, or use, or end is there in all these things?

Cri. We worship God, we praise and pray to Him: not because we think that He is proud of our worship, or fond of our praise or prayers, and affected with them as mankind are; or that all our service can contribute in the least degree to His happiness or good; but because it is good for us to be so disposed towards God: because it is just and right, and suitable to the nature of things, and becoming the relation we stand in to our supreme Lord and Governor.

Alc. If it be good for us to worship God, it should seem that the Christian religion, which pretends to teach men the knowledge and worship of God, was of some use and benefit to mankind.

Cri. Doubtless.

Alc. If this can be made appear, I shall own myself very much mistaken.

Cri. It is now near dinner-time. Wherefore, if you please, we will put an end to this conversation for the present, and tomorrow morning resume our subject.

THE SEVENTH DIALOGUE

1. The philosophers having resolved to set out for London next morning, we assembled at break of day in the library. Alciphron began with a declaration of his sincerity, assuring us he had very maturely and with a most unbiassed mind considered all that had been said the day before. He added that upon the whole he could not deny several probable reasons were produced for embracing the Christian faith. But, said he, those reasons being only probable, can never prevail against absolute certainty and demonstration. If, therefore, I can demonstrate your religion to be a thing altogether absurd and inconsistent, your probable arguments in its defence do from that moment lose their force, and with it all right to be answered or considered. The concurring testimony of sincere and able witnesses hath without question great weight in human affairs. I will even grant that things odd and unaccountable to human judgment or experience may sometimes claim our assent on that sole motive. And I will also grant it possible for a tradition to be conveyed with moral evidence through many centuries. But at the same time you will grant to me that a thing demonstrably and palpably false is not to be admitted on any testimony whatever, which at best can never amount to demonstration. To be plain, no testimony can make nonsense sense: no moral evidence can make contradictions consistent. Know, then, that as the strength of our cause doth not depend upon, so neither is it to be decided by any critical points of history, chronology, or languages. You are not to wonder, if the same sort of tradition and moral proof which governs our assent with respect to fact in civil or natural history is not admitted as a sufficient voucher for metaphysical absurdities and absolute impossibilities. Things obscure and unaccountable in

116

human affairs or the operations of nature may yet be possible, and, if well attested, may be assented unto; but religious assent or faith can be evidently shown in its own nature to be impracticable, impossible, and absurd. This is the primary motive to infidelity. This is our citadel and fortress, which may, indeed, be graced with outworks of various erudition, but, if those are demolished, remains in itself and of its own proper strength impregnable.

Euph. This, it must be owned, reduceth our inquiry within a narrow compass: do but make out this, and I shall have nothing more to say.

Alc. Know, then, that the shallow mind of the vulgar, as it dwells only on the outward surface of things, and considers them in the gross, may be easily imposed on. Hence a blind reverence for religious faith and mystery. But when an acute philosopher comes to dissect and analyse these points, the imposture plainly appears; and as he has no blindness, so he has no reverence for empty notions, or, to speak more properly, for mere forms of speech, which mean nothing, and are of no use to mankind.

2. Words are signs: they do or should stand for ideas; which so far as they suggest they are significant. But words that suggest no ideas are insignificant. He who annexeth a clear idea to every word he makes use of speaks sense; but where such ideas are wanting, the speaker utters nonsense. In order therefore to know whether any man's speech be senseless and insignificant, we have nothing to do but lay aside the words, and consider the ideas suggested by them. Men, not being able immediately to communicate their ideas one to another, are obliged to make use of sensible signs or words; the use of which is to raise those ideas in the hearer which are in the mind of the speaker; and if they fail of this end they serve to no purpose. He who really thinks hath a train of ideas succeeding each other and connected in his mind; and when he expresseth himself by discourse each word suggests a distinct idea to the hearer or reader; who by that means hath the same train of ideas in his which was in the mind of the speaker or writer. As far as this effect is produced, so far the discourse is intelligible, hath sense and meaning. Hence it follows that whoever can be supposed to understand what he reads or hears must have a train of ideas raised in his mind, correspondent to the train of words read or heard. These plain truths, to which

men readily assent in theory, are but little attended to in practice, and therefore deserve to be enlarged on and inculcated, however obvious and undeniable. Mankind are generally averse from thinking, though apt enough to entertain discourse either in themselves or others: the effect whereof is that their minds are rather stored with names than ideas, the husk of science rather than the thing. And yet these words without meaning do often make distinctions of parties, the subject-matter of their disputes, and the object of their zeal. This is the most general cause of error, which doth not influence ordinary minds alone, but even those who pass for acute and learned philosophers are often employed about names instead of things or ideas, and are supposed to know when they only pronounce hard words without a meaning.

3.   Though it is evident that, as knowledge is the perception of the connexion or disagreement between ideas, he who doth not distinctly perceive the ideas marked by the terms, so as to form a mental proposition answering to the verbal, cannot possibly have knowledge. No more can he be said to have opinion or faith; which imply a weaker assent, but still it must be to a proposition, the terms of which are understood as clearly, although the agreement or disagreement of the ideas may not be so evident, as in the case of knowledge. I say, all degrees of assent, whether founded on reason or authority, more or less cogent, are internal acts of the mind, which alike terminate in ideas as their proper object; without which there can be really no such thing as knowledge, faith, or opinion. We may perhaps raise a dust and dispute about tenets purely verbal; but what is this at bottom more than mere trifling? All which will be easily admitted with respect to human learning and science; wherein it is an allowed method to expose any doctrine or tenet by stripping them of the words, and examining what ideas are underneath, or whether any ideas at all? This is often found the shortest way to end disputes, which might otherwise grow and multiply without end, the litigants neither understanding one another nor themselves. It were needless to illustrate what shines by its own light, and is admitted by all thinking men. My endeavour shall be only to apply it in the present case. I suppose I need not be at any pains to prove that the same rules of reason and good sense which obtain in all other subjects ought to take place in religion. As for those who consider faith and reason as two distinct provinces,

and would have us think good sense has nothing to do where it is most concerned, I am resolved never to argue with such men, but leave them in quiet possession of their prejudices.

And now, for the particular application of what I have said, I shall not single out any nice disputed points of school divinity, or those that relate to the nature and essence of God, which, being allowed infinite, you might pretend to screen them under the general notion of difficulties attending the nature of infinity.

4. Grace is the main point in the Christian dispensation; nothing is oftener mentioned or more considered throughout the New Testament; wherein it is represented as somewhat of a very particular kind, distinct from anything revealed to the Jews, or known by the light of nature. This same grace is spoken of as the gift of God, as coming by Jesus Christ, as reigning, as abounding, as operating. Men are said to speak through grace, to believe through grace. Mention is made of the glory of grace, the riches of grace, the stewards of grace. Christians are said to be heirs of grace, to receive grace, grow in grace, be strong in grace, to stand in grace, and to fall from grace. And lastly, grace is said to justify and to save them. Hence Christianity is styled the covenant or dispensation of grace. And it is well known that no point hath created more controversy in the church than this doctrine of grace. What disputes about its nature, extent, and effects, about universal, efficacious, sufficient, preventing, irresistible grace, have employed the pens of Protestant as well as Popish divines, of Jansenists and Molinists, of Lutherans, Calvinists, and Arminians, as I have not the least curiosity to know, so I need not say. It sufficeth to observe, that there have been and are still subsisting great contests upon these points. Only one thing I should desire to be informed of, to wit, What is the clear and distinct idea marked by the word grace? I presume a man may know the bare meaning of a term, without going into the depth of all those learned inquiries. This surely is an easy matter, provided there is an idea annexed to such term. And if there is not, it can be neither the subject of a rational dispute, nor the object of real faith. Men may indeed impose upon themselves or others, and pretend to argue and believe, when at bottom there is no argument or belief, further than mere verbal trifling. Grace taken in the vulgar sense, either for beauty, or favour, I can easily understand. But when it denotes an active, vital, ruling principle,

influencing and operating on the mind of man, distinct from every natural power or motive, I profess myself altogether unable to understand it, or frame any distinct idea of it; and therefore I cannot assent to any proposition concerning it, nor consequently have any faith about it: and it is a self-evident truth, that God obligeth no man to impossibilities. At the request of a philosophical friend, I did cast an eye on the writings he showed me of some divines, and talked with others on this subject, but after all I had read or heard could make nothing of it, having always found, whenever I laid aside the word grace, and looked into my own mind, a perfect vacuity or privation of all ideas. And, as I am apt to think men's minds and faculties are made much alike, I suspect that other men, if they examine what they call grace with the same exactness and indifference, would agree with me, that there was nothing in it but an empty name. This is not the only instance where a word often heard and pronounced is believed intelligible, for no other reason but because it is familiar. Of the same kind are many other points reputed necessary articles of faith. That which in the present case imposeth upon mankind I take to be partly this. Men speak of this holy principle as of something that acts, moves, and determines, taking their ideas from corporeal things, from motion and the force or *momentum* of bodies, which, being of an obvious and sensible nature, they substitute in place of a thing spiritual and incomprehensible, which is a manifest delusion. For, though the idea of corporeal force be never so clear and intelligible, it will not therefore follow that the idea of grace, a thing perfectly incoporeal, must be so too. And though we may reason distinctly, perceive, assent, and form opinions about the one, it will by no means follow that we can do so of the other. Thus, it comes to pass that a clear sensible idea of what is real produceth, or rather is made a pretence for, an imaginary spiritual faith that terminates in no object; a thing impossible! For there can be no assent where there are no ideas: and where there is no assent there can be no faith: and what cannot be, that no man is obliged to. This is as clear as anything in Euclid![1]

5.⋆ The same method of reasoning may be applied by any man of sense to confute all other the most essential articles of the

[1] [The following three sections, numbered here 5.⋆, 6.⋆ and 7.⋆, were omitted in 1752.]

Christian faith. You are not therefore to wonder that a man who proceeds on such solid grounds, such clear and evident principles, should be deaf to all you can say from moral evidence, or probable arguments, which are nothing in the balance against demonstration.

Euph. The more light and force there is in this discourse, the more you are to blame for not having produced it sooner. For my part, I should never have said one word against evidence. But let me see whether I understand you rightly. You say every word in an intelligible discourse must stand for an idea; which ideas as far as they are clearly and distinctly apprehended, so far the discourse hath meaning, without which it is useless and insignificant.

Alc. I do.

Euph. For instance, when I hear the words *man, triangle, colour* pronounced, they must excite in my mind distinct ideas of those things whereof they are signs, otherwise I cannot be said to understand them?

Alc. Right.

Euph. And this is the only true use of language?

Alc. That is what I affirm.

Euph. But every time the word *man* occurs in reading or conversation, I am not conscious that the particular distinct idea of a man is excited in my mind. For instance, when I read in St Paul's Epistle to the Galatians these words, 'If a man thinketh himself to be something when he is nothing, he deceiveth himself,' methinks I comprehend the force and meaning of this proposition, although I do not frame to myself the particular distinct idea of a man.

Alc. It is very true you do not form in your mind the particular idea of Peter, James, or John, of a fair or a black, a tall or a low, a fat or a lean, a straight or a crooked, a wise or a foolish, a sleeping or waking man, but the abstract general idea of man, prescinding from and exclusive of all particular shape, size, complexion, passions, faculties, and every individual circumstance. To explain this matter more fully, you are to understand there is in the human mind a faculty of contemplating the general nature of things, separate from all those particularities which distinguish the individuals one from another. For example, in Peter, James, and John, you may observe in each a certain collection of stature, figure, colour, and other peculiar properties by

121

which they are known asunder, distinguished from all other men and, if I may so say, individuated. Now leaving out of the idea of a man that which is peculiar to the individual, and retaining only that which is common to all men, you form an abstract universal idea of man or human nature, which includes no particular stature, shape, colour or other quality whether of mind or body. After the same manner, you may observe particular triangles to differ one from another, as their sides are equal or unequal, and their angles greater or lesser; whence they are denominated equilateral, equicrural or scalenum, obtusangular, acutangular or rectangular. But the mind, excluding out of its idea all these peculiar properties and distinctions, frameth the general abstract idea of a triangle, which is neither equilateral, equicrural nor scalenum, neither obtusangular, acutangular or rectangular, but all and none of these at once.[2] The same may be said of the general abstract idea of colour, which is something distinct from and exclusive of blue, red, green, yellow, and every other particular colour, including only that general essence in which they all agree. And what has been said of these three general names and the abstract general ideas they stand for may be applied to all others. For you must know that, particular things or ideas being infinite, if each were marked or signified by a distinct proper name, words must have been innumerable and language an endless impossible thing. Hence it comes to pass that appellative or general names stand immediately and properly not for particular but for abstract general ideas, which they never fail to excite in the mind as oft as they are used to any significant purpose. And without this there could be no communication or enlargement of knowledge, no such things as universal science or theorems of any kind. Now for understanding any proposition or discourse it is sufficient that distinct ideas are thereby raised in your mind, correspondent to those in the speaker's, whether the ideas so raised are particular or only abstract and general ideas. Forasmuch, nevertheless, as these are not so obvious and familiar to vulgar minds, it happens that some men may think they have no idea at all when they have not a particular idea; but the truth is, you had the abstract general idea of man in the instance assigned wherein you thought you had none. After the same manner, when it is said that the three angles of a triangle

[2] See Locke, *On Human Understanding*, bk. iv, ch. 7.

are equal to two right ones, or that colour is the object of sight, it is evident the words do not stand for this or that triangle or colour, but for abstract general ideas, excluding everything peculiar to the individuals, and including only the universal nature common to the whole kind of triangles or of colours.

6.★ *Euph.* Tell me, Alciphron, are those abstract general ideas clear and distinct?

Alc. They are above all others clear and distinct, being the only proper object of science, which is altogether conversant about universals.

Euph. And do you not think it very possible for any man to know whether he has this or that clear and distinct idea or no?

Alc. Doubtless. To know this he needs only examine his own thoughts and look into his own mind.

Euph. But upon looking into my own mind I do not find that I have or can have these general abstract ideas of a man or a triangle abovementioned, or of colour prescinded from all particular colours.[3] Though I shut mine eyes and use mine utmost efforts, and reflect on all that passeth in my own mind, I find it utterly impossible to form such ideas.

Alc. To reflect with due attention and turn the mind inward upon itself is a difficult task, and not everyone's talent.

Euph. Not to insist on what you allowed, that everyone might easily know for himself whether he has this or that idea or no, I am tempted to think nobody else can form those ideas any more than I can. Pray, Alciphron, which are those things you would call absolutely impossible?

Alc. Such as include a contradiction.

Euph. Can you frame an idea of what includes a contradiction?

Alc. I cannot.

Euph. Consequently, whatever is absolutely impossible you cannot form an idea of.

Alc. This I grant.

Euph. But can a colour or triangle, such as you describe their abstract general ideas, really exist?

Alc. It is absolutely impossible such things should exist in nature.

Euph. Should it not follow, then, that they cannot exist in

[3] See the Introduction to a *Treatise concerning the Principles of Human Knowledge*, printed in the year 1710, where the absurdity of abstract ideas is fully considered.

your mind, or, in other words, that you cannot conceive or frame an idea of them?

Alc. You seem, Euphranor, not to distinguish between pure intellect and imagination. Abstract general ideas I take to be the object of pure intellect, which may conceive them although they cannot perhaps be imagined.

Euph. I do not perceive that I can by any faculty, whether of intellect or imagination, conceive or frame an idea of that which is impossible and includes a contradiction. And I am very much at a loss to account for your admitting that in common instances, which you would make an argument against divine faith and mysteries.

7.* *Alc.* There must be some mistake in this. How is it possible there should be general knowledge without general propositions, or these without general names, which cannot be without general ideas, by standing for which they become general?

Euph. But may not words become general by being made to stand indiscriminately for all particular ideas which from a mutual resemblance belong to the same kind, without the intervention of any abstract general idea?

Alc. Is there then no such thing as a general idea?

Euph May we not admit general ideas, though we should not admit them to be made by abstraction, or though we should not allow of general abstract ideas? To me it seems a particular idea may become general by being used to stand for or represent other ideas; and that general knowledge is conversant about signs or general ideas made such by their signification, and which are considered rather in their relative capacity, and as substituted for others, than in their own nature or for their own sake. A black line, for instance, an inch long, though in itself particular, may yet become universal, being used as a sign to stand for any line whatsoever.

Alc. It is your opinion, then, that words become general by representing an indefinite number of particular ideas?

Euph. It seems so to me.

Alc. Whenever, therefore, I hear a general name, it must be supposed to excite some one or other particular idea of that species in my mind?

Euph. I cannot say so neither. Pray, Alciphron, doth it seem to you necessary that as often as the word *man* occurs in reading or discourse, you must form in your mind the idea of a particular man?

Alc. I own it doth not; and not finding particular ideas always suggested by the words, I was led to think I had abstract general ideas suggested by them. And this is the opinion of all thinking men who are agreed the only use of words is to suggest ideas. And, indeed, what other use can we assign them?

5. *Euph.* Be the use of words or names what it will, I can never think it is to do things impossible. Let us then inquire what it is? and see if we can make sense of our daily practice. Words, it is agreed, are signs: it may not therefore be amiss to examine the use of other signs, in order to know that of words. Counters, for instance, at a card-table are used, not for their own sake, but only as signs substituted for money, as words are for ideas. Say now, Alciphron, is it necessary every time these counters are used throughout the progress of a game, to frame an idea of the distinct sum or value that each represents?

Alc. By no means: it is sufficient the players at first agree on their respective values, and at last substitute those values in their stead.

Euph. And in casting up a sum, where the figures stand for pounds, shillings, and pence, do you think it necessary, throughout the whole progress of the operation, in each step to form ideas of pounds, shillings, and pence?

Alc. I do not; it will suffice if in the conclusion those figures direct our actions with respect to things.

Euph. From hence it seems to follow, that words may not be insignificant, although they should not, every time they are used, excite the ideas they signify in our minds; it being sufficient that we have it in our power to substitute things or ideas for their signs when there is occasion. It seems also to follow, that there may be another use of words besides that of marking and suggesting distinct ideas, to wit, the influencing our conduct and actions; which may be done either by forming rules for us to act by, or by raising certain passions, dispositions, and emotions in our minds. A discourse, therefore, that directs how to act or excites to the doing or forbearance of an action may, it seems, be useful and significant, although the words whereof it is composed should not bring each a distinct idea into our minds.

Alc. It seems so.

ALCIPHRON

Euph. Pray tell me, Alciphron, is not an idea altogether inactive?

Alc. It is.

Euph. An agent therefore, an active mind, or spirit, cannot be an idea, or like an idea. Whence it should seem to follow that those words which denote an active principle, soul, or spirit do not, in a strict and proper sense, stand for ideas. And yet they are not insignificant neither; since I understand what is signified by the term *I*, or *myself*, or know what it means, although it be no idea, nor like an idea, but that which thinks, and wills, and apprehends ideas, and operates about them. [4]Certainly it must be allowed that we have some notion, that we understand, or know what is meant by, the terms *myself, will, memory, love, hate* and so forth; although to speak exactly, these words do not suggest so many distinct ideas.

Alc. What would you infer from this?

Euph. What hath been inferred already – that words may be significant, although they do not stand for ideas.[5] The contrary whereof having been presumed seems to have produced the doctrine of abstract ideas.

Alc. Will you not allow then that the mind can abstract?

Euph. I do not deny it may abstract in a certain sense; inasmuch as those things that can really exist, or be really perceived asunder, may be conceived asunder, or abstracted one from the other; for instance, a man's head from his body, colour from motion, figure from weight. But it will not thence follow that the mind can frame abstract general ideas, which appear to be impossible.

Alc. And yet it is a current opinion that every substantive name marks out and exhibits to the mind one distinct idea separate from all others.

Euph. Pray, Alciphron, is not the word *number* such a substantive name?

Alc. It is.

Euph. Do but try now whether you can frame an idea of number in abstract, exclusive of all signs, words, and things numbered. I profess for my own part I cannot.

Alc. Can it be so hard a matter to form a simple idea of number, the object of a most evident demonstrable science? Hold,

[4] [The following sentence was added in 1752.]
[5] See the *Principles of Human Knowledge*, sect. 135, and the Introduction, sect. 20.

126

let me see if I cannot abstract the idea of number from the numerical names and characters, and all particular numerical things. Upon which Alciphron paused awhile, and then said, To confess the truth I do not find that I can.

Euph. But, though it seems neither you nor I can form distinct simple *ideas* of number, we can nevertheless make a very proper and significant use of numeral names. They direct us in the disposition and management of our affairs, and are of such necessary use, that we should not know how to do without them. And yet, if other men's faculties may be judged of by mine, to obtain a precise simple abstract idea of number, is as difficult as to comprehend any mystery in religion.

6. But, to come to your own instance, let us examine what idea we can frame of force abstracted from body, motion, and outward sensible effects. For myself I do not find that I have or can have any such idea.

Alc. Surely everyone knows what is meant by force.

Euph. And yet I question whether everyone can form a distinct idea of force. Let me entreat you, Alciphron, be not amused by terms: lay aside the word force, and exclude every other thing from your thoughts, and then see what precise idea you have of force.

Alc. Force is that in bodies which produces motion and other sensible effects.

Euph. Is it then something distinct from those effects?

Alc. It is.

Euph. Be pleased now to exclude the consideration of its subject and effects, and contemplate force itself in its own precise idea.

Alc. I profess I find it no such easy matter.

Euph. Take your own advice, and shut your eyes to assist your meditation. Upon this, Alciphron, having closed his eyes and mused a few minutes, declared he could make nothing of it.

And that, replied Euphranor, which it seems neither you nor I can frame an idea of, by your own remark of men's minds and faculties being made much alike, we may suppose others have no more an idea of than we.

Alc. We may.

Euph. But, notwithstanding all this, it is certain there are many speculations, reasonings, and disputes, refined subtilties, and nice distinctions about this same force. And to explain its

127

nature, and to distinguish the several notions or kinds of it, the terms *gravity, reaction, vis inertiæ, vis insita, vis impressa, vis mortua, vis viva, impetus, momentum, solicitatio, conatus,* and divers other such-like expressions, have been used by learned men: and no small controversies have arisen about the notions or definitions of these terms. It has puzzled men to know whether force is spiritual or corporeal; whether it remains after action; how it is transferred from one body to another. Strange paradoxes have been framed about its nature, properties, and proportions: for instance, that contrary forces may at once subsist in the same quiescent body: that the force of percussion in a small particle is infinite. For which, and other curiosities of the same sort, you may consult Borellus 'De Vi Percussionis', the 'Lezioni Academiche' of Torricelli, the 'Exercitations' of Hermanus, and other writers. It is well known to the learned world what a controversy hath been carried on between mathematicians, particularly Monsieur Leibnitz and Monsieur Papin, in the Leipsic 'Acta Eruditorum', about the proportion of forces: whether they be each to other in a proportion compounded of the simple proportions of the bodies and the celerities, or in one compounded of the simple proportion of the bodies and the duplicate proportion of the celerities? A point, it seems, not yet agreed: as indeed the reality of the thing itself is made a question. Leibnitz distinguisheth between the *nisus elementaris,* and the *impetus* which is formed by a repetition of the *nisus elementaris,* and seems to think they do not exist in nature, but are made only by an abstraction of the mind. The same author, treating of original active force, to illustrate his subject, hath recourse to the substantial forms and *entelecheia* of Aristotle. And the ingenious Torricelli saith of force and impetus, that they are subtle abstracts and spiritual quintessences; and concerning the *momentum* and the velocity of heavy bodies falling, he saith they are *un certo che,* and *un non so che;* that is, in plain English, he knows not what to make of them. Upon the whole, therefore, may we not pronounce that – excluding body, time, space, motion, and all its sensible measures and effects – we shall find it as difficult to form an idea of force as of grace?

Alc. I do not know what to think of it.

7. *Euph.* And yet, I presume, you allow there are very evident propositions or theorems relating to force, which contain useful truths: for instance, that a body with conjunct forces

describes the diagonal of a parallelogram, in the same time that it would the sides with separate. Is not this a principle of very extensive use? Doth not the doctrine of the composition and resolution of forces depend upon it, and, in consequence thereof, numberless rules and theorems directing men how to act, and explaining phenomena throughout the mechanics and mathematical philosophy? And if, by considering this doctrine of force, men arrive at the knowledge of many inventions in mechanics, and are taught to frame engines, by means of which things difficult and otherwise impossible may be performed; and if the same doctrine which is so beneficial here below serveth also as a key to discover the nature of the celestial motions; shall we deny that it is of use, either in practice or speculation, because we have no distinct idea of force? Or that which we admit with regard to *force*, upon what pretence can we deny concerning *grace*? If there are queries, disputes, perplexities, diversity of notions and opinions about the one, so there are about the other also: if we can form no precise distinct idea of the one, so neither can we of the other. Ought we not therefore, by a parity of reason, to conclude there may be divers true and useful propositions concerning the one as well as the other? And that grace may, for aught you know, be an object of our faith, and influence our life and actions, as a principle destructive of evil habits and productive of good ones, although we cannot attain a distinct idea of it, separate or abstracted from God the author, from man the subject, and from virtue and piety its effects?

8.   Shall we not admit the same method of arguing, the same rules of logic, reason, and good sense, to obtain in things spiritual and things corporeal, in faith and science? and shall we not use the same candour, and make the same allowances, in examining the revelations of God and the inventions of men? For aught I see, that philosopher cannot be free from bias and prejudice, or be said to weigh things in an equal balance, who shall maintain the doctrine of force and reject that of grace, who shall admit the abstract idea of a triangle, and at the same time ridicule the Holy Trinity. But, however partial or prejudiced other minute philosophers might be, you have laid it down for a maxim, that the same logic which obtains in other matters must be admitted in religion.

Lys.   I think, Alciphron, it would be more prudent to abide by the way of wit and humour than thus to try religion by the dry test of reason and logic.

Alc. Fear not: by all the rules of right reason, it is absolutely impossible that any mystery, and least of all the Trinity, should really be the object of man's faith.

Euph. I do not wonder you thought so, as long as you maintained that no man could assent to a proposition without perceiving or framing in his mind distinct ideas marked by the terms of it. But, although terms are signs, yet having granted that those signs may be significant, though they should not suggest ideas represented by them, provided they serve to regulate and influence our wills, passions, or conduct, you have consequently granted that the mind of man may assent to propositions containing such terms, when it is so directed or affected by them, notwithstanding it should not perceive distinct ideas marked by those terms. Whence it seems to follow that a man may believe the doctrine of the Trinity, if he finds it revealed in Holy Scripture that the Father, the Son, and the Holy Ghost, are God, and that there is but one God, although he doth not frame in his mind any abstract or distinct ideas of trinity, substance, or personality; provided that this doctrine of a Creator, Redeemer, and Sanctifier makes proper impressions on his mind, producing therein love, hope, gratitude, and obedience, and thereby becomes a lively operative principle, influencing his life and actions, agreeably to that notion of saving faith which is required in a Christian. This, I say, whether right or wrong, seems to follow from your own principles and concessions. But, for further satisfaction, it may not be amiss to inquire whether there be anything parallel to this Christian faith in the minute philosophy. Suppose a fine gentleman or lady of fashion, who are too much employed to think for themselves, and are only free-thinkers at second-hand, have the advantage of being betimes initiated in the principles of your sect, by conversing with men of depth and genius, who have often declared it to be their opinion, the world is governed either by fate or by chance, it matters not which; will you deny it possible for such persons to yield their assent to either of these propositions?

Alc. I will not.

Euph. And may not their assent be properly called *faith*?

Alc. It may.

Euph. And yet it is possible those disciples of the minute philosophy may not dive so deep as to be able to frame any abstract, or precise, or any determinate idea whatsoever, either of fate or of chance?

Alc. This too I grant.

Euph. So that, according to you, this same gentleman or lady may be said to believe or have faith where they have not ideas?

Alc. They may.

Euph. And may not this faith or persuasion produce real effects, and show itself in the conduct and tenor of their lives, freeing them from the fears of superstition, and giving them a true relish of the world, with a noble indolence or indifference about what comes after?

Alc. It may.

Euph: And may not Christians, with equal reason, be allowed to believe the Divinity of our Saviour, or that in Him God and man make one Person, and be verily persuaded thereof, so far as for such faith or belief to become a real principle of life and conduct? inasmuch as, by virtue of such persuasion, they submit to His government, believe His doctrine, and practise His precepts, although they frame no abstract idea of the union between the Divine and human nature; nor may be able to clear up the notion of person to the contentment of a minute philosopher? To me it seems evident that if none but those who had nicely examined, and could themselves explain, the principle of individuation in man, or untie the knots and answer the objections which may be raised even about human personal identity, would require of us to explain the Divine mysteries, we should not be often called upon for a clear and distinct idea of person in relation to the Trinity, nor would the difficulties on that head be often objected to our faith.

Alc. Methinks, there is no such mystery in personal identity.

Euph. Pray, in what do you take it to consist?

Alc. In consciousness.

Euph. Whatever is possible may be supposed?

Alc. It may.

Euph. We will suppose now (which is possible in the nature of things, and reported to be fact) that a person, through some violent accident or distemper, should fall into such a total oblivion as to lose all consciousness of his past life and former ideas. I ask, is he not still the same person?

Alc. He is the same man, but not the same person. Indeed

you ought not to suppose that a person loseth its former consciousness; for this is impossible, though a man perhaps may; but
then he becomes another person. In the same person, it must be
owned, some old ideas may be lost, and some new ones got; but
a total change is inconsistent with identity of person.

Euph. Let us then suppose that a person hath ideas and is
conscious during a certain space of time, which we will divide
into three equal parts, whereof the later terms are marked by the
letters A, B, C. In the first part of time, the person gets a certain
number of ideas, which are retained in A: during the second part
of time, he retains one-half of his old ideas, and loseth the other
half, in place of which he acquires as many new ones: so that in
B his ideas are half old and half new. And in the third part, we
suppose him to lose the remainder of the ideas acquired in the
first, and to get new ones in their stead, which are retained in
C, together with those acquired in the second part of time. Is
this a possible fair supposition?

Alc. It is.

Euph. Upon these premises, I am tempted to think one may
demonstrate that personal identity doth not consist in consciousness.

Alc. As how?

Euph. You shall judge: but thus it seems to me. The persons
in A and B are the same, being conscious of common ideas by
supposition. The person in B is (for the same reason) one and
the same with the person in C. Therefore, the person in A is the
same with the person in C, by that undoubted axiom, *Quæ
conveniunt uni tertio conveniunt inter se.*[6] But the person in C hath
no idea in common with the person in A. Therefore personal
identity doth not consist in consciousness. What do you think,
Alciphron, is not this a plain inference?

Alc. I tell you what I think: you will never assist my faith,
by puzzling my knowledge.

9. *Euph.* There is, if I mistake not, a practical faith, or
assent, which showeth itself in the will and actions of a man,
although his understanding may not be furnished with those
abstract, precise, distinct ideas, which, whatever a philosopher
may pretend, are acknowledged to be above the talents of
common men; among whom, nevertheless, may be found, even

[6] [That is: 'Things equal to a third are equal to one another.']

according to your own concession, many instances of such practical faith, in other matters which do not concern religion. What should hinder, therefore, but that doctrines relating to heavenly mysteries might be taught, in this saving sense, to vulgar minds, which you may well think incapable of all teaching and faith, in the sense you suppose?

Which mistaken sense, said Crito, has given occasion to much profane and misapplied raillery. But all this may very justly be retorted on the minute philosophers themselves, who confound Scholasticism with Christianity, and impute to other men those perplexities, chimeras, and inconsistent ideas which are often the workmanship of their own brains, and proceed from their own wrong way of thinking. Who doth not see that such an ideal abstracted faith is never thought of by the bulk of Christians, husbandmen, for instance, artisans, or servants? Or what footsteps are there in the Holy Scripture to make us think that the wiredrawing of abstract ideas was a task enjoined either Jews or Christians? Is there anything in the law or the prophets, the evangelists or apostles, that looks like it? Everyone whose understanding is not perverted by science falsely so-called may see the saving faith of Christians is quite of another kind, a vital operative principle, productive of charity and obedience.

Alc. What are we to think then of the disputes and decisions of the famous Council of Nice, and so many subsequent Councils? What was the intention of those venerable Fathers – the *homoousians* and the *homoiousians*? Why did they disturb themselves and the world with hard words, and subtle controversies?

Cri. Whatever their intention was, it could not be to beget nice abstracted ideas of mysteries in the minds of common Christians, this being evidently impossible. Nor doth it appear that the bulk of Christian men did in those days think it any part of their duty to lay aside the words, shut their eyes, and frame those abstract ideas; any more than men now do of force, time, number, or several other things, about which they nevertheless believe, know, argue, and dispute. To me it seems that, whatever was the source of these controversies, and howsoever they were managed, wherein human infirmity must be supposed to have had its share, the main end was not, on either side, to convey precise positive ideas to the minds of men, by the use of those contested terms,

133

but rather a negative sense, tending to exclude Polytheism on the one hand, and Sabellianism on the other.[7]

Alc. But what shall we say to so many learned and ingenious divines, who from time to time have obliged the world with new explications of mysteries, who, having themselves professedly laboured to acquire accurate ideas, would recommend their discoveries and speculations to others for articles of faith?

Cri. To all such innovators in religion I would say with Jerome, 'Why after so many centuries do you pretend to teach us what was untaught before? Why explain what neither Peter nor Paul thought necessary to be explained?'[8] And it must be owned that the explication of mysteries in divinity, allowing the attempt as fruitless as the pursuit of the philosopher's stone in chemistry or the perpetual motion in mechanics, is no more than they, chargeable on the profession itself, but only on the wrongheaded professors of it.

10. It seems, that what hath been now said may be applied to other mysteries of our religion. Original sin, for instance, a man may find it impossible to form an idea of in abstract, or of the manner of its transmission; and yet the belief thereof may produce in his mind a salutary sense of his own unworthiness, and the goodness of his Redeemer: from whence may follow good habits, and from them good actions, the genuine effects of faith; which, considered in its true light, is a thing neither repugnant nor incomprehensible, as some men would persuade us, but suited even to vulgar capacities, placed in the will and affections rather than in the understanding, and producing holy lives rather than subtle theories. Faith, I say, is not an indolent perception, but an operative persuasion of mind, which ever worketh some suitable action, disposition, or emotion in those who have it; as it were easy to prove and illustrate by innumerable instances taken from human affairs. And, indeed, while the Christian religion is considered an institution fitted to ordinary minds, rather than to the nicer talent, whether improved or puzzled, of speculative men; and our notions about faith are accordingly taken from the commerce of the world, and practice of mankind, rather than from the peculiar systems of refiners; it will, I think, be no difficult matter to conceive and justify the meaning and use of

[7] *Vide* Sozomen, lib. ii, cap. 8.
[8] Hieronym., *Ad Pammachium et Oceanum, de Erroribus Origenis.*

our belief of mysteries, against the most confident assertions and objections of the minute philosophers, who are easily to be caught in those very snares which they have spun and spread for others. And that humour of controversy, the mother and nurse of heresies, would doubtless very much abate, if it was considered that things are to be rated, not by colour, shape, or stamp, so truly as by the weight. If the moment of opinions had been by some litigious divines made the measure of their zeal, it might have spared much trouble both to themselves and others. Certainly one that takes his notions of faith, opinion, and assent from common sense, and common use, and has maturely weighed the nature of signs and language, will not be so apt to controvert the wording of a mystery, or to break the peace of the church, for the sake of retaining or rejecting a term.[9]

But, to convince you by a plain instance of the efficacious necessary use of faith without ideas: we will suppose a man of the world, a minute philosopher, prodigal and rapacious, one of large appetites and narrow circumstances, who shall have it in his power at once to seize upon a great fortune by one villainous act, a single breach of trust, which he can commit with impunity and secrecy. Is it not natural to suppose him arguing in this manner? All mankind in their senses pursue their interest. The interests of this present life are either of mind, body, or fortune. If I commit this act my mind will be easy (having nought to fear here or hereafter); my bodily pleasure will be multiplied; and my fortune enlarged. Suppose now, one of your refined theorists talks to him about the harmony of mind and affections, inward worth, truth of character, in one word, the beauty of virtue; which is the only interest he can propose to turn the scale against all other secular interests and sensual pleasures; would it not, think you, be a vain attempt?[10] I say, in such a juncture what can the most plausible and refined philosophy of your sect offer to dissuade such a man from his purpose, more than assuring him that the abstracted delight of the mind, the enjoyments of an interior moral sense, the τὸ καλὸν, are what constitute his true interest? And what effect can this have on a mind callous to all those things, and at the same time strongly affected with a sense

[9] [The following paragraph was not in 1732a.]
[10] [In 1732b edition this sentence read: 'On the other hand, possess him with a thorough belief or persuasion that he shall forfeit eternal happiness, or incur eternal misery; and this alone may suffice to turn the scale.']

ALCIPHRON

of corporeal pleasures, and the outward interest, ornaments, and conveniences of life? Whereas that very man, do but produce in him a sincere belief of a future state, although it be a mystery, although it be what eye hath not seen, nor ear heard, nor hath it entered into the heart of man to conceive, he shall, nevertheless, by virtue of such belief, be withheld from executing his wicked project: and that for reasons which all men can comprehend though nobody can [comprehend] the object of them. I will allow the points insisted on by your refined moralists to be as lovely and excellent as you please to a reasonable, reflecting, philosophical mind. But I will venture to say that, as the world goes, few, very few, will be influenced by them. We see, therefore, the necessary use, as well as the powerful effects of faith, even where we have not ideas.

11. *Alc.* It seems, Euphranor, and you would persuade me into an opinion, that there is nothing so singularly absurd as we are apt to think in the belief of mysteries; and that a man need not renounce his reason to maintain his religion. But, if this were true, how comes it to pass that, in proportion as men abound in knowledge, they dwindle in faith?

Euph. O Alciphron, I have learned from you that there is nothing like going to the bottom of things, and analysing them into their first principles. I shall therefore make an essay of this method, for clearing up the nature of faith: with what success, I shall leave you to determine; for I dare not pronounce myself, on my own judgment, whether it be right or wrong: but thus it seems to me. The objections made to faith are by no means an effect of knowledge, but proceed rather from an ignorance of what knowledge is; which ignorance may possibly be found even in those who pass for masters of this or that particular branch of knowledge. Science and faith agree in this, that they both imply an assent of the mind: and, as the nature of the first is most clear and evident, it should be first considered in order to cast a light on the other. To trace things from their original, it seems that the human mind, naturally furnished with the ideas of things particular and concrete, and being designed, not for the bare intuition of ideas, but for action and operation about them, and pursuing her own happiness therein, stands in need of certain general rules or theorems to direct her operations in this pursuit; the supplying which want is the true, original, reasonable end of

136

studying the arts and sciences. Now, these rules being general, it follows that they are not to be obtained by the mere consideration of the original ideas, or particular things, but by the means of marks and signs, which, being so far forth universal, become the immediate instruments and materials of science. It is not, therefore, by mere contemplation of particular things, and much less of their abstract general ideas, that the mind makes her progress, but by an apposite choice and skilful management of signs: for instance, force and number, taken in concrete, with their adjuncts, subjects, and signs, are what everyone knows; and considered in abstract, so as making precise ideas of themselves, they are what nobody can comprehend. That their abstract nature, therefore, is not the foundation of science is plain: and that barely considering their ideas in concrete, is not the method to advance in the respective sciences is what everyone that reflects may see; nothing being more evident than that one, who can neither write nor read, in common use understands the meaning of numeral words, as well as the best philosopher or mathematician.

12. But here lies the difference: the one who understands the notation of numbers, by means thereof is able to express briefly and distinctly all the variety and degrees of number, and to perform with ease and despatch several arithmetical operations by the help of general rules. Of all which operations as the use in human life is very evident, so it is no less evident that the performing them depends on the aptness of the notation. If we suppose rude mankind without the use of language, it may be presumed they would be ignorant of arithmetic. But the use of names, by the repetition whereof in a certain order they might express endless degrees of number, would be the first step towards that science. The next step would be, to devise proper marks of a permanent nature, and visible to the eye, the kind and order whereof must be chosen with judgment, and accommodated to the names. Which marking or notation would, in proportion as it was apt and regular, facilitate the invention and application of general rules to assist the mind in reasoning and judging, in extending, recording, and communicating its knowledge about numbers: in which theory and operations, the mind is immediately occupied about the signs or notes, by mediation of which it is directed to act about things, or number in concrete (as the logicians call it) without ever considering the simple,

abstract, intellectual, general idea of number.[11] The signs, indeed, do in their use imply relations or proportions of things: but these relations are not abstract general ideas, being founded in particular things, and not making of themselves distinct ideas to the mind, exclusive of the particular ideas and the signs. I imagine one need not think much to be convinced that the science of arithmetic in its rise, operations, rules, and theorems, is altogether conversant about the artificial use of signs, names, and characters. These names and characters are universal, inasmuch as they are signs. The names are referred to things, and the characters to names, and both to operation. The names being few, and proceeding by a certain analogy, the characters will be more useful, the simpler they are, and the more aptly they express this analogy. Hence the old notation by letters was more useful than words written at length. And the modern notation by figures, expressing the progression or analogy of the names by their simple places, is much preferable to that, for ease and expedition, as the invention of algebraical symbols is to this, for extensive and general use. As arithmetic and algebra are sciences of great clearness, certainty, and extent, which are immediately conversant about signs, upon the skilful use and management whereof they entirely depend, so a little attention to them may possibly help us to judge of the progress of the mind in other sciences, which, though differing in nature, design, and object, may yet agree in the general methods of proof and inquiry.

13. If I mistake not, all sciences, so far as they are universal and demonstrable by human reason, will be found conversant about signs as their immediate object, though these in the application are referred to things. The reason whereof is not difficult to conceive. For, as the mind is better acquainted with some sort of objects, which are earlier offered to it, strike it more sensibly, or are more easily comprehended than others, it seems naturally led to substitute those objects for such as are more subtle, fleeting, or difficult to conceive. Nothing, I say, is more natural, than to make the things we know a step towards those we do not know; and to explain and represent things less familiar by others which are more so. Now, it is certain we imagine before we reflect, and we perceive by sense before we imagine, and of all our

---

[11] [The next sentence 'The signs, indeed . . . ideas and the signs.' (five lines) was inserted in 1752.]

senses the sight is the most clear, distinct, various, agreeable, and comprehensive. Hence it is natural to assist the intellect by the imagination, the imagination by sense, and the other senses by sight. Hence figures, metaphors, and types. We illustrate spiritual things by corporeal; we substitute sounds for thoughts, and written letters for sounds; emblems, symbols, and hieroglyphics, for things too obscure to strike, and too various or too fleeting to be retained. We substitute things imaginable for things intelligible, sensible things for imaginable, smaller things for those that are too great to be comprehended easily, and greater things for such as are too small to be discerned distinctly, present things for absent, permanent for perishing, and visible for invisible. Hence the use of models and diagrams. Hence right lines are substituted for time, velocity, and other things of very different natures. Hence we speak of spirits in a figurative style, expressing the operations of the mind by allusions and terms borrowed from sensible things, such as *apprehend, conceive, reflect, discourse,* and such-like: and hence those allegories which illustrate things intellectual by visions exhibited to the fancy. Plato, for instance, represents the mind presiding in her vehicle by the driver of a winged chariot, which sometimes moults and droops: and is drawn by two horses, the one good and of a good race, the other of a contrary kind; symbolically expressing the tendency of the mind towards the Divinity, as she soars or is borne aloft by two instincts like wings, the one in the intellect towards truth, the other in the will towards excellence, which instincts moult or are weakened by sensual inclinations; expressing also her alternate elevations and depressions, the struggles between reason and appetite, like horses that go on unequal pace, or draw different ways, embarrassing the soul in her progress to perfection. I am inclined to think the doctrine of signs a point of great importance, and general extent, which, if duly considered, would cast no small light upon things, and afford a just and genuine solution of many difficulties.

14.   Thus much, upon the whole, may be said of all signs: that they do not always suggest ideas signified to the mind: that when they suggest ideas, they are not general abstract ideas: that they have other uses besides barely standing for and exhibiting ideas, such as raising proper emotions, producing certain dispositions or habits of mind, and directing our actions in pursuit of

that happiness, which is the ultimate end and design, the primary spring and motive, that sets rational agents at work: [12]that signs may imply or suggest the relations of things; which relations, habitudes or proportions, as they cannot be by us understood but by the help of signs, so being thereby expressed and confuted, they direct and enable us to act with regard to things: that the true end of speech, reason, science, faith, assent, in all its different degrees, is not merely, or principally, or always, the imparting or acquiring of ideas, but rather something of an active operative nature, tending to a conceived good; which may sometimes be obtained, not only although the ideas marked are not offered to the mind, but even although there should be no possibility of offering or exhibiting any such idea to the mind: for instance, the algebraic mark, which denotes the root of a negative square, hath its use in logistic operations, although it be impossible to form an idea of any such quantity. And what is true of algebraic signs is also true of words or language, modern algebra being in fact a more short, apposite, and artificial sort of language, and it being possible to express by words at length, though less conveniently, all the steps of an algebraical process. And it must be confessed that even the mathematical sciences themselves, which above all others are reckoned the most clear and certain, if they are considered, not as instruments to direct our practice, but as speculations to employ our curiosity, will be found to fall short in many instances of those clear and distinct ideas, which, it seems, the minute philosophers of this age, whether knowingly or ignorantly, expect and insist upon in the mysteries of religion.

15. Be the science or subject what it will, whensoever men quit particulars for generalities, things concrete for abstractions, when they forsake practical views, and the useful purposes of knowledge for barren speculation, considering means and instruments as ultimate ends, and labouring to attain precise ideas which they suppose indiscriminately annexed to all terms, they will be sure to embarrass themselves with difficulties and disputes. Such are those which have sprung up in geometry about the nature of the angle of contact, the doctrine of proportions, of indivisibles, infinitesimals, and divers other points; notwithstanding all which, that science is very rightly esteemed an excellent and useful one, and is really found to be so in many occasions of human life,

[12] [From this point to 'that the true end' was inserted in 1752.]

wherein it governs and directs the actions of men, so that by the aid or influence thereof those operations become just and accurate which would otherwise be faulty and uncertain. And, from a parity of reason, we should not conclude any other doctrines which govern, influence, or direct the mind of man to be, any more than that, the less true or excellent, because they afford matter of controversy, and useless speculation to curious and licentious wits: particularly those articles of our Christian faith, which, in proportion as they are believed, persuade, and, as they persuade, influence the lives and actions of men. As to the perplexity of contradictions and abstracted notions, in all parts whether of human science or Divine faith, cavillers may equally object, and unwary persons incur, while the judicious avoid it. There is no need to depart from the received rules of reasoning to justify the belief of Christians. And if any pious men think otherwise, it may be supposed an effect, not of religion, or of reason, but only of human weakness. If this age be singularly productive of infidels, I shall not therefore conclude it to be more knowing, but only more presuming, than former ages: and their conceit, I doubt, is not the effect of consideration. To me it seems that the more thoroughly and extensively any man shall consider and scan the principles, objects, and methods of proceeding in arts and sciences, the more he will be convinced there is no weight in those plausible objections that are made against the mysteries of faith; which it will be no difficult matter for him to maintain or justify in the received method of arguing, on the common principles of logic, and by numberless avowed parallel cases, throughout the several branches of human knowledge, in all which the supposition of abstract ideas creates the same difficulties.[13]

Alc. According to this doctrine, all points may be alike maintained. There will be nothing absurd in Popery, not even transubstantiation.

Cri. Pardon me. This doctrine justifies no article of faith which is not contained in Scripture, or which is repugnant to human reason, which implies a contradiction, or which leads to idolatry or wickedness of any kind – all which is very different from our not having a distinct or an abstract idea of a point.

16. *Alc.* I will allow, Euphranor, this reasoning of yours to

[13] [The following two speeches appeared first in 1732b.]

have all the force you meant it should have. I freely own there may be mysteries; that we may believe where we do not understand; and that faith may be of use, although its object is not distinctly apprehended. In a word, I grant there may be faith and mysteries in other things, but not in religion: and that for this plain reason, because it is absurd to suppose there should be any such thing as religion; and, if there is no religion, it follows there cannot be religious faith or mysteries. Religion, it is evident, implies the worship of a God, which worship supposeth rewards and punishments, which suppose merits and demerits, actions good and evil, and these suppose human liberty a thing impossible: and, consequently, religion, a thing built thereon, must be an unreasonable absurd thing. There can be no rational hopes or fears where there is no guilt, nor any guilt where there is nothing done but what unavoidably follows from the structure of the world and the laws of motion. Corporeal objects strike on the organs of sense, whence ensues a vibration in the nerves, which, being communicated to the soul or animal spirit in the brain or root of the nerves, produceth therein that motion called volition: and this produceth a new determination in the spirits, causing them to flow into such nerves as must necessarily by the laws of mechanism produce such certain actions. This being the case, it follows that those things which vulgarly pass for human actions are to be esteemed mechanical, and that they are falsely ascribed to a free principle. There is therefore no foundation for praise or blame, fear or hope, reward or punishment; nor consequently for religion, which, as I observed before, is built upon and supposeth those things.

Euph. You imagine, Alciphron, if I rightly understand you, that man is a sort of organ played on by outward objects, which, according to the different shape and texture of the nerves, produce different motions and effects therein.

Alc. Man may, indeed, be fitly compared to an organ: but a puppet is the very thing. You must know that certain particles, issuing forth in right lines from all sensible objects, compose so many rays, or filaments, which drive, draw, and actuate every part of the soul and body of man, just as threads or wires do the joints of that little wooden machine vulgarly called a *puppet*: with this only difference, that the latter are gross, and visible to common eyes, whereas the former are too fine and subtle to be discerned by any but a sagacious free-thinker. This admirably accounts for all those operations which we have been taught to ascribe to a thinking principle within us.

Euph. This is an ingenious thought, and must be of great use in freeing men from all anxiety about moral notions; as it transfers the principle of action from the human soul to things outward and foreign. But I have my scruples about it. For, you suppose the mind in a literal sense to be moved, and its volitions to be mere motions. Now, if another should affirm, as it is not impossible some or other may, that the soul is incorporeal, and that motion is one thing and volition another, I would fain know how you could make your point clear to such a one. It must be owned very clear to those who admit the soul to be corporeal, and all her acts to be but so many motions. Upon this supposition, indeed, the light wherein you place human nature is no less true than it is fine and new. But, let anyone deny this supposition, which is easily done, and the whole superstructure falls to the ground. If we grant the above-mentioned points, I will not deny a fatal necessity must ensue. But I see no reason for granting them. On the contrary, it seems plain that motion and thought are two things as really and as manifestly distinct as a triangle and a sound. It seems, therefore, that, in order to prove the necessity of human actions, you suppose what wants proof as much as the very point to be proved.

17. *Alc.* But, supposing the mind incorporeal, I shall, nevertheless, be able to prove my point. Not to amuse you with far-fetched arguments, I shall only desire you to look into your own breast and observe how things pass there, when an object offers itself to the mind. First, the understanding considers it: in the next place, the judgment decrees about it, as a thing to be chosen or rejected, to be omitted or done, in this or that manner: and this decree of the judgment doth necessarily determine the will, whose office is merely to execute what is ordained by another faculty: consequently, there is no such thing as freedom of the will. For, that which is necessary cannot be free. In freedom there should be an indifference to either side of the question, a power to act or not to act, without prescription or control: and without this indifference and this power, it is evident the will cannot be free. But it is no less evident that the will is not indifferent in its actions, being absolutely determined and governed by the judgment. Now, whatever moves the judgment, whether the greatest

present uneasiness, or the greatest apparent good or whatever else it be, it is all one to the point in hand. The will, being ever concluded and controlled by the judgment, is in all cases alike under necessity. There is, indeed, throughout the whole of human nature, nothing like a principle of freedom, every faculty being determined in all its acts by something foreign to it. The understanding, for instance, cannot alter its idea, but must necessarily see it such as it presents itself. The appetites by a natural necessity are carried towards their respective objects. Reason cannot infer indifferently anything from anything, but is limited by the nature and connexion of things, and the eternal rules of reasoning. And, as this is confessedly the case of all other faculties, so it equally holds with respect to the will itself, as hath been already shown. And, if we may credit the divine Characterizer of our times, this above all others must be allowed the most slavish faculty. 'Appetite (saith that noble writer), which is elder brother to Reason, being the lad of stronger growth, is sure, on every contest, to take the advantage of drawing all to his own side. And Will, so highly boasted, is but at best a football or top between these youngsters, who prove very unfortunately matched; till the youngest, instead of now and then a kick or lash bestowed to little purpose, forsakes the ball or top itself, and begins to lay about his elder brother.'[14]

Cri. This beautiful parable for style and manner might equal those of a known English writer in low life, renowned for allegory, were it not a little incorrect, making the weaker lad find his account in laying about the stronger.

Alc. This is helped up by supposing the stronger lad the greater coward. But, be that as it will, so far as it relates to the point in hand, this is a clear state of the case. The same point may be also proved from the prescience of God. That which is certainly foreknown will certainly be. And what is certain is necessary. And necessary actions cannot be the effect of free-will. Thus you have this fundamental point of our free-thinking philosophy demonstrated different ways.

Euph. Tell me, Alciphron, do you think it implies a contradiction that God should make a creature free?

Alc. I do not.

Euph. It is then possible there may be such a thing?

[14] [*Characteristics*, vol. i., p. 187.]

Alc. This I do not deny.

Euph. You can therefore conceive and suppose such a free agent?

Alc. Admitting that I can; what then?

Euph. Would not such an one think that he acted?

Alc. He would.

Euph. And condemn himself for some actions, and approve himself for others?

Alc. This too I grant.

Euph. Would he not think he deserved reward or punishment?

Alc. He would.

Euph. And are not all these characters actually found in man?

Alc. They are.

Euph. Tell me now, what other character of your supposed free agent may not actually be found in man? For, if there is none such, we must conclude that man hath all the marks of a free agent.

Alc. Let me see! I was certainly overseen in granting it possible, even for Almighty power, to make such a thing as a free agent. I wonder how I came to make such an absurd concession, after what had been, as I observed before, demonstrated so many different ways.

Euph. Certainly whatever is possible may be supposed: and whatever doth not imply a contradiction is possible to an Infinite Power: therefore, if a natural agent implieth no contradiction, such a being may be supposed. Perhaps, from this supposition, I might infer man to be free. But I will not suppose him that free agent; since it seems, you pretend to have demonstrated the contrary.[15]. O Alciphron! it is vulgarly observed that men judge of others by themselves. But, in judging of me by this rule, you may be mistaken. Many things are plain to one of your sagacity, which are not so to me, who am often puzzled rather than enlightened by those very proofs that with you pass for clear and evident. And, indeed, be the inference never so just, yet, so long as the premises are not clear, I cannot be thoroughly convinced. You must give me leave therefore to propose some questions, the solution of which may perhaps show what at present I am not able to discern.

Alc. I shall leave what hath been said with you, to consider

---

[15] [From the beginning of Euphranor's speech to this point first appeared in 1732b.]

and ruminate upon. It is now time to set out on our journey: there is, therefore, no room for a long string of question and answer.

18. *Euph.* I shall then only beg leave, in a summary manner, to make a remark or two on what you have advanced. In the first place, I observe you take that for granted which I cannot grant, when you assert whatever is certain the same to be necessary. To me, certain and necessary seem very different; there being nothing in the former notion that implies constraint, nor consequently which may not consist with a man's being accountable for his actions. If it is foreseen that such an action shall be done, may it not also be foreseen that it shall be an effect of human choice and liberty? In the next place, I observe that you very nicely abstract and distinguish the actions of the mind, judgment, and will: that you make use of such terms as power, faculty, act, determination, indifference, freedom, necessity, and the like, as if they stood for distinct abstract ideas: and that this supposition seems to ensnare the mind into the same perplexities and errors, which, in all other instances, are observed to attend the doctrine of abstraction. It is self-evident that there is such a thing as motion: and yet there have been found philosophers, who, by refined reasoning, would undertake to prove that there was no such thing. Walking before them was thought the proper way to confute those ingenious men. It is no less evident that man is a free agent: and though, by abstracted reasonings, you would puzzle me, and seem to prove the contrary, yet, so long as I am conscious of my own actions, this inward evidence of plain fact will bear me up against all your reasonings, however subtle and refined. The confuting plain points by obscure ones may perhaps convince me of the ability of your philosophers, but never of their tenets. I cannot conceive why the acute Cratylus should suppose a power of acting in the appetite and reason, and none at all in the will? Allowing, I say, the distinction of three such beings in the mind, I do not see how this could be true. But, if I cannot abstract and distinguish so many beings in the soul of man so accurately as you do, I do not find it necessary; since it is evident to me, in the gross and concrete, that I am a free agent. Nor will it avail to say, the will is governed by the judgment, or determined by the object, while, in every sudden common cause, I cannot discern nor abstract the decree of the

146

judgment from the command of the will; while I know the sensible object to be absolutely inert: and lastly, while I am conscious that I am an active being, who can and do determine myself. If I should suppose things spiritual to be corporeal, or refine things actual and real into general abstracted notions, or by metaphysical skill split things simple and individual into manifold parts, I do not know what may follow. But, if I take things as they are, and ask any plain untutored man, whether he acts or is free in this or that particular action, he readily assents, and I as readily believe him from what I find within. And thus, by an induction of particulars, I may conclude man to be a free agent, although I may be puzzled to define or conceive a notion of freedom in general and abstract. And if man be free, he is plainly accountable. But, if you shall define, abstract, suppose, and it shall follow that, according to your definitions, abstractions, and suppositions, there can be no freedom in man, and you shall thence infer that he is not accountable, I shall make bold to depart from your metaphysical abstracted sense, and appeal to the common sense of mankind.

19. If we consider the notions that obtain in the world of guilt and merit, praise and blame, accountable and unaccountable, we shall find the common question, in order to applaud or censure, acquit or condemn a man, is, whether he did such an action? and whether he was himself when he did it? which comes to the same thing. It should seem, therefore, that, in the ordinary commerce of mankind, any person is esteemed accountable simply as he is an agent. And, though you should tell me that man is inactive, and that the sensible objects act upon him, yet my own experience assures me of the contrary. I know I act; and what I act I am accountable for. And, if this be true, the foundation of religion and morality remains unshaken. Religion, I say, is concerned no further than that man should be accountable: and this he is according to my sense, and the common sense of the world, if he acts; and that he doth act is self-evident. The grounds, therefore, and ends of religion are secured, whether your philosophic notion of liberty agrees with man's actions or no; and whether his actions are certain or contingent; the question being not, whether he did it with a free will? or what determined his will? not, whether it was certain or foreknown that he would do

it? but only, whether he did it wilfully? as what must entitle him to the guilt or merit of it.

Alc. But still, the question recurs, whether man be free?

Euph. In my opinion, a man is said to be free, so far forth as he can do what he will. Is this so, or is it not?

Alc. It seems so.

Euph. Man, therefore, acting according to his will, is to be accounted free.

Alc. This I admit to be true in the vulgar sense. But a philosopher goes higher, and inquires whether man be free to will?

Euph. That is, whether he can will as he wills? I know not how philosophical it may be to ask this question, but it seems very idle. The notions of guilt and merit, justice and reward, are in the minds of men antecedent to all metaphysical disquisitions; and, according to those received natural notions, it is not doubted that man is accountable, that he acts, and is self-determined.

20. But a minute philosopher shall, in virtue of wrong suppositions, confound things most evidently distinct; body, for instance, with spirit; motion with volition; certainty with necessity. And an abstractor or refiner shall so analyse the most simple instantaneous act of the mind as to distinguish therein divers faculties and tendencies, principles and operations, causes and effects; and, having abstracted, supposed, and reasoned upon principles, gratuitous and obscure, he will conclude it is no act at all, and man no agent, but a puppet, or an organ played on by outward objects, and his will a top or a football. And this passeth for philosophy and free-thinking. Perhaps this may be what it passeth for, but it by no means seems a natural or just way of thinking. To me it seems that, if we begin from things particular and concrete, and thence proceed to general notions and conclusions, there will be no difficulty in this matter. But, if we begin with generalities, and lay our foundation in abstract ideas, we shall find ourselves entangled and lost in a labyrinth of our own making. I need not observe, what everyone must see, the ridicule of proving man no agent, and yet pleading for free thought and action, of setting up at once for advocates of liberty and necessity. I have hastily thrown together these hints or remarks, on what you call a fundamental article of the minute philosophy, and your method of proving it, which seems to furnish an admirable specimen of the sophistry of abstract ideas.

If, in this summary way, I have been more dogmatical than became me, you must excuse what you occasioned, by declining a joint and leisurely examination of the truth.

Alc. I think we have examined matters sufficiently.

Cri. To all you have said against human liberty, it is a sufficient answer to observe that your arguments proceed upon an erroneous supposition, either of the soul's being corporeal, or of abstract ideas: not to mention other gross mistakes and gratuitous principles. You might as well suppose that the soul is red or blue as that it is solid. You might as well make the will anything else as motion. And whatever you infer from such premises, which (to speak in the softest manner) are neither proved nor probable, I make no difficulty to reject. You distinguish in all human actions between the last degree of the judgment and the act of the will. You confound certainty with necessity: you inquire, and your inquiry amounts to an absurd question – whether man can will as he wills? As evidently true as is this identical proposition, so evidently false must that way of thinking be which led you to make a question of it. You say the appetites have by necessity of nature a tendency towards their respective objects. This we grant; and withal that appetite, if you please, is not free. But you go further, and tell us that the understanding cannot alter its idea, nor infer indifferently anything from anything. What then? Can we not act at all if we cannot alter the nature of objects, and may we not be free in other things if we are not at liberty to make absurd inferences? You take for granted that the mind is inactive, but that its ideas act upon it: as if the contrary were not evident to every man of common sense, who cannot but know that it is the mind which considers its ideas, chooses, rejects, examines, deliberates, decrees, in one word acts about them, and not they about it. Upon the whole, your premises being obscure and false, the fundamental point, which you pretend to demonstrate so many different ways, proves neither sense nor truth in any.[16] And, on the other hand, there is not need of much inquiry to be convinced of two points, than which none are more evident, more obvious, and more universally admitted by men of all sorts, learned or unlearned, in all times and places, to wit, that man

---

[16] [The above passage, beginning 'not to mention other gross mistakes . . . nor truth in any' was, with one exception, inserted in 1732b. The exception is the passage 'You say the appetites . . . absurd inferences' which is found only in 1752.]

acts, and is accountable for his actions. Whatever abstractors, refiners, or men prejudiced to a false hypothesis may pretend, it is, if I mistake not, evident to every thinking man of common sense, that human minds are so far from being engines or foot-balls, acted upon and bandied about by corporeal objects, without any inward principle of freedom or action, that the only original true notions that we have of freedom, agent, or action are obtained by reflecting on ourselves, and the operations of our own minds. The singularity and credulity of minute philosophers, who suffer themselves to be abused by the paralogisms of three or four eminent patriarchs of infidelity in the last age, is, I think, not to be matched; there being no instance of bigoted superstition the ringleaders whereof have been able to seduce their followers more openly and more widely from the plain dictates of nature and common sense.

21. *Alc.* It has been always an objection against the dis-coverers of truth, that they depart from received opinions. The character of singularity is a tax on free-thinking: and as such we most willingly bear it, and glory in it. A genuine philosopher is never modest in a false sense, to the preferring authority before reason, or an old and common opinion before a true one. Which false modesty, as it discourages men from treading in untrodden paths, or striking out new light, is, above all other qualities, the greatest enemy to free-thinking.

Cri. Authority in disputable points will have its weight with a judicious mind, which yet will follow evidence wherever it leads. Without preferring, we may allow it a good second to reason. Your gentlemen, therefore, of the minute philosophy may spare a world of common-place upon reason, and light, and discoveries. We are not attached to authority against reason, nor afraid of untrodden paths that lead to truth, and are ready to follow a new light when we are sure it is no *ignis fatuus*. Reason may oblige a man to believe against his inclinations: but why should a man quit salutary notions for others not less unreason-able than pernicious? Your schemes, and principles, and boasted demonstrations have been at large proposed and examined. You have shifted your notions, successively retreated from one scheme to another, and in the end renounced them all. Your objections have been treated in the same manner, and with the same event. If we except all that relates to the errors and faults of particular persons, and difficulties which, from the nature of things, we are not obliged to explain; it is surprising to see, after such magnificent threats, how little remains that can amount to a pertinent objection against the Christian religion. What you have produced has been tried by the fair test of reason; and though you should hope to prevail by ridicule when you cannot by reason, yet, in the upshot, I apprehend you will find it impracticable to destroy all sense of religion. Make your countrymen ever so vicious, ignorant, and profane, men will still be disposed to look up to a Supreme Being. Religion, right or wrong, will subsist in some shape or other, and some worship there will surely be either of God or the creature. As for your ridicule, can anything be more ridiculous than to see the most unmeaning men of the age set up for free-thinkers, men so strong in assertion, and yet so weak in argument; advocates for freedom introducing a fatality; patriots trampling on the laws of their country; and pretenders to virtue destroying the motives of it? Let any impartial man but cast an eye on the opinions of the minute philosophers, and then say if anything can be more ridiculous than to believe such things and at the same time laugh at credulity.

22. *Lys.* Say what you will, we have the laughers on our side; and as for your reasoning I take it to be another name for sophistry.

Cri. And I suppose by the same rule you take your own sophisms for arguments. To speak plainly, I know no sort of sophism that is not employed by minute philosophers against religion. They are guilty of a *petitio principii*, in taking for granted that we believe contradictions; of *non causa pro causa*, in affirming that uncharitable feuds and discords are the effects of Christianity; of *ignoratio elenchi*, in expecting demonstrations where we pretend only to faith. If I was not afraid to offend the delicacy of polite ears, nothing were easier than to assign instances of every kind of sophism, which would show how skilful your own philosophers are in the practice of that sophistry you impute to others.

Euph. For my own part, if sophistry be the art or faculty of deceiving other men, I must acquit these gentlemen of it. They seem to have led me a progress through atheism, libertinism, enthusiasm, fatalism, not to convince me of the truth of any of them, so much as to confirm me in my own way of thinking. They have exposed their fairy ware not to cheat but divert us.

As I know them to be professed masters of ridicule, so in a serious sense I know not what to make of them.

Alc. You do not know what to make of us! I should be sorry you did. He must be a superficial philosopher that is soon fathomed.

23. *Cri.* The ambiguous character is, it seems, the sure way to fame and esteem in the learned world, as it stands constituted at present. When the ingenious reader is at a loss to determine whether his author be atheist or deist or polytheist, Stoic or Epicurean, sceptic or dogmatist, infidel or enthusiast, in jest or in earnest, he concludes him without hesitation to be enigmatical and profound. In fact, it is true of the most admired writers of the age, that no man alive can tell what to make of them, or what they would be at.

Alc. We have among us moles that dig deep under ground, and eagles that soar out of sight. We can act all parts and become all opinions, putting them on or off with great freedom of wit and humour.

Euph. It seems then you are a pair of inscrutable, unfathomable, fashionable philosophers.

Lys. It cannot be denied.

Euph. But, I remember, you set out with an open dogmatical air, and talked of plain principles, and evident reasoning, promised to make things as clear as noonday, to extirpate wrong notions and plant right in their stead. Soon after, you began to recede from your first notions, and adopt others; you advanced one while and retreated another, yielded and retracted, said and unsaid. And after having followed you through so many untrodden paths and intricate mazes I find myself never the nearer.

Alc. Did we not tell you the gentlemen of our sect are great proficients of raillery?

Euph. But, methinks, it is a vain attempt for a plain man of any settled beliefs or principles, to engage with such slippery, fugitive, changeable philosophers. It seems as if a man should stand still in the same place, while his adversary chooses and changes his situation, has full range and liberty to traverse the field, and attack him on all sides and in all shapes, from a nearer or further distance, on horseback or on foot, in light or heavy armour, in close fight or with missive weapons.

Alc. It must be owned, a gentleman hath great advantage over a strait-laced pedant or bigot.

Euph. But, after all, what am I the better for the conversation of two such knowing gentlemen? I hoped to have unlearned my errors, and to have learned truths from you, but, to my great disappointment, I do not find that I am either untaught or taught.

Alc. To unteach men their prejudices is a difficult task; and this must first be done, before we can pretend to teach them the truth. Besides, we have at present no time to prove and argue.

Euph. But suppose my mind white paper; and, without being at any pains to extirpate my opinions, or prove your own, only say what you would write thereon, or what you would teach me in case I were teachable. Be for once in earnest, and let me know some one conclusion of yours before we part; or I shall entreat Crito to violate the laws of hospitality towards those who have violated the laws of philosophy, by hanging out false lights to one benighted in ignorance and error. I appeal to you (said he, turning to Crito), whether these philosophical knight-errants should not be confined in this castle of yours, till they make reparation.

Euphranor has reason, said Crito, and my sentence is, that you remain here in durance till you have done something towards satisfying the engagement I am under – having promised, he should know your opinions from yourselves, and you also agreed to.

24. *Alc.* Since it must be so, I will now reveal what I take to be the sum and substance, the grand arcanum and ultimate conclusion of our sect, and that in two words, ΠΑΝΤΑ ΥΠΟΛΗΨΙΣ.[17]

Cri. You are then a downright sceptic. But, sceptic as you are, you own it probable there is a God, certain that the Christian religion is useful, possible it may be true, certain that, if it be, the minute philosophers are in a bad way. This being the case, how can it be questioned what course a wise man should take? Whether the principles of Christians or infidels are truest may be made a question; but which are safest can be none. Certainly if you doubt of all opinions you must doubt of your own; and then, for aught you know, the Christians may be true. The more doubt the more room there is for faith, a sceptic of all men

[17] [That is: Everything is assumption.]

153

having the least right to demand evidence. But, whatever uncertainty there may be in other points, thus much is certain: – either there is or is not an agent: the soul is or is not immortal. If the negatives are not sure, the affirmatives are possible. If the negatives are improbable, the affirmatives are probable. In proportion as any of your ingenious men finds himself unable to prove any one of these negatives, he hath grounds to suspect he may be mistaken. A minute philosopher, therefore, that would act a consistent part, should have the diffidence, the modesty, and the timidity, as well as the doubts of a sceptic; not pretend to an ocean of light, and then lead us to an abyss of darkness. If I have any notion of ridicule, this is most ridiculous. But your ridiculing what, for aught you know, may be true, I can make no sense of. It is neither acting as a wise man with regard to your own interest, nor as a good man with regard to that of your country.

25.   Tully saith somewhere, *Aut undique religionem tolle, aut usque-quaque conserva:* Either let us have no religion at all, or let it be respected. If any single instance can be shown of a people that ever prospered without some religion, or if there be any religion better than the Christian, propose it in the grand assembly of the nation to change our constitution, and either live without religion, or introduce that new religion. A sceptic, as well as other men, is member of a community, and can distinguish between good and evil, natural or political. Be this then his guide as a patriot, though he be no Christian. Or, if he doth not pretend even to this discernment, let him not pretend to correct or alter what he knows nothing of: neither let him that only doubts behave as if he could demonstrate. Timagoras is wont to say, I find my country in possession of certain tenets; they appear to have a useful tendency, and as such are encouraged by the legislature; they make a main part of our constitution; I do not find these innovators can disprove them, or substitute things more useful and certain in their stead: out of regard therefore to the good of mankind and the laws of my country, I shall acquiesce in them. I do not say Timagoras is a Christian, but I reckon him a patriot. Not to inquire in a point of so great concern is folly, but it is still a higher degree of folly to condemn without inquiring.

Lysicles seemed heartily tired of this conversation. It is now late, said he to Alciphron, and all things are ready for our departure. Everyone hath his own way of thinking; and it is as impossible for me to adopt another man's as to make his complexion and features mine.

Alciphron pleaded that, having complied with Euphranor's conditions, they were now at liberty: and Euphranor answered that, all he desired having been to know their tenets, he had nothing further to pretend.

26.   The philosophers being gone, I observed to Crito how unaccountable it was that men so easy to confute should be so difficult to convince.

This, said Crito, is accounted for by Aristotle, who tells us that arguments have not an effect on all men, but only on them whose minds are prepared by education and custom, as land is for seed.[18] Make a point never so clear, it is great odds that a man whose habits and the bent of whose mind lie in a contrary way shall be unable to comprehend it. So weak a thing is reason in competition with inclination.

I replied, this answer might hold with respect to other persons and other times; but when the question was of inquisitive men, in an age wherein reason was so much cultivated, and thinking so much in vogue, it did not seem satisfactory.

I have known it remarked, said Crito, by a man of much observation, that in the present age thinking is more talked of but less practised than in ancient times; and that since the revival of learning men have read much and wrote much but thought little: insomuch that with us to think closely and justly is the least part of a learned man, and none at all of a polite man. The free-thinkers, it must be owned, make great pretensions to thinking, and yet they show but little exactness in it. A lively man, and what the world calls a man of sense, are often destitute of this talent; which is not a mere gift of nature, but must be improved and perfected by much attention and exercise on very different subjects; a thing of more pains and time than the hasty men of parts in our age care to take. Such were the sentiments of a judicious friend of mine. And if you are not already sufficiently convinced of these truths, you need only cast an eye on the dark and confused, but nevertheless admired, writers of this famous sect; and then you will be able to judge whether those who are led by men of such wrong heads can have very good ones of their own. Such, for instance, was Spinosa, the great leader of

[18] *Ethic. ad Nicom.*, lib. x, cap. 9.

our modern infidels, in whom are to be found many schemes and notions much admired and followed of late years: – such as undermining religion under the pretence of vindicating and explaining it: the maintaining it not necessary to believe in Christ according to the flesh: the persuading men that miracles are to be understood only in a spiritual and allegorical sense: that vice is not so bad a thing as we are apt to think: that men are mere machines impelled by fatal necessity.

I have heard, said I, Spinosa represented as a man of close argument and demonstration.

He did, replied Crito, demonstrate; but it was after such a manner as any one may demonstrate anything. Allow a man the privilege to make his own definitions of common words, and it will be no hard matter for him to infer conclusions which in one sense shall be true and in another false, at once seeming paradoxes and manifest truisms. For example, let but Spinosa define natural right to be natural power, and he will easily demonstrate that 'whatever a man can do' he hath a right to do.[19] Nothing can be plainer than the folly of his proceeding: but our pretenders to the *lumen siccum* are so passionately prejudiced against religion, as to swallow the grossest nonsense and sophistry of weak and wicked writers for demonstration.

27. And so great a noise do these men make, with their thinking, reasoning, and demonstrating, as to prejudice some well-meaning persons against all use and improvement of reason. Honest Demea, having seen a neighbour of his ruined by the vices of a free-thinking son, contracted such a prejudice against thinking that he would not suffer his own to read Euclid, being told it might teach him to think; till a friend convinced him the epidemical distemper was not thinking, but only the want and affectation of it. I know an eminent free-thinker who never goes to bed without a gallon of wine in his belly, and is sure to replenish before the fumes are off his brain, by which means he has not had one sober thought these seven years; another, that would not for the world lose the privilege and reputation of free-thinking, who games all night, and lies in bed all day: and as for the outside or appearance of thought in that meagre minute philosopher Ibycus, it is an effect, not of thinking, but of carking, cheating, and writing in an office. Strange, said he, that such

[19] *Tractat. Polit.*, cap. 2.

men should set up for free-thinkers! But it is yet more strange that other men should be out of conceit with thinking and reasoning, for the sake of such pretenders.

I answered, that some good men conceived an opposition between reason and religion, faith and knowledge, nature and grace; and that, consequently, the way to promote religion was to quench the light of nature and discourage all rational inquiry.

28. How right the intentions of these men may be, replied Crito, I shall not say; but surely their notions are very wrong. Can anything be more dishonourable to religion than the representing it as an unreasonable, unnatural, ignorant institution? God is the Father of all lights, whether natural or revealed. Natural concupiscence is one thing, and the light of nature another. You cannot therefore argue from the former against the latter: neither can you from science, falsely so called, against real knowledge. Whatever, therefore, is said of the one in Holy Scripture is not to be interpreted of the other.

I insisted that human learning in the hands of divines had, from time to time, created great disputes and divisions in the church.

As abstracted metaphysics, replied Crito, have always a tendency to produce disputes among Christians, as well as other men, so it should seem that genuine truth and knowledge would allay this humour, which makes men sacrifice the undisputed duties of peace and charity to disputable notions.

After all, said I, whatever may be said for reason, it is plain the sceptics and infidels of the age are not to be cured by it.

I will not dispute this point, said Crito: in order to cure a distemper, you should consider what produced it. Had men reasoned themselves into a wrong opinion, one might hope to reason them out of it. But this is not the case; the infidelity of most minute philosophers seeming an effect of very different motives from thought and reason. Little incidents, vanity, disgust, humour, inclination, without the least assistance from reason, are often known to make infidels. Where the general tendency of a doctrine is disagreeable, the mind is prepared to relish and improve everything that with the least pretence seems to make against it. Hence the coarse manners of a country curate, the polite manners of a chaplain, the wit of a minute philosopher, a jest, a song, a tale can serve instead of a reason for infidelity. Bupalus preferred a rake in the church, and then made use of him as an argument against it. Vice, indolence, faction, and fashion produce minute philosophers, and mere petulancy not a few. Who then can expect a thing so irrational and capricious should yield to reason? It may, nevertheless, be worth while to argue against such men, and expose their fallacies, if not for their own sake, yet for the sake of others; as it may lessen their credit, and prevent the growth of their sect, by removing a prejudice in their favour, which sometimes inclines others as well as themselves to think they have made a monopoly of human reason.

29. The most general pretext which looks like reason is taken from the variety of opinions about religion. This is a resting-stone to a lazy and superficial mind. But one of more spirit and a juster way of thinking makes it a step whence he looks about, and proceeds to examine, and compare the differing institutions of religion. He will observe which of these is the most sublime and rational in its doctrines, most venerable in its mysteries, most useful in its precepts, most decent in its worship? which createth the noblest hopes, and most worthy views? He will consider their rise and progress: which oweth least to human arts or arms? which flatters the senses and gross inclinations of men? which adorns and improves the most excellent part of our nature? which hath been propagated in the most wonderful manner? which hath surmounted the greatest difficulties, or showed the most disinterested zeal and sincerity in its professors? He will inquire, which best accords with nature and history? He will consider, what savours of the world and what looks like wisdom from above? He will be careful to separate human alloy from that which is Divine; and, upon the whole, form his judgment like a reasonable free-thinker. But instead of taking such a rational course, one of these hasty sceptics shall conclude without demurring that there is no wisdom in politics, no honesty in dealings, no knowledge in philosophy, no truth in religion; and all by one and the same sort of inference, from the numerous examples of folly, knavery, ignorance, and error which are to be met with in the world. But, as those who are unknowing in everything else imagine themselves sharpsighted in religion, this learned sophism is oftenest levelled against Christianity.

30. In my opinion, he that would convince an infidel who can be brought to reason ought in the first place clearly to convince him of the being of a God; it seeming to me, that any man

who is really a Theist, cannot be an enemy to the Christian religion; and that the ignorance or disbelief of this fundamental point is that which at bottom constitutes the minute philosopher. I imagine they who are acquainted with the great authors in the minute philosophy need not be told of this. The being of a God is capable of clear proof, and a proper object of human reason: whereas the mysteries of His nature, and indeed whatever there is of mystery in religion, to endeavour to explain and prove by reason is a vain attempt. It is sufficient if we can show there is nothing absurd or repugnant in our belief of those points, and, instead of framing hypotheses to explain them, we use our reason only for answering the objections brought against them. But, on all occasions, we ought to distinguish the serious, modest, ingenuous man of sense, who hath scruples about religion, and behaves like a prudent man in doubt, from the minute philosophers, those profane and conceited men, who must needs proselyte others to their own doubts. When one of this stamp presents himself, we should consider what species he is of: whether a first or a second-hand philosopher, a libertine, scorner, or sceptic? Each character requiring a peculiar treatment. Some men are too ignorant to be humble, without which there can be no docility. But though a man must in some degree have thought, and considered, to be capable of being convinced, yet it is possible the most ignorant may be laughed out of his opinions. I knew a woman of sense reduce two minute philosophers, who had long been a nuisance to the neighbourhood, by taking her cue from their predominant affectations. The one set up for being the most incredulous man upon earth, the other for the most unbounded freedom. She observed to the first, that he who had credulity sufficient to trust the most valuable things, his life and fortune, to his apothecary and lawyer, ridiculously affected the character of incredulous by refusing to trust his soul, a thing in his own account but a mere trifle, to his parish priest. The other, being what you call a beau, she made sensible how absolute a slave he was in point of dress, to him the most important thing in the world, while he was earnestly contending for a liberty of thinking, with which he never troubled his head; and how much more it concerned and became him to assert an independency of fashion, and obtain scope for his genius where it was best qualified to exert itself. The minute philosophers at first hand are very few, and, considered in themselves, of small consequence: but their followers, who pin

159

their faith upon them, are numerous, and not less confident than credulous; there being something in the air and manner of these second-hand philosophers very apt to disconcert a man of gravity and argument, and much more difficult to be borne than the weight of their objections.

31. Crito having made an end, Euphranor declared it to be his opinion, that it would much conduce to the public benefit, if, instead of discouraging free-thinking, there was erected in the midst of this free country a Dianoetic Academy, or seminary for free-thinkers, provided with retired chambers, and galleries, and shady walks and groves, where, after seven years spent in silence and meditation, a man might commence a genuine free-thinker, and from that time forward have licence to think what he pleased, and a badge to distinguish him from counterfeits.

In good earnest, said Crito, I imagine that thinking is the great *desideratum* of the present age; and that the real cause of whatever is amiss may justly be reckoned the general neglect of education in those who need it most – the people of fashion. What can be expected where those who have the most influence have the least sense, and those who are sure to be followed set the worst example? where youth so uneducated are yet so forward? where modesty is esteemed pusillanimity, and a deference to years, knowledge, religion, laws, want of sense and spirit? Such untimely growth of genius would not have been valued or encouraged by the wise men of antiquity; whose sentiments on this point are so ill suited to the genuis of our times that it is to be feared modern ears could not bear them. But, however ridiculous such maxims might seem to our British youth, who are so capable and so forward to try experiments, and mend the constitution of their country, I believe it will be admitted by men of sense that, if the governing part of mankind would in these days, for experiment's sake, consider themselves in that old Homerical light as pastors of the people, whose duty it was to improve their flock, they would soon find that this is to be done by an education very different from the modern, and otherguess maxims than those of the minute philosophy. If our youth were really inured to thought and reflexion, and an acquaintance with the excellent writers of antiquity, we should see that licentious humour, vulgarly called *free-thinking*, banished from the presence of gentlemen, together with ignorance and ill taste; which as they are inseparable from vice, so men follow vice for the sake of pleasure, and fly from virtue through an abhorrence of pain. Their minds, therefore, betimes should be formed and accustomed to receive pleasure and pain from proper objects, or, which is the same thing, to have their inclinations and aversions rightly placed. Καλῶς χαίρειν ἢ μισεῖν. This, according to Plato and Aristotle, was the ὀρθὴ παιδεία, the right education.[20] And those who, in their own minds, their health, or their fortunes, feel the cursed effects of a wrong one, would do well to consider, they cannot better make amends for what was amiss in themselves than by preventing the same in their prosperity.

While Crito was saying this, company came in, which put an end to our conversation.

[20] Plato in *Protag.*, and Arist. *Ethic. ad Nicom.*, lib. ii, cap. 2, and lib. x, cap. 9.

From *Divine Analogy* (1733)
pp. 475–9, 521–5, 537–40

Peter Browne

This author [i.e. Berkeley] takes occasion from hence to say, *That it was indeed a current opinion in the schools, that even being* or existence *itself, should be attributed analogicaly to God and the creatures.*[1] But surely not according to *His singular* notion of analogy between things the very same in kind, and differing only in degree; so that a lower degree of *existence* should be analogous to a higher degree. No; but as he himself is obliged to own, *That they supposed not God to exist in the* same sence *with created beings; not that he exists less realy and truly than they;* and he adds *less properly and formaly than they.*[2] But to *exist properly and formaly* is a phrase of his own here, and not of the *Schoolmen*; who hold that tho' God doth exist *realy* and *truly*, yet the term *existence* is not to be applyed to him in the same *proper* and *formal* sence in which it is applyed to *man*. The *ratio formalis* of any thing in the sence of the schools is, what is so peculiarly essential to it as such, that thereby only it becomes *what it is*, and different from all other kinds of things whatsoever: and accordingly when a *word* is applyed to any thing so as to include and signify that intrinsic, peculiar, distinguishing essence or property of it; it is said to be applyed in a *formal sence*, and in its strict and *literal* propriety. Thus it is they say *existence* is applyed to God in a sence actualy *true* and *real*, but not *formaly* and *properly* and *literaly* as it is applyed to *man*; of whose existence and the manner of it we have a direct and immediate conception. This is what our author should have confuted; and not have blended his absurd notion together with it in one sentence, by slipping into it two words of his own utterly destructive of the Schoolmen's real meaning. Till he does confute it, it must be a current opinion among all men. For surely we are as far from any direct idea or

162

conception of the *true divine existence*, as we are of the divine *substance*; or at least as we are of those real *intrinsic* divine *attributes* which exist: and consequently the *manner* of *God's* existence, than by analogy with our own and that of other men whereof we have an immediate perception and consciousness; nor any other way of expressing it than by a word borrowed from thence. And tho' nothing is more true than that God doth not *exist* in the *same sence* with created beings; or that he hath not the same *kind* or *manner* of existence, but a kind and manner infinitely different from them all; yet we can affirm that *God is* or *exists*, with as much truth and reality as that we our selves exist.

The last of his Schoolmen is *Cajetan*, from whom the only material thing observed is this. *Knowlege*, says our author, *may be attributed to God in the proper and formal meaning of the word: for as we say that God is infinitely above man, so is the knowlege of God infinitely above the knowlege of man; this* says he, *is what* Cajetan *calls analogia proprie facta*, a proper analogy as he wrongly translates it. But word the sentence right, and you will do justice both to truth, and to Cajetan. We say, that as the *nature* of God is infinitely above the *nature* of man; so is the *nature* or *kind* of his *knowlege* infinitely above the nature or kind of *knowlege* in man; and consequently no proportion of *degrees only* can be signifyed by that term when attributed to God: so that it cannot be attributed to him in the *proper*, or *formal*, or *literal* sence of the word; but by that *analogy* only which is founded on such a real correspondency and similitude as may be between two things different in nature or *kind*. This is *analogia proprie facta, analogy properly formed*, or *what is properly analogy*; and not *analogia propria*, the short and mistaken turn given to the words of Cajetan in this author's translation of them.

I here appeal to the reader whether, as our author confesseth this to have been *his first fault* in medling with the *Schoolmen*; he is not bound in conscience to keep *his promise, that it shall be the last of the kind*. To induce him to be as good as his word, I shall observe to him; that men of sence in the present age are already surfeited of treatises full of *curtailed, perverted, mistranslated, misapplyed* and *impertinent quotations*: and begin to nauseate them, as temperate sober men do the dishes that are served up with a very little substantial food; but stuffed with forcemeats, and brimful of unwholesom and pernicious sauces. Nothing is more void of real improvement and instruction to the mind, and more fulsom, than heaps of quotations, and tedious disquisitions what opinions such and such men were of, in relation to matters properly determinable only by right reason and Scripture; and inquiries how far they at first maintained those opinions, or how far they receded from them afterwards. Whereas the stating any of those opinions of importance distinctly and fairly; explaining them clearly and fully; and producing the best reasons and arguments for or against them either from our selves or others, with that brevity and perspicuity which may save men the irksome trouble of frequently raking over a large dunghill before they find one jem; would be of real service to mankind in general, as well as to the more *polite* part of them in particular.

The substance of his first answer [to the infidels or freethinkers] is, that whereas the objection supposeth every *general* term in an intelligible discourse, to stand for a distinct *abstract* general idea; he proceeds to shew, very justly indeed, how groundless and false that notion is, of men's forming any *universal* ideas by *abstracting* intirely from all the *particulars* of any kind of thing whatsoever. The application he makes of it is this. That men are as little capable of forming *abstract* ideas or conceptions even of things *natural* and *sensible*, as they are of things *divine* and *supernatural*; that they can form no such general abstract idea of *number* and *force*, any more than they can of *grace*: and his consequence is, that both being upon the same level with respect to our forming any abstract conception or idea of them; it is unreasonable that men should insist upon having such an idea of grace, when they cannot have the like idea of number or force. But to what purpose is all this? For the objection, as it is stated by infidels supposeth no such thing; nor doth he himself mention *any* sort of *abstract* ideas in any part of it, to give even a colour to his being so prolix in discanting upon them in his answer. No, the whole strength of their objection is resolved into this; that they can obtain no ideas, either general or particular, either in the abstract or in the concrete, either clear or obscure, distinct or indeterminate, of things divine and spiritual contained in the gospel mysteries; *different* from the ideas of common worldly objects: nor of grace in particular, different from that of human grace or favour; and therefore they reject it as an insignificant term, without any real and useful meaning when taken in a divine and religious sence. They do not insist upon ideas of things divine and spiritual, rendred general by *abstraction* from all the *particulars*; nor upon such as become general by *one* of the particulars being made to *stand for* an *indefinite number* of things of the same kind, which is the true abstraction: no nor upon an idea of divine grace abstracted from the *cause* operating, from the *subject* operated upon, and from the *effects* produced; as he groundlessly supposes in his answer. But what they demand is, *any* ideas of them as different from all the ideas and conceptions of things sensible and human, as these are from things imperceptible and divine: and accordingly they tell you that when they look inward for such ideas to annex to the terms, their mind is an empty void; and therefore they look no farther than the strictly proper and formal and literal acceptation of those words.

But should we grant that the objection did realy proceed upon a supposition that men cannot have as clear and distinct an *abstract* idea of grace, as they imagine they have of number and force: yet the tacit supposition upon which his whole answer manifestly proceeds, and which is an unavoidable consequence of his supposing the divine and human attributes to be the same in kind, is absolutely false. Namely, that we have as *direct* and *immediate* ideas or conceptions of things divine and spiritual, as we have of things sensible and human, tho' we have no abstract ideas of either; and that we have as *direct* an idea of grace in particular, as we have of number or force: for tho', says he, we cannot form any idea of number in the *abstract*, or exclusive of all things numbred; nor of force *prescinded*, as he speaks, from body, motion, time, and place; yet we can form a clear and distinct *direct* idea of each of them in the *concrete*. But surely we can form no *direct immediate* idea or conception of divine grace, either *abstracted* from God the author, from man the subject, and from virtue and piety its effects; or *even in the concrete* and *in conjunction with them*: because as the *operation it self* is inconceivable directly, so neither can we have any direct and immediate conception or idea of the divine *spirit* which operates, or of any thing the same in kind with it. What are we to do then here? The very same that we are obliged to do in respect of all other things divine and spiritual, even the very attributes of God; that is to substitute the clear and distinct and *direct* conception of a natural and human operation in the *concrete*, as an analogical representation of (what is otherwise inconceivable) the divine grace or influence in the

165

concrete also; or inclusive of the holy Spirit, the human mind, and the happy effects. So that the true ground of men's delusion in rejecting the conceptions and faith of things divine and spiritual contained in the gospel mysteries; and all real and useful signification of the terms by which we express them, and of *grace* in particular; is not the intire want of such an *abstract* idea of it as they falsely imagine they have of number and force, which is this author's wrong solution of the matter: but their not discerning that tho' the thing it self were granted to be ever so true and real; yet it is absurd to expect that the mind of man can obtain *direct* and *immediate* ideas or conceptions of such kinds of objects as are out of the direct reach of all their faculties; or that it can have *natural* ideas of things *supernatural*. And therefore that if there *is* any such thing as grace, or an immediate assisting influence of the divine spirit upon the mind of man (which is plainly revealed, and impossible for them to disprove) there can be no other way of conceiving it but by the influence of an human and natural cause: because such divine operation must unavoidably be as inconceivable with respect to its *real nature*, as the spirit it self which operates. And their fatal error is, that upon their principle they must necessarily reject the *truth* and *reality* of every thing that is thus *inconceivable to us as it is in it self*; and of whatever is not otherwise conceivable than by analogy with things natural and human; even the attributes of God included.

The last and most extraordinary step taken by our author for solving the preceding grand objection of infidels is, by telling them *that the true end of speech, reason, science, faith, assent; is not always the imparting or acquiring of ideas: but something of an operative nature, tending to a conceived good; which may be obtained – altho' there should be no possibility of offering or exhibiting any such idea to the mind.*[3] Surely more confusion and absurdity could not possibly have been crowded into the compass of one short period. *The end of speech is not always the imparting or acquiring ideas*, conceptions, or notions; tho' without some of these affixed to the words or excited by them as *signs*, it is no *speech*, but insignificant empty *noise*. Tho' it be evidently plain that speech could serve no rational end; if it did not suggest and impart some of these: tho' this is the very point, wherein human language differs from the irrational instinctive sounds of birds and beasts, and even of insects. And tho' if you exclude this use, no man living can assign any other for words or speech: in which it would be impossible there should be either propriety or figure; or any thing tending to excite us to a rational *operation*. Insomuch that our conversing like mutes, and denoting the ideas and conceptions of the mind by signs upon the fingers; would, according to his notion, be of more real advantage to mankind, and upon all accounts vastly preferable to any sounds variously articulated by the different organs of voice. *The true end of reason*. But surely one true end and use of reason, is to acquire and impart a perception of the agreements and disagreements of our ideas, conceptions, and notions; which it could never perform, unless the *ideas*, conceptions, and notions themselves are acquired, or exhibited to the mind: without this it could never influence us to *act* or *operate* like men; nor to obtain our ultimate end, which is true rational happiness. *The true end of science*. But surely each rational science must be conversant about some *ideas*, conceptions, or notions of things; and these must be acquired or exhibited to the mind, and imparted by the terms and signs used in it: or it would be impossible to understand or teach any of the sciences; or to render them useful to any rational *end* or *operation*. Otherwise the true end of all science would be to talk much, but to learn and know and practise nothing: there would be in reality but one science in the world; that is a very learned method of multiplying such marks and words only, as were most agreeable to the eye and harmonious to the ear. Upon this author's principle, there might be some use of *singing* indeed; but it would be to no purpose for any man to speak who could not perform it melodiously. *The true end of faith*. Religion then is placed upon the same absurd foot with science; faith (according to him) may answer a true and excellent and operative end, without our always acquiring any idea or conception or notion of *what* we believe, or having it any way exhibited to the mind; and *we may believe* (as this author himself words it) *where we do not understand*. The bare words in which we express our faith, may be vital ruling principles to rational creatures; tho' they are not always animated by any ideas or conceptions affixed to them, and exhibited to the mind: and tho' faith in words only for its object, is no other than believing in certain sounds and syllables. You may profess indeed to believe in *father, son*, and *spirit*; in the *grace* of God; and in the *mediation* and *intercession* of Christ; but yet it is not always *necessary* or *possible* for you to

167

acquire, or exhibit to your mind, any *ideas*, conceptions or notions
of the things marked out by those words: tho' by this rule you
may as well be said to have faith in the noise of sounding brass
or a tinkling cymbal. Nay your believing a God would be very
useful; tho' upon his scheme it may be no more than faith in a
monosyllable. You may commendably believe in what you *hear*,
tho' you do not *understand* any thing of it. Thus all faith would
terminate in the ear; and no point of it could ever reach the head
or the heart, or influence us to any rational action. *The true end
of assent.* The *end* of assent indeed is not the imparting or acquiring
ideas, conceptions, or notions: but surely some of these must
necessarily be acquired or exhibited to the mind for the *object* of
our assent; otherwise it would be just such another useful assent
as one *parrot* may yield to another.

NOTES

1 [Browne is quoting from *Alciphron* IV. 20.]
2 [See *Alciphron* IV. 20.]
3 *Alciphron* VII. 14.

'Additions and Corrections'
from *Inquiry into Beauty and Virtue* (4th edn, 1738)

Francis Hutcheson

P. 45. *upon the penult. Paragraph*, note. 'Tis surprising to see the ingenious author of *Alciphron* alledging, that all beauty observed is solely some *use* perceived or imagined; for no other reason than this, that the apprehension of the use intended, occurs continually, when we are judging of the forms of chairs, doors, tables, and some other things of obvious use; and that we like those forms most, which are *fittest for the use*. Whereas we see, that in these very things *similitude* of parts is regarded, where unlike parts would be equally useful: thus the feet of a chair would be of the same use, tho' unlike, were they equally long; tho' one were strait, and the other bended; or one bending outwards, and the other inwards: a coffin-shape for a door would bear a more manifest aptitude to the human shape, than that which artists require. And then what is the *use* of these *imitations of nature* or of its works, in *architecture*? Why should a pillar please which has some of the human proportions? Is the *end* or *use* of a pillar the same as of a man? Why the imitation of other natural or well-proportioned things in the entablature? Is there then a *sense of imitation*, relishing it where there is no other use than this, that it naturally pleases? Again; is no man pleased with the shapes of any animals, but those which he expects use from? The shapes of the horse or the ox may promise use to the owner; but is he the only person who relishes the beauty? And is there no beauty discerned in plants, in flowers, in animals, whose use is to us unknown? But what is still more surprising, is his representing *Aristotle* as giving the ἐπαινετὸν, for the notion of the καλὸν: when he has so often told us, 'that the καλὸν is prior to it; that we love praise from others, as it gives testimony to, and confirms our opinion of, our being possessed of virtue, or the καλὸν; and

169

that the superior excellency of this, which we antecedently perceive, is the reason why we love praise'. *See Ethic. ad Nicom. Lib.
i. c.* 5, and often elsewhere. 'Tis true, that the καλὸν is laudable,
and, as *Plato* asserts, all-wise, ἡδὺ καὶ ὠφέλιμον, at last; and so
does every one maintain who asserts a *moral sense*, in that very
assertion. And yet the doctor has found out the art of making
this an objection to a *moral sense*.

From *Philosophical Works* (1754), vol. 1, pp. 176–81

Lord Bolingbroke

I could wish that Alciphron and Lysicles had made this observation to Euphranor, and had applied it to shew him why they admitted the word force, and rejected the word grace. The task would not have been hard, since it would not have been hard to shew him real causes sufficiently known, and sufficiently marked by words, of the effects ascribed by him to a cause supposed unknown, and marked by a distinct word appropriated to this purpose. They might have shewn these causes to be the influence of a religious education, a warm head, and a warmer heart; hope, fear, grief, joy, strong passions turned by prejudice and habit to devotion, devotion itself nursing its own principles, the effect in its turn becoming a cause uniform and constant, or redoubling its force, on the least failure, in acts of attrition, contrition, mortification, and repentance. They might have proved not only by probable reasons, but by indubitable facts, the sufficiency of these and other known causes to produce all the effects commonly ascribed to grace, even the most astonishing that ever appeared in saints, confessors, or martyrs. Nay, they might have shewn that effects more astonishing, and many of them better vouched, than most of these, have been, and are still daily, produced in men, whom it would be blasphemous to repute under the divine influence. Alciphron might have illustrated this argument in his serious character, by quoting the saints, confessors, and martyrs of idolatry and heresy; and Lysicles in his gayer character, by quoting those of atheism, and of the most abominable vices, as well as the most indifferent customs; of paederasty, for instance, and of long beards.

I am thinking what Euphranor would have replied to the minute philosophers; and can discover no reply worthy of that solidity and that candor which render him equally admirable and amiable. He might have said indeed that he was misunderstood by them, that the parity he insisted on was not meant to 'consist in a proof of grace, as well as force, from the effects; that it was only meant to answer an objection against the doctrine of grace, supposing it proved from revelation, and not to prove its existence; that therefore if the parity was sufficient to prove the possibility of believing grace without an idea of it, the objection they had made was answered, and he aimed at no more.' But I think that as minute philosophers as I am willing to allow Alciphron and Lysicles to have been, they would have maintained very easily the pertinence of their objection, and the insufficiency of Euphranor's answer.

They might have said, there is not even the parity you now suppose between force and grace. Our objection against the latter did in effect anticipate your reply: and if we allowed your reply to be a good one, it would neither strengthen your cause, nor weaken ours. The parity between force and grace, which you confine now to a possibility of believing one as well as the other, is not sufficient; because it is not real. The possibility of believing force, is nothing more than the possibility of believing that every effect has a cause, tho' the cause be unknown to us, and the propriety of the word consists in the application of it to no other cause. The disparity and impropriety do not arise from our having no idea of grace; for it is true that we have none of force: but they arise from hence, that there is not the same possibility of believing a cause, whereof we have no idea, and which cannot be ascertained by its effects, as there is of believing one whereof we have no idea indeed, but which may be ascertained by its effects. You assume grace as a cause of one particular kind, an immediate influence of God on the mind; and you apply to it effects that may have causes of several kinds. Should a word be invented to signify a moral cause of effects purely physical, or a physical cause of effects purely moral, you would laugh at the invention; and you would be in the right. But is it a jot less ridiculous to assign a particular cause, either natural or supernatural, of effects that may be produced by any, or all, of these; and to think to save the absurdity by saying that the word, invented to denote this cause, has no idea attached to it, no more than that of force?

The use of the word force can have no equivocal consequence:

the use of the word grace may. The testimony, nay, the conviction, of men, that they felt the influence of this unknown cause, would not take off the equivocation. How should it, after all the examples that may be brought from daily experience? A real enthusiast doubts no more of his perceptions of the operations of grace, informing his mind, and determining his will, than he doubts of his perceptions of the action of outward objects on his senses, and perhaps less.

Another thing, which I imagine that the minute philosophers would have said to Euphranor, is this. Since the parity you endeavour to establish between force and grace, cannot be so established as to answer your purpose on any principles of reason; it remains that the notion of grace cannot be received, nor the word employed, on any other authority, than that of implicit faith in the revelation by which you suppose the existence of grace proved. That authority obliges us to believe an action or an influence of God on his elect, the manner of which no human idea can reach: but on what authority, Euphranor, do you answer our 'objection against the doctrine of grace, by supposing it proved by revelation?' If you have proved this fact, that the Christian revelation, in which the doctrine of grace is contained, was made by God to mankind, as all facts, and especially one of this importance, ought to be proved, for every other kind of proof proves nothing; we will agree, tho' there be not the same reason for admitting grace as for admitting force, that both are to be received alike. Our objection was insufficient; but your answer then was unnecessary: for surely nothing can be more unnecessary, than to go about to establish on probable arguments what is already established on demonstration: and the real existence of grace has been already demonstrated, if the truth of the revelation, in every part of it, has been so; since no proposition can be more demonstrated than this, that a doctrine taught by infinite wisdom and truth is a true doctrine. If you have not proved this fact, and we think you have scarce attempted it, by the proper proofs, your argument is a pure sophism. When we urge that the doctrine of grace, or any other Christian doctrine, is inconceivable, or that it is pregnant with absurd consequences, and therefore unworthy of God; this is urged, in strictness, *ex abundantia*; for we do not give up the fundamental point, which is, that the authenticity of your scriptures, in the whole and in every part of them, and the truth by consequence of your revelation, has not been yet proved. When you suppose the contrary, therefore, in disputing with us, you beg the question about a principle, in order to confirm a consequence. Thus it seems to me that the dispute between Euphranor and the minute philosophers would have ended. What I have said upon it can be scarce called a digression; since this comparison of force and grace serves admirably well to exemplify what has been said concerning the art and artifice of the mind in the proper and improper use of words, to which no determinate ideas are annexed.

From 'Berkeley's Life and Writings' (1871)[1]

J. S. Mill

Besides Berkeley's properly metaphysical writings, some notice must be taken of his strictly polemical performances – his attacks on the freethinkers, and on the mathematicians. The former controversy pervades more or less all his writings, and is the special object of the longest of them, the series of dialogues entitled *Alciphron, or the Minute Philosopher*. Of this it may be said with truth, that were it not the production of so eminent a man, it would have little claim to serious attention. As a composition, indeed, it has great merit; and, together with the dialogues on Matter, entitle Berkeley to be regarded as the writer who, after Plato, has best managed the instrument of controversial dialogue. The opinions, however, which he puts into the mouths of freethinkers are mostly such as no one would now think worth refuting, for the excellent reason that nobody holds them; it may be permitted to doubt whether they were even held by any one worth answering. The freethinkers in the dialogues are two in number – Alciphron, who is intended to represent a disciple of Shaftesbury; and Lysicles, a follower of Mandeville, or rather a man of pleasure who avails himself of Mandeville in defending his own way of life. Alciphron stands for sentimental, Lysicles for sensual infidelity; the latter (with whom Alciphron also at first seemed to agree) denying all moral distinctions, and professing a doctrine of pure selfishness. Now Mandeville himself did neither of these, nor are such doctrines known to have been ever professed, even by those who, so far as they dared, acted on them. It is most likely that Berkeley painted freethinkers from no actual acquaintance with them, and in the case of 'sceptics and atheists' without any authentic knowledge of their arguments; for few, if any, writers in his time avowed either scepticism or atheism, and,

175

before Hume, nobody of note had attempted, even as an intellectual exercise, to set out the case on the atheistical side. Like most other defenders of religion in his day, though we regret to have it to say of a man of his genius and virtues, Berkeley made no scruple of imputing atheism on mere surmise – to Hobbes, for example, who never speaks otherwise than as a believer in God, and even in Christianity; and to the 'god-intoxicated' Spinoza. We may judge that he replied to what he supposed to be in the minds of infidels, rather than to what they anywhere said; and, in consequence, his replies generally miss the mark. Indeed, with the exception of his own special argument for Theism, already commented upon, he has much more to say for the usefulness of religion than for its truth; and even on that he says little more than what is obvious on the surface.

NOTE

1 *Fortnightly Review* LIX, N.S., pp. 519–20.

From *English Thought in the Eighteenth Century* (1876)

Leslie Stephen

IX.45

Berkeley's 'Minute Philosopher' is the least admirable perform-
ance of that admirable writer. The most characteristic part is
the attempt to erect a proof of theology upon his own peculiar
metaphysical theory. The remainder consists for the most part of
the familiar commonplaces, expressed in a style of exquisite grace
and lucidity, but not implying any great originality. The general
tendency of his remarks, both upon Mandeville and Shaftesbury,
may be described as utilitarian. Although, as already noticed, he
seems to be incapable of detecting the economical fallacy involved
in Mandeville's eulogy upon extravagance, he, of course, sees,
and has no difficulty in proving, that vice is prejudicial to a
community. He establishes with rather superfluous care that
immorality of all kinds is ruinous to the constitution of individuals, and destructive to a state. Virtue is not a mere fashion,
but implies obedience to the laws upon which men's physical and
spiritual health depends. Shaftesbury is condemned on the same
grounds. Admitting Shaftesbury's leading principle of the beauty
of virtue, Berkeley argues that our sense of beauty consists essentially in our perception of the right adaptation of means to ends.
The beauty of the universe consists, therefore, in the existence of
an intelligent principle, governing all things, punishing the
wicked, protecting the virtuous. 'In such a system, vice is madness, cunning is folly, wisdom and virtue all the same thing';[77]
and whatever seems amiss, will, in the last act, be ultimately
wound up according to the strictest rules of wisdom and justice.
Shaftesbury's ruling mind must, therefore, be either the Christian
Deity, or another name for blind Fate. In the latter case, a man
must be a 'Stoic or a Knight-errant'[77] to be virtuous; the 'minute
philosopher' is the devotee of 'an inexplicable enthusiastic notion

of moral beauty',[78] or, as Lysicles, the representative of Mandeville, puts it, his doctrine 'hath all the solid inconveniences, without the amusing hopes and prospects, of the Christians'.[79]

NOTES

77 Dial, III. sect. 10.
78 Ibid. sect. 12.
79 Ibid. sect. 7.

Berkeley on beauty

J. O. Urmson

In the history of thought it is almost always pointless to ascribe even an approximate date to the beginning of any movement or enterprise, both because antecedents can always be found and because such movements and enterprises are not easily individuated. But, with such an acknowledgement and allowing ourselves the licence of including 1699, the year of publication of Shaftesbury's *Inquiry Concerning Virtue*, in the eighteenth century, we may reasonably ascribe the beginnings of aesthetics as we know the discipline today to British philosophers of the eighteenth century, most notably to Shaftesbury, Hutcheson, Hume and Reid. It was these philosophers who first systematically discussed such questions as what in the twentieth century might be called the analysis of aesthetic judgements and the criteria of aesthetic excellence, though they would more likely have framed their questions as being concerned with the definition of beauty and of the standard of taste. Our modern discussions of aesthetics are no doubt in many ways different from but are surely continuous with theirs to a degree far greater than with any earlier work.

Berkeley contributed briefly to this movement of thought. While his discussion of the nature of beauty and of criteria of judgement of aesthetic merit is motivated by theological considerations and put to theological use, and while he makes no contribution not found elsewhere in the philosophers of the eighteenth century, nevertheless the major problems are there raised in an acute form with all Berkeley's familiar clarity and directness. At least in a tercentennial year his contribution is worthy of notice.

In the earlier portion of the Third Dialogue of the *Alciphron* Alciphron presents the views of those freethinkers whom he regards as 'men of curious contemplation, not governed by such

179

gross things as sense and custom' (sect. 3) on morality and beauty. He offers a version of the position taken by Shaftesbury and Hutcheson; but it is surely wrong for Jessop to claim, as he does in his edition of the *Alciphron* (p. 116n), that Alciphron either faithfully presents or is meant faithfully to present the ideas of Shaftesbury, though Shaftesbury, clearly referred to under the name of Cratylus in the dialogue, is represented as being of the same school of thought. Berkeley makes no clear reference to Hutcheson's *Inquiry into the Origin of Ideas of Beauty and Virtue* which had been published seven years before *Alciphron* and he appears to have, at any rate, made no close study of it.

Alciphron commences by claiming that 'there is an idea of Beauty natural to the mind of man'. Beauty is discerned by all men by instinct and it 'attracts without a reason'. There is corporeal beauty and there is moral beauty, and 'as the eye perceiveth the one, so the mind doth, by a certain inner sense, perceive the other'. Thus moral beauty is rather to be felt than understood, it is 'an object, not of the discursive faculty, but of a peculiar sense, which is properly called the *moral sense*, being adapted to the perception of moral beauty as the eye to colours, or the ear to sounds' (sect. 5). There is an odd asymmetry in this; while there is a peculiar, i.e. special, sense of moral beauty which feels rather than understands, physical beauty is said to be directly perceived by the eye and should therefore be a, no doubt, complex idea of sense alongside of such ideas as those of colour and shape. This asymmetry, not found in Shaftesbury, Hutcheson, and Hume, will, as we shall see, be disastrous for Alciphron.

In the dialogue Alciphron is motivated largely by a desire to explain morality without an appeal to theology; for Alciphron morality is not, as it is for Berkeley, obedience to the will of God and motivated by a desire to avoid punishment for transgressions against that will. It is a brute fact of human nature that moral beauty is perceived in some things by men and pleases them, even if they are sometimes led by self-seeking to disregard it. Like Shaftesbury, Alciphron claims that his morality is true morality, while theocentric morality, so called, is mercenary and banausic. But the view had also other attractions and it is quite similar to Hume's discussion of the perception of virtue and vice in his *Treatise of Human Nature*, Book III, Part I.[1] The theological motivation is dispensable.

At this stage Euphranor, the Christian apologist, professes himself unable to understand this claim to a physical sense of corporeal beauty and an internal sense of moral beauty. Regarding it as unwise to attempt to discuss both claims at once, Euphranor proposes that they should discuss only the sense of corporeal beauty, and asks what it is that we call beauty in objects of sense. Alciphron feels compelled to answer the question, and, having already incautiously spoken of moral beauty as being 'an order, a symmetry, and comeliness, in the moral world' (sect. 3), now answers analogously that corporeal beauty is a 'certain symmetry or proportion pleasing to the eye' (sect. 8).

Why, one might reasonably ask, only to the eye? At Euphranor's prompting Alciphron has ruled out mere pleasing smells and tastes as not beautiful, since they scarcely could be said to have symmetry and proportion, thus reminding us of Kant's rejection of such pleasures as not aesthetic. So Alciphron says that 'beauty is, to speak properly, perceived only by the eye.' This clearly rules out beauty in music and in literature, which is surely arbitrary and not required by the argument to date, since it is not unreasonable to claim that symmetry and proportion may be discerned in both these fields as well as by vision. The explanation seems to be that Berkeley limits his discussion to natural beauty, and the beauty of artefacts, a contrary limitation to that of many modern writers on aesthetics who limit their discussion to the arts. Berkeley's limitation clearly excludes literature, and natural sounds might be thought to lack the necessary structure.

But, to return to exposition, Alciphron now agrees that symmetry and proportion vary with different kinds of object and that symmetry and proportion is what makes 'the whole complete and perfect in its kind'. Thus the proportions we admire in a horse are different from those we admire in a door and in each case appropriate to the perfection of its kind. Euphranor now leads Alciphron to agree that a thing is 'perfect in its kind when it answers the end for which it was made'. This disastrous admission completes Alciphron's downfall; he cannot possibly claim that the eye determines whether a thing answers to the end for which it was made and admits that this is the work of reason. Euphranor can now claim that 'beauty, in your sense of it, is an object, not of the eye, but of the mind'; we see the object but discern its beauty with the aid of reason.

Euphranor's theological strategy now becomes clear; by analogy the notion of moral beauty, based on order and symmetry in social and personal relationships, must require the notions of end and purpose. So we cannot interpret the world in terms of chance, but must allow a providence that has ends and purposes.

In some respects, no doubt, this is an unsatisfactory and contrived end to the discussion. If beauty is, indeed, fitness for an end, then our perception of beauty has to be limited not merely to objects of the eye but to such of those which we may discern by reason to answer to an end. Even by highly anthropocentric criteria this is limiting. If we allow that a horse is made for an end discernible by Berkeley and Euphranor, and if the atheist Alciphron can at any rate allow that men treat horses as serving a human purpose, it is hard to see that we have here an account of beauty applicable to sunsets and roses. Berkeley and Euphranor may be sure that God made them for a purpose, but would be surely arrogant to claim that they knew what it was.

But we cannot simply dismiss Alciphron's view as merely contrived by Berkeley to give Euphranor an easy theological victory. No doubt Alciphron was disastrously incautious to identify symmetry and order with being made for an end, but much of his view was to remain standard in the eighteenth century. Thus Hume in his *Treatise* (p. 299) says that 'if we consider all the hypotheses which have been formed either by philosophy or common reason, to explain the difference betwixt beauty and deformity, we shall find that all of them resolve into this, that beauty is such an order and construction of parts, as, either by the *primary constitution* of our nature, by *custom*, or by *caprice*, is fitted to give pleasure and satisfaction to the soul.' If Hume would not dream of specifying the order and construction of which he speaks in terms of being made for an end, as Alciphron was led to do, he is ready enough to specify it in terms of utility, of it serving our ends, or, in the case of animals, their welfare. Thus 'that shape which produces strength is beautiful in one animal: and that which is a sign of agility, in another.' This remained Hume's view to the end, and in the *Enquiry concerning the Principles of Morals* the beauty of certain forms of ships, buildings, doors and windows is explained in terms of their utility.[2] Hume is also too canny a Scot to identify beauty simply with rationally discerned utility, as Euphranor persuades Alciphron to do; 'the power of producing pain and pleasure', he tells us, 'makes . . . the essence of beauty and deformity'. Thus for Hume beauty is

182

something other than order and construction of parts and other than utility; it is merely a well-founded observation that these bring about that special kind of pleasure in which the sense of beauty consists. In this Hume was following in the steps of Hutcheson. Hutcheson recognized two special senses: the moral sense which Alciphron following Shaftesbury, had also recognized, and also a sense of beauty.

Euphranor's attack against Alciphron would have been ineffective against Hutcheson and Hume. They could readily have admitted that reason, reflecting on the evidence of sense-perception, recognized order, symmetry, unity amidst variety (Hutcheson's preferred version), or whatever else was the ground of the peculiar aesthetic pleasure; but the pleasure itself was an ultimate fact of human nature and not to be explained by theological or any other considerations. Euphranor's attack would indeed have been ineffective if it had been launched directly against Alciphron's account of morality. For Alciphron had postulated, like Shaftesbury, Hutcheson, and Hume, a special moral sense; so he could have readily agreed with Euphranor that social order and harmony were recognized by reason and still claimed that morality was a matter of sense, something 'rather to be felt than understood'.

Alciphron, in fact, misstates the position he is supposed to defend; he fails to make a true parallel between the sense of beauty and the moral sense. Having claimed that order and symmetry are the ground both of aesthetic and/or moral delight, he appears to present a neat parallel: 'as the eye perceiveth the one, so the mind doth, by a certain interior sense, perceive the other' (sect. 3). But it is clear that Alciphron's interior sense does not perceive order and symmetry in the social world – if it did it would not be an interior sense – but is rather the feeling induced by this order and symmetry; by making the sense of beauty a matter of sense-perception he brings ruin on himself and he is forced to identify beauty with something external to himself. The true parallel would be to have two inner senses, the moral sense and the sense of beauty, each triggered by a different kind of symmetry and order.

So Berkeley failed to state the theory of the peculiar senses of beauty and morality, through Alciphron's mouth, in a satisfactory form. So Euphranor's attack, whatever force it may have against Alciphron, leads only to an unsatisfactory victory. It was to be left to Reid to begin the assault on this characteristic eighteenth-century theory which eventually led to its disappearance.

One final reaction. We have seen how not merely Alciphron and Euphranor, in Berkeley's writings, but also Hume, linked the order that brought the response of the sense of beauty or the moral sense with finality – the notion of an end or purpose. We have seen how Hume avoided the theological implications suggested by Euphranor by relativizing the notion of utility; we use horses for an end and there is no need to inquire into the end or function of a horse *sub specie aeternitatis*. But still the notion of an end was powerless to deal with the beauty of the many things which we find beautiful but for which we have no use and which scarcely have ends of their own – flowers and the creations of the fine arts, for example. Can it be that Kant's doctrine of the beautiful having the form of finality can be seen as a sophistication and generalization of the line of thought which had appealed to the British philosophers of the eighteenth century? If so, it would not be an isolated case.

NOTES

1 References to Hume's *Treatise* are to the Selby-Bigge edition (Clarendon Press, Oxford, 1888).
2 *Enquiries*, ed. Selby-Bigge (Clarendon Press, Oxford, 1902), 212–13.

Berkeley's divine language
argument

A. David Kline

I. INTRODUCTION

Dean Berkeley wrote *Alciphron* during his somewhat impatient stay in Newport. He wanted to get on with the Bermuda project. Students of Berkeley have been impatient with the *Alciphron* – too much apologetics and too little philosophy. There is one apparent exception. The fourth dialogue, on The Truth of Theism, contains a proof of God's existence. But on a closer look many have found an unexciting version of the design argument, a version easily slain by Hume. T. E. Jessop, not one to underestimate Berkeley, puts it bluntly: . . . the proof is the usual one from effect to cause, not the one peculiar to Berkeley.[1]

In a recent paper, 'Berkeley's Argument from Design',[2] Michael Hooker has argued persuasively that the inattention to Dialogue IV is undeserved. In this paper the structure of Berkeley's argument will be explored. After an overview of the textual argumentation, three interpretations offered by Hooker will be considered. Out of their critical treatment a new interpretation will be generated. The argument is not the traditional design argument nor a version of the passivity or continuity arguments found in the *Principles* and *Three Dialogues*, respectively.[3] The argument is an inference to the best explanation parallel to the Cartesian argument for other minds.

II. OVERVIEW OF THE ARGUMENT

There are two phases in the discussion of God's existence. In the first, Alciphron, the free-thinker, begins with a methodological prolegomenon. The ontological and cosmological proofs, and

185

appeals to authority and to utility are out. The former, though they may puzzle, never convince; the latter, though perhaps suitable for the cleric or statesman, scarcely deserve mention to the philosopher. Alciphron insists on a proof based on sense-perception.

Euphranor, Berkeley's spokesman, gets Alciphron to admit that men have souls, yet this knowledge is inferred from sense-experience. In a similar manner Euphranor suggests that we can have knowledge of God's existence:

> From motions, therefore, you infer a mover as cause; and from reasonable motions (or such as appear calculated for a reasonable end) a rational cause, soul or spirit? . . . The soul of man actuates but a small body, an insignificant particle, in respect of the great masses of nature, the elements, and the heavenly bodies and system of the world. And the wisdom that appears in those motions which are the effect of human reason is incomparably less than that which discovers itself in the structure and use of organized natural bodies, animal or vegetable. A man with his hand can make no machine so admirable as the hand itself; nor can any of those motions by which we trace out human reason approach the skill and contrivance of those wonderful motions of the heart, brain, and other vital parts, which do not depend on the will of man . . . Doth it not follow, then that from natural motions, independent of man's will, may be inferred both power and wisdom incomparably greater than that of the human soul? (*Alc.* IV. 4–5).

Alciphron admits that there is something to the argument. But he insists that Euphranor's proof of God's existence is much weaker than Euphranor's proof that Alciphron exists. After all, Alciphron stands before him in the flesh.

Euphranor stresses that the argument for another's soul does have the same structure as the argument for God's existence. Alciphron the person, i.e. an individual thinking thing, should not be confused with Alciphron's body. Alciphron's soul is no more nor less given in sense-experience than God is:

> . . . in the self-same manner, it seems to me that, though I cannot with eyes of flesh behold the invisible God, yet I do in the strictest sense behold and perceive by all my

senses such signs and tokens, such effects and operations, as suggest, indicate, and demonstrate an invisible God, as certainly, and with the same evidence, at least, as any other signs perceived by sense do suggest to me the existence of your soul . . . (*Alc.* IV. 5)

The structure of the argument for other minds and the argument for God's existence appear to be analogical. We need not examine the fine structure of these analogical arguments, for, as we shall see, the discussion advances to arguments of an improved form.

The second phase begins with Alciphron's admission that he was initially nonplussed by the previous discussion. But upon further reflection he recognizes that the previous argument was really not successful.

At first methought a particular structure, shape, or motion was the most certain proof of a thinking reasonable soul. But a little attention satisfies me that these things have no necessary connexion with reason, knowledge, and wisdom; and that allowing them to be certain proofs of a living soul, they cannot be so of a thinking and reasonable one. (*Alc.* IV. 6)

Though the previous proofs will not do, Alciphron now asserts what on reflection does justify one's belief in other minds:

Upon this point, I have found that nothing so much convinces me of the existence of another person as his speaking to me. It is my hearing you talk that, in strict philosophical truth, is to me the best argument for your being.

This argument has the form of an inference to the best explanation. One is not justified in believing in another mind because the other body looks like his or moves like his, etc. One is justified because the other body exhibited linguistic behavior and the only adequate explanation of such behavior is the existence of a mind.[4]

Alciphron challenges Euphranor to produce an argument of similar structure for God's existence – you (Euphranor) wouldn't 'pretend that God speaks to man in the same clear and sensible manner as one man doth to another'.

Euphranor wants to be sure he understands exactly what needs to be shown:

[If] intervention and use of arbitrary, outward, sensible signs, having no resemblance or necessary connexion with the things they stand for and suggest; if it shall appear that, by innumerable combinations of these signs, or endless variety of things is discovered and made known to us; and that we are thereby instructed or informed in their different natures; that we are taught and admonished what to shun, and what to pursue; and are directed how to regulate our motions, and how to act with respect to things distant from us, as well in time and place will this content you? (*Alc.* IV. 7)

Alciphron agrees that such a demonstration would satisfy him. Berkeley's central point of the fourth dialogue is that nature constitutes just such a language.

III. HOOKER'S INTERPRETATIONS

Michael Hooker believes that the text can be used to support three interpretations, which he treats as being equally plausible. For facility in discussion I name them as follows: the analogical design argument, the orderliness of sense-experience argument, and the sense-experience/world-connection argument.

Consider first the suggestion that Berkeley was giving an analogical design argument (D-argument):

According to that interpretation, our senses inform us just as the spoken language of another informs us, so the data of our senses can be viewed as a kind of language. Since tokens of spoken language each have intelligent speakers behind them, so too must the language of our sense have an intelligent 'speaker' behind it.[5]

In evaluating the D-argument Hooker rehearses the Humean criticism of arguments by analogy.

Supposedly on the first interpretation the argument has the following structure:

Spoken language has the property of being informative and having a mind behind it.
Sense-data have the property of being informative.
Therefore, sense-data have a mind behind them.

This interpretation suffers from at least two difficulties: (1) The

D-argument is a very weak analogical argument. Analogical arguments will be stronger as the 'objects' of the analogy share more properties. The D-argument only mentions one property. (2) More importantly, the interpretation does not bring into relief how the theological argument is parasitic on the argument for other minds, a point emphasized by Berkeley. Furthermore, it undermines their similarity of structure. The linguistic argument for other minds was clearly an argument to the best explanation. Informativeness is only one of the many marks of something being a language. It is the linguistic behavior of a man that requires explanation by a mind and it is the linguistic behavior of nature that requires explanation by a Divine Mind. That Berkeley intends his theistic argument to be an inference to the best explanation is evident in his summation of the discussion: 'It [sense-data language] cannot be accounted for by mechanical principles by atoms, attraction, or effluvia . . . being utterly inexplicable and unaccountable by the laws of motion . . . doth set forth and testify the immediate operation of a spirit.' (*Alc.* IV. 14)

The next two interpretations, the orderliness of sense-experience argument (O-argument) and the sense-experience/world-connection argument (C-argument) rest on a distinction between the epistemological and ontological dimensions of the sign relation.[6] The idea is simple: one idea of sense signifying another idea of sense – e.g. the sight of fire signifies the feeling of warmth – is the epistemological sign relation. When an idea of sense signifies an object in the world the relation is ontological.[7]

What follows is Hooker's O-argument interpretation. It is based on the epistemological dimension of the sign relation.

Viewed from the first perspective an argument to the effect that God preserves the connection between contingent ideas of sense is not straightforwardly an analogical argument from design. What is needed is an explanation of why contingently connected sense data show the remarkably regular co-occurrence that they do. Without the assurance of some ordering force behind the world of sense data, we should not expect the feeling of warmth to accompany the sight of fire. But it does, with remarkable regularity, so there must be an ordering force. By this mode of arguing, then, God is posited as the best explanation of the uniformity of experience.[8]

Hooker correctly points out that on the O-argument Berkeley's view is not unlike the theistic argument of *Principles*. Evaluating the arguments begins by assuring oneself that the phenomenon *needs* explanation, then considering the power of alternative explanations.

Before considering the merits of the O-argument as an interpretation of Berkeley, let us finish the survey by stating the account that rests on the ontological dimension of the sign relation:

> In *Alciphron*, though he refers obliquely to the immaterialist doctrine of his developed philosophy, Berkeley is speaking to the philosophically unsophisticated. His audience will hold a common sense view of our senses as giving us information about a world that is really out there and represented to us by the data of our senses. However, and this is the important point, there is no guarantee in virtue of a necessary connection that our senses do accurately inform us. But because we think we are informed, we must suppose that something exists as the guarantor of the reliability of our cognitive sensory faculties. Hence we conclude that God exists. The analogy to language is just this: In the case of language there is a contingent or conventional connection between words and the things they signify; in the case of the language of nature there is similarly a contingent connection between our experiences and the worldly things they signify. In the case of spoken language it is the speaker's intention that ensures the reference relationship, and in the case of the language of nature it is the theophonic deity, always speaking to us through our senses, who ensures the reference of our sense experience.[9]

It is clear from the quotation above and other remarks of Hooker's that on the C-argument interpretation God is invoked to avoid the scepticism generated by Lockean realism. If we assume that real bodies exist outside the mind independently of being perceived, what reason is there to believe that our sense-experience, even if it is caused by bodies, accurately represents them or provides us with information about them? The answer is that God guarantees that sense-experience is informative of the real world.

It will be useful to begin with this reading and work back to the O-argument. The C-argument contains some very suspicious assumptions about the philosophy of language: the referring and informing relation are the same relation and *a* speaker maintains by *his* intentions the reference relationship. But we need not pursue those issues, for there is a blunt objection.

How are we to understand 'real world?' If we understand the notion in accord with Berkeley's mature philosophy, i.e. as a set of appearances, then the C-argument degenerates into the O-argument. God is preserving connections among sense-data.

Can we understand 'real world' in the Lockean sense? Hooker realizes that it is extraordinary to propose that Berkeley is assuming a version of Lockean realism. But Hooker is willing to swallow this on the explanation that Berkeley's audience is the unsophisticated. He supposedly has put his idealism in the closet and will show the uninitiated the 'truth' about God. There are two things wrong with this: (1) Lockean realism is not a vulgar doctrine. (2) It is simply preposterous to hold that a thinker of Berkeley's ability and character would attempt to persuade others by premises he believed to be false. In the course of the dialogue Euphranor criticizes Alciphron for being a lazy thinker, only wanting to get the discussion over and not having the intellectual stamina to get matters right. We should look for a better interpretation than to suppose that Berkeley's discussion of God's existence is not even intended as a sound argument.[10]

We are left with the O-argument. It has at least three problems: (1) According to the argument God maintains the orderliness of sense-data – all sense-data. But Berkeley explicitly denies that there is a Divine Language of smell or odor. Yet he insists that the sense-data of smell and odor are orderly. So if he is giving an inference to the best explanation, it cannot be the explanation for orderliness simpliciter. The O-argument is not subtle enough. Berkeley is up to something this argument does not illustrate.

(2) The O-argument does not do justice to Berkeley's lengthy and complex discussion of other minds. If he is ultimately giving an O-argument, the preliminaries are at best fat and in effect confusing. One should get on with it. There is orderliness and it needs explanation. A better interpretation would make sense of the preliminaries.

(3) It is very odd that Berkeley would give the O-argument independently of his immaterialist weapons. Standing alone it is not going to convince anyone, especially those in Berkeley's audience. Inferences to the best explanation are evaluated in the

context of their competitors. The free-thinkers have an obvious competitor – materialism. Materialism can explain mere orderliness. We have certainly nothing more than a stand-off. An interpretation is needed that would speak less naively to Berkeley's opponents.

IV. THE DIVINE LANGUAGE ARGUMENT

How then should we read the text? The objections to the O-argument provide adequacy conditions for an interpretation: it (i) must illuminate the primacy of a *visual* Divine Language, (ii) must make sense of the other minds discussion, (iii) must give Berkeley something powerful to answer his opponents.

The key is the second adequacy condition. Once it is met the others fall out. Recall that Berkeley rejects what appears to be an analogical argument for other minds, then accepts a certain inference to the best explanation. He, curiously, does not spell out exactly what features of another's linguistic behavior demand explanation by non-materialistic causes. He takes the need for a non-materialistic explanation as obvious. I suspect that the reason he does this is because he is relying on the Cartesian proof of other minds. Berkeley takes that argument as sound and, better yet, he takes his readers as accepting the argument. (It is Alciphron who balks at the analogical argument and suggests the linguistic move.)

This is a very powerful ploy on Berkeley's part. He can build a demonstration of God's existence for free-thinkers on the basis of shared strategy. I do not want to go too far astray with historical details. But a few rough remarks are in order given my claims.

Berkeley was of course familiar with much of Descartes' work. He refers to Descartes (sometimes by name) on numerous occasions. In Dialogue IV when, as we shall see, he criticizes a view on the nature of distance perception, that view is unmistakably identified with the one defended by Descartes in *Dioptrics*.[11]

Alciphron according to its subtitle is 'an apology for the Christian religion against those who are called free-thinkers.' As Jessop points out, Berkeley's text is embedded in the 'anti-deistic controversy that absorbed much of the attention of the orthodox during the first half of the eighteenth century'.[12] Berkeley would not regard Descartes as a free-thinker and deist. But undoubtedly

Descartes' emphasis on rationalism and mechanism inspired free-thinking and deism. Berkeley appreciated this historical point.

Free-thinking is a complex and diverse tradition, but two figures Berkeley must have had in mind in composing *Alciphron* were John Toland and Anthony Collins. Toland's *Christianity not Mysterious* received a rejoinder from Peter Browne, the Provost of Berkeley's college.[13] Collins's *Discourse on Free Thinking* was very widely known. It is a clear and urbane work. Now the important point for us is that each of these figures was inspired by Cartesianism.[14] Collins goes so far as to list Descartes among the roll of illustrious free-thinkers.[15]

My claim is that Berkeley knew Descartes and his free-thinking audience well. On many occasions Berkeley had to criticize a Cartesian position in order to make way for his own. In *Alciphron*, Dialogue IV, matters are different. He will use the Cartesian argument for other minds to build a proof for the existence of God. Given his audience, he expects little resistance on the other minds issue, but then he believes the theistic conclusion will be unavoidable.

In a passage well known to contemporary philosophers, Descartes states that even if a machine looked like a man we could tell that it was not a *real* man:

> . . . they could never use words or other constructed signs, as we do to declare our thoughts to others. It is quite conceivable that a machine should be so made as to utter words, and even utter them in connection with physical events that cause a change in one of its organs; so that, e.g., if it is touched in one part, it asks what you want to say to it, and if touched in another, it cries out that it is hurt; but not that it should be so made as to arrange words variously in response to the meaning of what is said in its presence, as even the dullest men can do.[16]

Descartes makes three important points in this passage: (i) language is composed of *constructed* signs; (ii) linguisitic behavior exhibits rich *generative* powers – we are able to combine signs in many diverse ways; (iii) linguistic behavior is *appropriate* to the background environment. Descartes believes that (i) gives an essential property of language and that (ii) and (iii) can only be explained by minds.

If Berkeley is constructing a proof of God's existence in a

parallel fashion to Descartes' discussion of other minds, we would expect Berkeley to emphasize similar points about the Divine Language. This is precisely what we find. Berkeley agrees with Descartes that language is a constructed set of signs. The choice of marks or sounds for a given word is arbitrary. And there is no necessary connection between the sign and the thing signified: 'God speaks to men by the intervention and use of arbitrary, outward, sensible signs, having no resemblance or necessary connexion with the things they stand for and suggest.'

For Berkeley a thing looking little and faint is a sign of its being at a great distance. But there is no necessary connexion here. One must by experience make the connection just as by experience one makes the connection between 'dog' and dog. Berkeley in Dialogue IV anticipates a Cartesian objection to his thesis and hence repeats some of the basic argument found earlier in *An Essay towards a New Theory of Vision*. Some writers on optics (Descartes for one) held that distance was judged by a kind of natural geometry. According to this view there is a necessary connection between certain 'apprehended' angles and the distances of objects. The details are unimportant here. But clearly Berkeley must refute this view in order to maintain that the Divine Language is a *language*. His lengthy effort along these lines is further evidence that he is addressing an audience familiar with the Cartesian moves.

Like Descartes, Berkeley also emphasizes the generative feature of language. Descartes often compares the 'language' of brutes with real language. Brutes begin with a small set of primitives. Furthermore, their ability to combine them to form new signs is very impoverished. Man does not suffer this liability. And according to Berkeley neither does the Divine Language. The language of sense-data exhibits 'innumerable combinations of these signs'. (See also my discussion of the first adequacy condition.)

For Descartes a certain giveaway that a brute is really a simple, albeit gooey, machine is a breakdown in the appropriateness of its behavior. In a humorous example he describes an episode familiar to any cat owner.[17] The beast carefully prepares a hole for its excrement only to miss the hole, but nevertheless carefully covers up the original area. Such behavior is not the mark of a mind. Linguistic behavior in brutes is a more specific version of the general failing. Your parrot may utter 'good morning' when you arise for breakfast, but it also gives this cheery greeting when you return from an evening concert. In modern terms the behavior in the cat example and the behavior of 'talking' parrots is tropistic.

Can a case be made for the natural language being appropriate? When we speak of an object's behavior being appropriate we must be able to distinguish the object from its environment and then assign goals to the object. If, as the environment changes, the object behaves in accord with its goals we can speak of the behavior being appropriate. Imagine a small shop owner's device to indicate the presence of a customer – perhaps an appropriately located electric eye attached to a buzzer. The object is the electric eye. Its goal is to mark the presence of customers. The device's behavioral repertoire is to buzz or not. If a customer transgresses the space the buzzer sounds.

Modifications of the environment reveal the crudeness of the device. The buzzer sounds when a mailman, a dog, or a falling sycamore leaf approaches. The device gives away its stupidity or mindlessness. Again the issue is to show that natural language, in a way similar to the customer detector, exhibits appropriate behavior but does not break down as the customer detector does, and in fact is so agile that its behavior carries the mark of mind.

The 'object' in the natural language case is God. Berkeley tells us His goals – to inform, to teach, to entertain, to direct, and to admonish us. The informational goal is primary. (*Alc.* IV. 7). For simplicity of disussion I shall restrict God's goals to that of informing us. Relevant behaviors are various natural signs. What constitutes the environment? There is an apparent rub here, especially if we interpret all of nature as God's signs as Hooker does in the O-argument. We need a behavior/environment distinction if the parallel to the customer detector is to be exhibited.

The way clear of the rub is to realize that God's language is a *visible* language and that God's language is informative of the tangible properties of objects.[18]

> Upon the whole, it seems the proper objects of sight are light and colours, with their several shades and degrees; all of which being infinitely diversified and combined, form a language wonderfully adapted to suggest and exhibit to us the distances, figures, situations, dimensions, and various qualities of tangible objects . . . (*Alc.* IV. 10)

The visible appearance/tangible property distinction constitutes the linguistic behavior/environment distinction. So the parallel with Descartes' cat and parrot and my customer detector is complete!

Do visible appearances appropriately inform us of tangible properties? Berkeley, quite plausibly, thinks they do. But does natural language, like the customer detector, break down (act inappropriately) and hence reveal not a mind but a dull device? More importantly, does it make sense to test nature? What sort of interference *might* unmask nature as tropistic?

Suppose Fred is chasing a butterfly. We might arrange for various hurdles to plague him – having someone walk in his way, release a playful dog, spray the butterfly with a chemical that excites it to fly faster, etc. The visual language unlike the customer detector does not keep saying the same thing. Nature appropriately speaks anew to Fred, consistent with the goal of informing him. In virtue of that information Fred may successfully negotiate the obstacles, judge the distances and speeds accurately, and grasp the butterfly. So it is conceptually sensible to *attempt* to unmask nature. As it turns out, nature is a sophisticated show.

Berkeley's lengthy discussion of the other minds problem is not just fluff. He, as I have argued, believes the reader to accept or be persuaded by the Cartesian position on other minds. By showing the reader that just those features of human language that cry out for explanation are also features of nature's language, he hopes to force the reader to see the necessity of a Divine Mind.

Returning to the first adequacy condition, we have already seen some evidence for the primacy of visual language, but more can be said. Alciphron having heard Berkeley's argument remains perplexed. He then offers a *reductio* of visual signs forming a Divine Language:

> I cannot help thinking that some fallacy runs throughout this whole ratiocination, though perhaps I may not readily point it out. It seems to me that every other sense may as well be deemed a language as that of vision. Smells and tastes for instance, are signs that inform us of other qualities to which they have neither likeness nor necessary connexion. (*Alc.* IV. 12)

Alciphron's suggestion is that given Euphranor's characterization of nature's language, smell and taste would form a Divine

Language. That is absurd, hence the characterization of those features sufficient for a language must be mistaken. One might expect Berkeley to dig in and assert that smells and tastes do form a language. But he does not. His answer is more interesting:

> That they are signs is certain, as also that language and all other signs agree in the general nature of sign, or so far forth as signs. But it is as certain that all signs are not language: not even all significant sounds, such as the natural cries of animals, or the inarticulate sounds and interjections of men. It is the articulation, combination, variety and copiousness, extensive and general use and easy application of signs (all which are commonly found in vision) that constitutes the true nature of language. Other senses may indeed furnish signs: and yet those signs have no more right than inarticulate sounds to be thought a language.

I understand Berkeley not to be emphasizing orderliness simpliciter in the above. There is a certain orderliness between the cry an animal makes and the animal being in pain or a certain bitter taste and unsweetened chocolate on the palate. These signs do not fail as language because they are necessarily connected with the thing signified or because there is a lack of orderliness in the relation. They fail because of the generative condition. Basic smells and tastes only combine in very limited ways to form new signs. Their limited combining patterns restrict their informative power. But colors and shapes form endless complex and informative new patterns. The impoverishment of the former appearances takes away their license as a real language.

According to the third adequacy condition we should adopt an interpretation that at least *prima facie* gives Berkeley something interesting and powerful to say to his opponents. Neither the D-, O- or C-arguments do that. The D-argument is very weak logically. The O-argument is a throwback to the *Principles*. And both the O- and C-arguments have obvious materialistic replies. The Divine Language argument being based on the Cartesian proof of other minds is much more powerful. If Berkeley can persuade his opponent that sense–data form a language, which he has tried to do by emphasizing the Cartesian features of language, there can be little disagreement on how to explain it.

My primary purpose throughout this chapter has been to provoke a discussion of the structure of Berkeley's argument.

A. DAVID KLINE

There remains a problem I have side-stepped that demands comment.

The difficulty arises when we consider Berkeley from a contemporary point of view. He assumes that linguistic behavior requires mentalistic explanation. Berkeley does not attempt to defend this claim. (My interpretation explains his silence.) Nevertheless, the received view in philosophy of mind has it that complex performances (e.g. linguistic behavior or problem solving) do not require non-materialistic explanation. The last holdout for any form of non-materialism is not sapience but sentience, e.g., having a certain sensation. The features Descartes and Berkeley draw our attention to were and are explanatorily opaque. The search for an adequate theory is not likely to appeal to seventeenth-and eighteenth-century minds, but that does not minimize the insight that *simple* mechanical paradigms will not do either.

NOTES

1 From Jessop's Introduction to *Alciphron*, p. 13.
2 Michael Hooker, 'Berkeley's Argument from Design', in *Berkeley Critical and Interpretive Essays*, ed. Colin M. Turbayne (Minneapolis: University of Minnesota Press, 1982), pp. 261–70.
3 These arguments are named and discussed in Jonathan Bennett's well-known paper, 'Berkeley and God', *Philosophy*, XL (1965), pp. 207–21.
4 For a discussion of the logic of inferences to the best explanation, see Gilbert Harman, 'The Inference to the Best Explanation', *Philosophical Review* 65 (1965), pp. 88–95; and Peter Achinstein, *Law and Explanation* (Oxford: Oxford University Press, 1971), pp. 119–24.
5 Hooker, p. 264.
6 Hooker traces this distinction to Robert Armstrong.
7 Hooker, pp. 265–6.
8 *Ibid.*, p. 266.
9 *Ibid.*, p. 269.
10 Furthermore, we should not forget that Hooker has no specific textual evidence for the C-argument, or any of his interpretations for that matter, that goes beyond the passages cited in the overview.
11 See Colin M. Turbayne, ed., *Works on Vision* (Indianapolis: Bobbs-Merrill, 1963), p. xxiii.
12 From Jessop's Introduction to *Alciphron*, p. 4.
13 *Ibid.*, p. 5. For a discussion of Browne and the deists including Toland and Collins, see Paul Olscamp, *The Moral Philosophy of George Berkeley* (The Hague: Martinus Nijhoff, 1970), pp. 184–222.
14 For one example of the Cartesian influence, see John Toland, *Christianity not Mysterious* (London, 1702), p. 58. Ernest Campbell Mossner,

'Deism', in *The Encyclopedia of Philosophy*, ed. by Paul Edwards, vol. 2 (New York: Macmillan, 1967), p. 328.

15 Ernest Campbell Mossner, 'Anthony Collins', in *The Encyclopedia of Philosophy*, ed. by Paul Edwards, vol. 2 (New York: Macmillan, 1967), p. 145.

16 René Descartes, *Discourse on the Method of Rightly Conducting the Reason*, in *Descartes: Philosophical Writings*, ed. by Elizabeth Anscombe and Peter Geach (London: Thomas Nelson & Sons, 1954), p. 43. Descartes gives another reason (p. 116) which appears to be a generalized version of the first. See Keith Gunderson, *Mentality and Machines* (Garden City, N.Y.: Anchor Books, 1971), pp. 7–17.

17 René Descartes, 'Letter to the Marquis of Newcastle', in *Materialism and the Mind-Body Problem*, ed. by David Rosenthal (Englewood Cliffs, N.J.: Prentice-Hall), pp. 22–3.

18 These ideas are not new to *Alciphron*. See *NTV*, 1–28, and *Principles*, 44.

Cognitive theology and emotive mysteries in Berkeley's *Alciphron*

David Berman

I

In 1732 Berkeley published *Alciphron: or the Minute Philosopher*, his most comprehensive statement on religion. During the next three years he wrote five shorter works which have a bearing on his theological system. The unity and strength of this system has not been appreciated, probably because commentators have concentrated on Berkeley's philosophical writings of 1709–13. My aim in this paper is exegetical rather than critical. By focusing on *Alciphron*, I hope to reveal one of the last great theological syntheses: a strong-minded defence of religion based on a revolutionary philosophy of language.

★ ★ ★

Religion, Berkeley clearly recognised, consists of more than rational theology. Christianity is concerned with grace, original sin, the doctrine of the Trinity, and an afterlife; these matters of faith and mystery are discussed in *Alciphron*, Dialogue VII.[1] Yet in order to believe sensibly in mysteries such as the Holy Trinity and the grace of God we must, according to Berkeley, first believe that there is a God. If the God of theism – a good, wise, provident creator of the world – did not exist then there would hardly be much point in speaking about His grace or His three-in-one nature. Hence in *Alciphron*, Dialogue IV, Berkeley carefully presents his proof that there is such a God. His argument moves as follows:

(1) There are some things which we know only by their effects. Berkeley mentions animal spirits and force, but the most crucial inferred entities are other human minds (*Alc.* IV. sections 4–5).

(2) The human mind is different from its physical embodiment, and we can know that there are other intelligent and wise minds only from their bodily effects. 'By the person . . . is meant an individual thinking Thing, and not the Hair, Skin, or visible Surface, or any Part of the outward form, colour, or shape of [that person; hence we do not see] that individual thinking Thing, but only such visible Signs and Tokens, as suggest and infer the Being of that invisible thinking Principle or Soul.' (sect. 5).

(3) But there are innumerable intelligent and wise effects in nature which are not assignable to human agents; consequently, if we are justified in inferring other (finite) human minds, we must also, *a fortiori*, infer an (infinite) divine mind.

At this point Berkeley's proof is largely a reworking from an epistemological point of view of the traditional cosmological and teleological proofs for a Deity. Berkeley had already formulated this line of argument in the *Principles of Human Knowledge* (1710), sects. 145–8. The novelty of his procedure is that it clearly brings to the fore, possibly for the first time in the history of Philosophy, the problem of other minds. Berkeley's readers are forced to choose between God and solipsism: between having the company of other minds, including God, or being entirely alone (apart from one's ideas) in the universe. The next phase of the demonstration is even more distinctively Berkeleian; it is taken largely from the *Essay Towards a New Theory of Vision* (1709), a revised version of which Berkeley appended to the first three editions of *Alciphron* (all published in 1732).[2]

(4) What most compels us to believe that there are other minds is that they talk to us. Hearing a man speak convinces us that he is 'a thinking and reasonable' mind (*Alc*. IV. 7).

(5) Hence, if our knowledge of God is really on the same level as our knowledge of other minds, it must be shown that God, too, speaks to us. (And this is precisely what Berkeley tries to do in sections 7 to 15. The most effective way of seeing the force of his argument is by listing the correspondences he provides between God's visual language and a language such as English.)

(5.1) Just as there is no necessary connection or resemblance between an audible or visible word and the thing it signifies, so there is no necessary connection or resemblance between visual data and the tangible objects that they stand for. Berkeley's justification of this fundamental doctrine draws on (i) direct experience, (ii) conceptual argument, and (iii) experimental evidence.

(i) He thinks that what we immediately experience by sight are light and colours, and that these are altogether different from what we touch. (ii) He also argues that heterogeneity of sight and touch is shown in the impossibility of quantifying a visual datum with a tactile datum.[3] (iii) Finally, in the *Theory of Vision, Vindicated and Explained* (1733), he appeals to the Chesselden experiment (reported in no. 402 of the *Philosophical Transactions* 1728) which seemed to support the conclusion that someone born blind and made to see would have no understanding of the things he immediately saw (see sect. 71).

(5.2) The collection or system of arbitrary signs both in English and in vision is orderly and coherent: an innumerable combination of signs can make known to us an endless variety of things. For example, a certain roundish green shape generally stands for a tangible apple; the smaller the patch of green, the further away the tactile object is likely to be; and similar things can be said about the information with which visible signs supply us concerning the size and texture of tangible objects.

(5.3) As there is a grammar and syntax in English so there are the laws of nature which contingently govern the orderly appearance of visual (as well as other) sense-data. According to Berkeley, our best understanding of this grammar of nature is provided by Newton's *Principia*. Moreover, we can understand and use the two languages – English and vision – even though we are ignorant of their grammars (see *Principles*, sects. 108–10).

(5.4) We must learn both languages. We are less aware of learning the visual language because (i) it is a language which all people – apart from those who are blind – learn, (ii) we start learning it at an age when we are barely able to reflect, and (iii) it is learned with little effort or pain.

(5.5) In both languages we are concerned primarily with what the signs signify; hence we sometimes say when reading a book that we see the notions and not the characters. Similarly we say that we see the tangible object, when all we in fact immediately see are light and colours. We are insensibly carried to what the signs signify; and this movement is more powerful in the optic language because it is virtually a universal language. But once we succeed in mentally putting ourselves in the position of someone born blind and made to see (as described in Molyneux's famous problem), we will then realise that such a person is like a Chinaman who hears English words for the first time.

(5.6) There are 'tricky' elements in both languages: as there are puns and homonyms in English, so there are illusions and the reflections of mirrors in vision; and these, incidentally, show there is no necessary connection in either language between sign and thing signified.[4]

(5.7) Both languages usefully direct our actions, attitudes, and emotions; they teach us 'how to act in respect of Things distant from us, as well in Time as Place' (sect. 7). Seeing a visual precipice before us is like hearing someone shouting out: 'Don't come any further; it's dangerous!'

(5.8) In both cases, context is important, and the actual meaning and import of a sign can be affected by extra-linguistic factors, such as emphasis and tone with English words and the unusual positioning of visible signs.[5]

(5.9) Both languages may afford amusement and exaltation as well as instruction; here we might compare the delight in a sunset with the delight in a poem. (Also see *Principles*, sect. 109.)

II

I have now listed some nine correspondences laid down by Berkeley between the conventional language of English and the Divine Language of vision. His conclusion is that ' . . . this visual Language proves, not a Creator merely, but a provident governor actually and intimately present and attentive to all our Interests' (*Alc.* IV. 14). He stresses that the optic language proves more than a distant deistic God. This is an important point, and it provides the transition to the second part of Dialogue IV, where he criticises certain accounts of God and His attributes which he thinks tend directly to atheism. Certain fideistic negative theologians had recently tried to protect the theistic conception of God from the charge of contradiction – e.g. with regard to God's prescience and man's free will – by arguing that God's nature is entirely unknowable. Their theory, as Berkeley saw it, amounted to saying that God is an 'unknown Subject of Attributes absolutely unknown' (*Alc.* IV. 17). Now, in *Principles* Berkeley had driven the materialists to admit that their conception of matter amounted to an 'unknown Support of unknown Qualities' (sect. 77). Hence he was all too aware of the unintelligibility and inutility of both conceptions. As he put it in *Alciphron* IV. 18:

. . . if this [conception of God] could once make its way, and obtain in the World, there would be an end of all natural or rational Religion, which is the Basis both of the Jewish and Christian: for he who comes to God, or enters himself in the Church of God, must first believe that there is a God, in some intelligible sense: and not only that there is something in general without any proper Notion, though never so inadequate, of any of its Qualities or Attributes: for this may be Fate, or Chaos, or Plastic Nature, or anything else as well as God.

Thus we have, in effect, 'God' without religion; and in the analogous conception of matter (in *Principles*, sect. 77) we have 'matter' without materialism. Berkeley took up the theological issue again in the *Theory of Vision Vindicated*, which contains (sects. 1–7) one of the shrewdest accounts of the rise of British freethought; in section 6 he suggests that this kind of negative fideistic theology, which was espoused by such well-meaning churchmen as Archbishop King and Bishop Browne, was being exploited by freethinkers, notably Anthony Collins, for atheistic ends.[6] Berkeley felt so strongly about the issue that, in addition to cautioning Browne in the *Theory of Vision Vindicated*, he wrote him a long letter on the subject, in which he presses him to admit that God is either literally wise or He is not; for there can be no medium.[7] Since God is at the basis of religion, any uncertainty or vagueness in our conception of Him must affect the stability of the rest of religion. One 'cannot prove, that God is to be loved for his Goodness, or feared for his Justice, or respected for his Knowledge . . . [if these] Attributes [are] admitted in no particular Sense, or in a Sense which no one can understand' (*Alc.* IV. 18). Our knowledge of God is for Berkeley essentially scientific knowledge: from the optic language he *knows* that God is wise, since 'this optic Language hath a necessary Connexion with Knowledge, Wisdom and Goodness' (*Alc.* IV. 14). 'The Being of God', he states in the penultimate section of *Alciphron*, 'is capable of clear Proof, and a proper Object of human Reason'. But this is not to say that all religious beliefs are like scientific judgements.

III

Berkeley was the first modern philosopher to formulate and support the thesis that words can be meaningful without informing or standing for ideas. He first publicly expressed this fruitful insight in section 20 of the Introduction to the *Principles*, where he enumerated three additional non-cognitive functions: the evoking of (1) emotions, (2) dispositions, and (3) actions. He re-states this emotive theory (as it is now generally called) in *Alciphron* VII: words or signs

> have other Uses besides barely standing for and exhibiting Ideas, such as raising proper Emotions, producing certain Dispositions or Habits of Mind, and directing our Actions in pursuit of that Happiness, which is . . . the primary Spring and Motive, that sets rational Agents at work . . . (vii. 14)

In *Alciphron* VII, 7–10, he uses this theory to explain the import and force of religious mysteries. He discusses four specific mysteries: grace in section 7, the Holy Trinity in section 8, and original sin and a future state, both in section 10, where he also expressly identifies faith with the three non-cognitive functions of language: 'Faith, I say, is not an indolent Perception, but an operative Persuasion of the Mind, which ever worketh some suitable Action, Disposition or Emotion in those who have it.'[8]

Consider for example the doctrine of the Trinity. Although a man may form no distinct idea of trinity, substance or personality, this does not imply, Berkeley maintains, that the mystery is meaningless, because it may well produce in his mind 'Love, Hope, Gratitude, and Obedience, and thereby become a lively operative Principle influencing his Life and Actions' (sect. 8). Berkeley deals in a similar way with grace, original sin, and a future state. He admits that they have little or no cognitive content, but that this does not prevent their meaningful use. Utterances become emotive, he argues elsewhere, by being associated with emotions, attitudes, and actions; so that merely hearing the former tends to evoke the latter.[9] Thus talk of grace has the tendency to produce good habits and piety; original sin can deter men from committing an evil deed, and a future state is likely to produce good habits and a salutary sense of one's unworthiness.

Religious mysteries are pragmatic; they are justified by their utility.

Because we know from the optic language that God is good, wise, knowing, and just, we must also realise that we ought to act and feel in certain ways. Because God is just, it is right to be fearful about doing the wrong thing; and it is imperative to develop such moral habits. Because God is good, it is right to love Him; because He is wise and knowing, it is appropriate to respect Him. Now in Berkeley's view, belief in the Christian mysteries is an excellent way of bringing about these ends. Nothing will so effectively make people fear God's justice as the mystery of a future state. Similarly, the best way of bringing people to love God is by means of the symbolism embodied in the Trinity.

Of course, if we did not believe that God was good and just, or if we had only a confused and distant idea of these attributes – as King and Browne believed – then there would be little point in talking about the Holy Trinity or a future state. For why should a bad man fear a being that is not literally just? Hence Berkeley's emotive account of mysteries rests squarely on his cognitive account of theology: Dialogue VII rests on Dialogue IV. It would be wrong, however, to give the impression that these two dialogues comprise all Berkeley had to say about religion. In dialogues V and VI he also argues for the truth of the Christian revelation. Here he makes use of the usual arguments. He tries to show that Jesus Christ did rise from the dead, that He did perform miracles, that the Old Testament prophecies were fulfilled by Him, and so on. In this way Berkeley has an additional reason for holding that the Christian mysteries in the Scriptures reveal the right and desirable symbology. Not only do these mysteries flow pragmatically from a scientifically proven theology, but they also follow from the authenticity of the Scriptures. I have made less of this second string to Berkeley's religious bow because it is not distinctively Berkeleian, and it has been shown to be intrinsically weak, in my opinion, by the so-called higher criticism.

Basic to Berkeley's distinctive theology is the linguistic distinction which he was the first to draw: between cognitive statements which inform – such as 'That cow is brown' – and emotive utterances which produce emotions, dispositions, and actions – for example: 'Cheer up', 'Life's a bore', and 'Get out!'[10] Statements of rational theology, particularly 'God exists and is wise', are for Berkeley cognitive statements; and they support emotive utterances such as those concerning grace and the Holy Trinity. Berkeley's commitment to the primary and regulative role of cognitive theology over emotive mysteries appears several times in *Alciphron*. In Section II, I have quoted one such statement and Berkeley makes the point also in *Alciphron* V. 27 and 29, as well as in some of his other writings, such as in his letter to Sir John James: 'Light and heat are both found in a religious mind duly disposed. Light in due order goes first. It is dangerous to begin with heat, that is with the affections . . . our affections shou'd grow from inquiry and deliberation.'[11]

IV

Berkeley's discovery of the emotive theory and its application to religious mysteries did not occur in an historical vacuum. It was occasioned, I believe, by the destructive use to which various freethinkers had put Locke's astringent theory of meaning and meaninglessness: that if a word does not signify a distinct idea, then it is meaningless.[12] Locke's freethinking disciples, especially John Toland and Anthony Collins, had notoriously applied this semantic touchstone to religious mysteries: since mysteries, such as the Holy Trinity, do not stand for distinct ideas, Toland and Collins argued that Christianity either employs meaningless doctrines, or it is not mysterious. This line of argument is fairly apparent even from the title of Toland's most famous book: *Christianity not Mysterious: or, a treatise shewing, that there is nothing in the Gospel contrary to reason, nor above it: and that no Christian doctrine can be properly call'd a mystery* (1696). The Christian mysteries were for Toland meaningless 'Blictri' words, because like 'Blictri' they did not stand for any distinct idea.[13]

Now Berkeley accepted part of Toland's claim, namely, that religious mysteries do not signify distinct ideas; but this does not imply, he urged, that they are meaningless. This conclusion only follows if one accepts the Lockean *either, or* – which at one time Berkeley did accept but which in *Alciphron* VII. 1 he calls 'the primary Motive to Infidelity' – that words *either* communicate ideas and are meaningful, *or* do not signify ideas and are meaningless. Once one realises the false restrictiveness of the Lockean *either, or*, one is no longer forced into the onerous, unnecessary, and absurd position of trying to provide ideas and reasons for things which, by one's own hypothesis, are above reason and beyond any human ideas. Then one can admit, with a good intellectual conscience, that the Holy Trinity and grace are emotive and not cognitive.

Berkeley's emotive accommodation of mysteries is, therefore, based on his expanded theory of meaning; but this is not to say that the theory came before the application. In my view, he discovered his revolutionary emotive theory of language while trying to find some way around Toland's irreligious but consistent application of Locke's cognitive theory of meaning. Theory followed or went together with practice. As Pope elegantly put it in a couplet suppressed from his *Essay on man*:

> What partly pleases, totally will shock:
> I question much if Toland would be Locke.[14]

My hypothesis about the genesis of Berkeley's theory is strongly supported by the first eight sections of Dialogue VII, where Alciphron (the freethinker) does indeed apply Locke's *either, or* to religious mysteries in the manner of Toland and Collins. Here, working from the Lockean theory of meaning, Alciphron confidently asserts: '. . . by all the Rules of right Reason, it is absolutely impossible that any Mystery, and least of all the Trinity, should really be the Object of Man's faith'. Berkeley's answer (through his champion Euphranor) is, in effect, an indictment of 'Locke-become-Toland': 'I do not wonder you thought so, as long as you maintained that no Man could assent to a Proposition without perceiving or framing in his Mind distinct Ideas marked by the terms of it' (*Alc.* VIII. 8).

V

The structure of Berkeley's theology can, therefore, be represented in the following way:

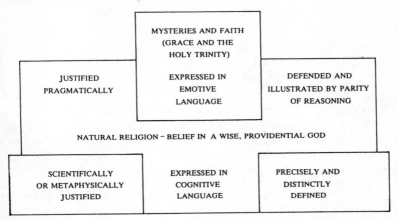

One feature of this diagram I have not as yet explained: the defence and illustration of mysteries by parity of reasoning. This line of reasoning – summed up in the proverb 'Sauce for the goose is also sauce for the gander' – constitutes an important part of Berkeley's theological strategy; he employs it in *Alciphron* and also in the *Analyst* (1734) and *Defence of Free-Thinking in Mathematics* (1735). He outlines his strategy in the penultimate, retrospective section of *Alciphron* VII. I have quoted the first part of this key passage, but it is worth quoting the whole because it provides the best single statement of his complete position:

> The Being of a God is capable of clear Proof, and a proper Object of human Reason: whereas the Mysteries of his Nature, and indeed whatever there is of Mystery in Religion, to endeavour to explain and prove by Reason, is a vain Attempt. It is sufficient if we can shew there is nothing absurd or repugnant in our Belief of those points, and, . . . use our reason only for answering the Objections brought against them (sect. 33).

By skilfully using some of the critical results of his early work in philosophy and philosophy of science, Berkeley tries to show that there is nothing 'absurd or repugnant' in Christian mysteries.

Thus he contends that while there seem to be difficulties and even contradictions in the Holy Trinity, there are similar difficulties in the received (Lockean) theory of personal identity.[15] And while it is hard to understand grace, it is not any harder than understanding the concept of force; although both 'grace' and 'force' are of considerable use.

Berkeley continued his *ad hominem* defence of mysteries in the *Analyst*, the tract in which he pointed out a serious flaw in Newton's method of fluxions. The apologetic aim of the pamphlet is stated in the subtitle: *wherein it is examined whether the object, principles, and inferences of the modern analysis are more distinctly conceived, or more evidently deduced, than religious mysteries and points of faith*. Berkeley's approach is less constructive and more sceptical, and the ten last questions appended to the *Analyst* deliver the sceptical sting. Thus he pointedly enquires:

> Whether Mathematicians, who are so delicate in religious Points, are strictly scrupulous in their own Science? Whether they do not submit to Authority, take things upon Trust, believe Points inconceivable? Whether they have not their Mysteries, and what is more, their Repugnances and Contradictions? (Qu. 64).

Berkeley had used the method of interrogatory, to a similar purpose, in *Alciphron* VII. 7 which is composed almost entirely of questions. He was to use it again in section 50 of the *Defence* (1735), which, along with sections 3 and 7, comprises his final defence of religious mysteries by parity of reasoning with mathematics. The interrogatory form nicely suited Berkeley's strategy, which was not to establish any interpretation of particular mysteries, but rather to undermine objections against mysteries. For every difficulty and obscurity in religion, he tries to show something comparable in the supposed paradigms of knowledge: mathematics, philosophy, and science.

Berkeley's defence of religious mysteries has, broadly speaking, three prongs or components. (i) Utterances about mysteries are shown to be essentially emotive; (ii) while justified pragmatically, by their effectiveness, they are also supported and evaluated by rational theology; (iii) their apparent obscurities and difficulties are shown to have parallels in the received theories of the most admired thinkers of the time – Locke and Newton. Hence one

210

must either accept religious mysteries or reject them along with cherished philosophical, mathematical, and scientific mysteries.

Berkeley's theology, one must acknowledge, was a magnificent achievement: possibly the last great and creative theological synthesis. Its greatness lies partly in the powerful theories of which it is constituted: that of the optic language, of emotive language, of other minds, as well as those theories embodied in the various arguments by parity of reasoning. Much (although by no means all) of the strength of Berkeley's philosophical position is here superbly displayed and marshalled; and yet there is also a remarkable degree of unity, even architectonic, in this theology. Finally, it is to Berkeley's credit that he accepted and tried to meet the legitimate challenges of freethought, rather than – as many later theologians have done – ignore them.

NOTES

1 I shall be referring to, and quoting from, the last authorised edition – the so-called 'Third edition' – published late in 1752 in London. It was the last work Berkeley saw through the press.

2 Berkeley's revisions in sections 147 and 152 make the theistic implications of the *New Theory of Vision* more explicit; see A. A. Luce's editorial note in *Works of George Berkeley* 1948–1957 (referred to hereafter as *Works*), vol. 1, p. 231.

3 See the *New Theory of Vision*, sect. 131: ' . . . A Blue, and Red Line I can conceive added together into one Sum, and making one continued Line: but to make, in my Thoughts, one continued Line of a visible and tangible Line added together is, I find, a Task . . . insurmountable . . .'

4 The possible double meaning and ambiguity of the visual language is dramatically used by Edgar Allen Poe in his short story, 'The sphinx'. Poe describes a highly strung man who looks out of a window and thinks that he sees an enormous animal 'Of hideous conformation'. The monster is *seen* as bigger than the 'large trees' on a 'distant hill'. But 'the monster' turns out to be an unusual insect, no longer than one-sixteenth of an inch, that is walking on a spider's web hanging from the window sash, less than an inch from the man's eyes.

5 See *New Theory of Vision*, sect. 73: 'Now, it is known, a Word pronounced with certain Circumstances, or in a certain Context with other Words, hath not always the same Import and Signification, that it hath when pronounced in some other Circumstances, or different Context of Words. [Similarly] the very same Visible Appearance as to Faintness and all other Respects, if placed on high, shall not suggest the same Magnitude that it would if it were seen at an equal Distance

on a level with the Eye. The Reason whereof is, that we are rarely accustomed to view Objects at a great Height.' Thus the faintness or indistinctness of the insect mentioned in the previous note could mean either extreme farness or extreme closeness. A comparable ambiguity in English would be irony.

6 See my 'Anthony Collins and the question of atheism in the early part of the eighteenth century', in the *Proceedings of the Royal Irish Academy*, 75C (5), pp. 85–102.

7 See 'A new letter by Berkeley to Browne on divine analogy', by J.-P. Pittion, A. A. Luce and the present writer, in *Mind* (1969), especially pp. 387–92. The immediate occasion of Berkeley's letter was the publication of Browne's *Things Divine and Supernatural Conceived by Analogy with Things Natural and Human* (1733) which contained an extensive attack (pp. 374–554) on *Alciphron* IV and – to a lesser extent – VII. Browne criticised Berkeley's natural theology (in *Alc.* IV) for being too literal and cognitive, and his account of mysteries (in *Alc.* VII) for not being literal and cognitive enough.

8 Compare Berkeley's similar, although less explicit, deployment of emotive theory in his *Sermon before the Society for the Propagation of the Gospel* (1732), in *Works* vii, especially p. 116. Berkeley has not generally been given credit for being the first to develop the emotive theory, and the first to apply it to religion, economics, and metaphysics. But there can be no doubt that he anticipates the emotive analysis of metaphysical language offered by such (former) Logical Positivists as Rudolf Carnap and A. J. Ayer. Of course, this is not to say that they were directly influenced by Berkeley's writings. (In a private letter of 5 May 1975, Professor Ayer informed me that Berkeley had not influenced his account of emotive language in *Language, Truth and Logic* (1936).)

9 This is Berkeley's view in the Draft Introduction (*c.* 1708) to the *Principles* where he examines the Pauline proposition that the 'good things' in Heaven are 'such as eye hath not seen nor ear heard', which he takes to be cognitively vacuous but capable of begetting 'in us a chearfulness and zeal and perseverance in well doing', once 'a customary connexion [grows up] betwixt . . . that proposition' and the desired emotions and dispositions (*Works* ii. pp. 137–8).

10 See C. L. Stevenson, *Facts and Values* (1963), esp. essay iii. Probably the most serious omission in Berkeley's account of emotive language is his failure to see that not only are words able to evoke emotions, for instance, but that emotions are able to evoke words, as in such *expressive* utterances as 'Bravo', 'Oh dear', and 'Damnation'.

11 See *Works* vii, pp. 146–7. This letter of 7 June 1741 contains Berkeley's objections to Roman Catholicism.

12 See *Essay Concerning Human Understanding* (1690), especially Book III; in Chap. ii. 2, e.g. Locke asserts that 'The use then of Words, is to be sensible Marks of *Ideas*'.

13 See *Christianity not Mysterious* (1696), especially sect. 3. 'Could that person justly value himself upon being wiser than his Neighbours [asks Toland], who having infallible Assurance that something call'd

Blictri had a Being in Nature, in the mean time knew not what this *Blictri* was?' (p. 133).

14 Quoted in *New Studies on Berkeley's Philosophy* (1966) ed. by W. Steinkraus, p. 25. The early evidence for my thesis is to be found in the Draft Introduction (*Works* ii, esp.pp. 137–40), Berkeley's first extant sermon which was delivered 11 January 1707/8 (*Works* ii, esp. pp. 12–13), the *Philosophical Commentaries*, esp. entry 720, and his 'Of infinites', read on 19 November 1707 (*Works* iv, esp. pp. 235–6). The evidence indicates that Berkeley discovered his emotive theory early in 1708.

15 In the *Essay* II. xxvii, Locke had maintained that personal identity consists in identity of consciousness. But, Berkeley argues in *Alciphron* VII.8, if we divide a person's conscious life into three parts – A, B, C – we may suppose that, although there are enough ideas in common between A and B, and B and C, there are few or no ideas in common between A and C. It will then follow, however, supposing the truth of the Lockean theory of personal identity, that A and C are *and* are not the same person.

Was Berkeley a precursor of Wittgenstein?

Antony Flew

I

Certainly it is altogether appropriate that a contribution to a volume in honour of Ernest Mossner should start from Hume. Yet it is surely no less appropriate that the discussion should then proceed to another great figure of the same century, and that it should relate to questions of continuing contemporary relevance. I start with Hume's acknowledgements to Berkeley, offered first near the beginning of the *Treatise* and again in the first *Enquiry*. I then go on to defend at length my own earlier hints that Hume's account here of what he owes to Berkeley significantly understates the scope and nature of the lesson which Berkeley had to teach. In a nutshell the story is that in the *Alciphron*, first published in 1732 with a second edition in the same year, Berkeley said things about meaning which make him a precursor of Wittgenstein; and that Hume, even if he did study this dialogue thoroughly,[1] was not ready to appreciate so radical a challenge to a fundamental of Locke's new way of ideas. This conclusion does perhaps very slightly diminish Hume. But Berkeley himself seems not to have seen that the innovations of the *Alciphron* may call for some rethinking of his own most characteristic positions; while even two centuries later Wittgenstein – no doubt for reasons of a different kind – appears never to have recognized Berkeley as a partial precursor.

II

In the *Treatise* Hume credits what he himself regards as 'one of the greatest and most valuable discoveries that has been made of late years in the republic of letters' to Dr Berkeley: 'A great philosopher . . . has asserted, that all general ideas are nothing but particular ones, annexed to a certain term, which gives them a more extensive signification, and makes them recall upon occasion other individuals, which are similar to them' (p. 64).

In the first *Enquiry* Hume appeals to the same putative discovery to support the contention that primary like secondary qualities 'exist not in the objects themselves, but are perceptions in the mind, without any external archetype or model, which they represent'. He maintains:

> Nothing can save us from this conclusion, but the asserting, that the ideas of those primary qualities are attained by abstraction, an opinion, which, if we examine it accurately, we shall find to be unintelligible, and even absurd. An extension, that is neither tangible nor visible, cannot possibly be conceived: and a tangible or visible extension, which is neither hard nor soft, black nor white, is equally beyond the reach of human conception. Let any man try to conceive a triangle in general, which is neither isosceles nor scalenum, nor has any particular length or proportion of sides; and he will soon perceive the absurdity of all the scholastic notions with regard to abstraction and general ideas.[2]

In a note to this second passage Hume remarks: 'This argument is drawn from Dr. Berkeley; and indeed most of the writings of that very ingenious author form the best lessons of scepticism, which are to be found among the antient or modern philosophers, Bayle not excepted. He professes, however, in his title-page (and undoubtedly with great truth) to have compos'd his book against the sceptics as well as against the atheists and free-thinkers'; and so on. The title-page referred to could be either that of *The Principles of Human Knowledge*, first published in 1710, or that of the *Three Dialogues*, published in 1713. A second edition of the former, the first and last to be revised by the author, had followed twenty-four years later in 1734. That Hume should have written 'his title-page' (singular) in a volume published in 1748 is remarkable. For by then all those of Berkeley's philosophical works which were to be printed in his lifetime had already appeared; and not just 'most of the writings of that very ingenious author'. Indeed everything but the marginal *Siris*, first published in 1744, had been available for some time before Book I of Hume's *Treatise* came out in 1739.

III

I have elsewhere suggested that 'as accounts of Berkeley's full contribution to the theory of meaning Hume's two summaries are utterly insufficient'.[3] For they ignore the *Alciphron*. There in Dialogue VII, Section 14, Berkeley's Euphranor argues that 'the algebraic mark, which denotes the root of a negative square, hath its use in logistic operations, although it be impossible to form an idea of any such quantity. And what is true of algebraic signs is also true of words and language; modern algebra being in fact a more short, apposite, and artificial sort of language, and it being possible to express by words at length, though less conveniently, all the steps of an algebraical process.'

This contention, I further suggested, constitutes a 'revolutionary and historically premature insight'. What Hume welcomed so enthusiastically in the *Treatise* was an elaboration of the received doctrine that the understanding of a word requires the occurrence of – or at least the possibility of summoning – corresponding mental imagery. But what Berkeley maintains here in the *Alciphron* flatly contradicts that received doctrine. The crux now is neither the actual nor the potential occurrence of mental imagery. What matters is not the (private) idea but the (public) use – 'its use in logistic operations'. And, furthermore, 'what is true of algebraic signs is also true of words and language'.

IV

I want in this present paper to develop these suggestions about the interpretation of Berkeley, and to defend them against the rival reading proposed by Professor J. F. Bennett. Bennett notices my suggestions, and continues: 'Berkeley here chooses an "algebraic mark", of which one *cannot* form a corresponding idea, and seems to say that "algebraic signs" are not, in the relevant respect, a special case . . . Isn't this impressive evidence that he thoroughly and radically rejects Locke's theory of meaning?'[4]

Bennett disagrees, and his disagreement is based primarily upon an insistence on a distinction between theoretical and practical uses of language: 'In the section from which the quoted bit is drawn, Berkeley is concerned with non-theoretical or practical uses of language. He thinks that mathematics is best considered not as a set of theoretical truths but rather as a practical instrument, as something which can help us to build bridges and the like'. Bennett then quotes the following and final sentence from Section 14 of Dialogue VII, but omitting the initial six concessive words: 'And it must be confessed that even the mathematical sciences themselves, which above all others are reckoned the most clear and certain, if they are considered, not as instruments to direct our practice, but as speculations to employ our curiosity, will be found to fall short in many instances of those clear and distinct ideas, which, it seems, the minute philosophers of this age, whether knowingly or ignorantly, insist upon in the mysteries of religion.'

A little later Bennett gives a further explanation of the distinction which he takes to be crucial here:

> Presumably the idea is that, just as 'The good things which God hath prepared . . . etc.' has the practical force of 'Cheer up and do better', so Pythagoras' Theorem has the practical force of 'If you want such and such a structure, cut your materials thus and so'. Even if it isn't helpful to bracket these together, treating them as instances of a single kind of phenomenon which might be called 'practical meaning' Berkeley thinks that it is. And in this section – which is simply an exercise in Christian apologetics – he is directly comparing them. Faced with the accusation that the 'mysteries of religion' cannot be presented as clean, clear theory, Berkeley is replying that the same is true of mathematics, and that the kind of intellectual respectability that mathematics *can* have is also available to the mysteries of religion. The section is a rather well-controlled *ad hominem* argument, directed against the 'minute philosophers' . . . It is the essence of this argument of Berkeley's that it divorces meaningfulness from ideas only in respect of practical mathematics and practical uses of language . . . The argument as a whole does not support the view that Berkeley had a 'revolutionary insight' into what it is for language – including theoretical language – to be meaningful.[5]

ANTONY FLEW

V

(a) Now, certainly, Berkeley did present the *Alciphron* as 'an
exercise in Christian apologetics'. It is on the original title-page
offered as 'Containing an apology for the Christian religion,
against those who are called free-thinkers'. But to say this is a
very different thing from saying that it is 'simply an exercise in
Christian apologetics'; and nothing else besides. It can in general
be a serious mistake to categorize something as a this, and thence
to infer that it cannot also be a that; unless this and that are in
truth mutually exclusive. (It was, for instance, presumably
because he had mentally pigeon-holed Hume's consideration of
evidence for the miraculous as simply anti-Christian apologetics
that R. G. Collingwood in *The Idea of History* altogether failed
to take account of it as also an important part of Hume's contribution to the philosophy of history.) But it is in particular a
serious mistake in interpreting Berkeley to insist upon a sharp
separation between what is philosophy and what is Christian
apologetics. To do both simultaneously is altogether characteristic
of Berkeley. Thus the title-page of the *Three Dialogues* tells us:
'The design . . . is plainly to demonstrate the reality and perfection of human knowledge, the incorporeal nature of the soul, and
the immediate providence of a Deity, in opposition to sceptics
and atheists.'

(b) Certainly too the final sentence of Section 14 does express
an *ad hominem* argument. But, first and less important, once the
initial six-word concessive clause is restored that sentence looks
much more like the Parthian shot which it is than an epitome
of what has gone immediately before. Second, and much more
important, even if the immediately preceding argument had been
ad hominem, that itself would not be enough to show that Berkeley
shared the assumption which required his opponents to make
what were to them disagreeable concessions. It is indeed precisely
because this final sentence does express an *ad hominem* argument
that we cannot derive from it any support for the conclusion that
Berkeley shares with 'the minute philosophers of this age' the
belief that 'clear and distinct ideas' are essential to theoretical
respectability – to what Bennett calls 'clean, clear theory'.

(c) It is, I submit, significant that the final sentence of Dialogue
VII, Section 14, is the only passage of the *Alciphron* which Bennett
deploys in confirmation of his reading. All the other Berkeley

218

citations in Bennett's section on 'Berkeley on Meaning and Understanding' are drawn from much earlier works. Of these the latest is the *Three Dialogues*, first published in 1713, with second and third editions in 1725 and 1734, respectively. The earliest is the *Philosophical Commentaries* of 1705–8. *The Principles* falls in between, with the first draft of the 'Introduction' dating back to perhaps the later months of 1708. Obviously, appeals to what was first written between nineteen and twenty-seven years earlier cannot be decisive in a dispute over the interpretation of what it is contended is a new insight in the *Alciphron*. One thing which we especially need to have if Bennett's reading of this section is to be established – a thing which he does not, and which I maintain that he cannot, provide – is evidence that, at the relevant time, Berkeley 'divorces meaningfulness from ideas only in respect of practical mathematics and practical uses of language'.

VI

(a) So let us now look again directly at the disputed Section 14 of Dialogue VII, and at its immediate context. Does that support the Bennett thesis that here 'Berkeley is concerned with non-theoretical or practical uses of language', and 'divorces meaningfulness from ideas only in respect of practical mathematics and practical uses of language'?

Section 14 begins: 'Thus much, upon the whole, may be said of all signs: – that they do not always suggest ideas signified to the mind: that when they suggest ideas, they are not general abstract ideas: that they have other uses besides barely standing for and exhibiting ideas – such as raising proper emotions, producing certain dispositions or habits of mind, and directing our actions in pursuit of that happiness which is the ultimate end and design, the primary spring and motive, that sets rational agents at work.'

At this point Bennett might be beginning to form the words: 'I told you so'. But this is exactly where Berkeley was careful to add, in the third edition of 1752: 'that signs may imply or suggest the relations of things; which relations, habitudes or proportions as they cannot be by us understood without the help of signs, so being thereby expressed and corrected, they enable us to act with regard to things'. Certainly there is a practical concern here. But the practice is to be guided by 'the relations of things'; 'which relations . . . cannot be by us understood without the help of signs'.

Berkeley's sentence continues: 'that the true end of speech, reason, science, faith, assent, in all its different degrees, is not merely, or principally, or always the imparting or acquiring of ideas, but rather something of an active operative nature, tending to a conceived good: which may sometimes be obtained, not only although the ideas marked are not offered to the mind, but even although there should be no possibility of offering or exhibiting any such idea to the mind: for instance, the algebraic mark, which denotes the root of a negative square, hath its use in logistic operations, although it be impossible to form an idea of any such quantity'. Again there is the same emphasis on 'something of an active operative nature, tending to a conceived good'. Yet the theoretical and the fact-stating are no more excluded by this emphasis than they are by contemporary references to 'language-games', or by the once-fashionable slogan: 'Don't ask for the meaning, ask for the use!'

It is, therefore, entirely appropriate for Berkeley to proceed, without any limiting qualification: 'and what is true of algebraic signs is also true of words or language; modern algebra being in fact a more short, apposite, and artificial sort of language, and it being possible to express by words at length, though less conveniently, all the steps of an algebraical process.'

(b) The rest of Dialogue VII is as unhelpful to Bennett's interpretation as is Section 14 itself. In the first four sections Alciphron expounds an extreme position: 'Words are signs: they do or should stand for ideas; which so far forth as they suggest they are significant'; and, consequently, the key term *grace* must be senseless. In the next sections Euphranor reveals progressively the extent of Berkeley's present disagreement with that view of meaning. In the original Sections 5–7, which Berkeley excised in the third edition, Euphranor protests first that 'every time the word *man* occurs in reading or conversation, I am not conscious that the particular distinct idea of a man is excited in my mind'. Alciphron agrees with this observation, but maintains that, in understanding, what is before the mind is 'the abstract general idea of man'. Euphranor replies that this certainly is not his own experience; and, furthermore, that such an idea cannot occur since it 'includes a contradiction'. He then offers a suggestion: 'To me it seems a particular idea may become general, by being used to stand for or represent other ideas'; afterwards adding the further point that to employ such a word with understanding you do not have always to have a relevant particular idea before your mind.

But from the third edition in 1752, thoroughly revised by the author and printed in the year before his death, all this is cut out. Berkeley thus deliberately excluded from what were to be his last words in philosophy what Hume thirteen years before had hailed as 'one of the greatest and most valuable discoveries that has been made of late years in the republic of letters'. Instead Berkeley preferred that his reply to Alciphron should begin, in what is now numbered as Section 5, with what had previously appeared as an addendum to that greatest and most valuable discovery: 'that words may not be insignificant, although they should not, every time they are used, excite the ideas they signify in our minds; it being sufficient that we have it in our power to substitute things or ideas for their signs when there is occasion'.

(c) This statement is immediately followed by a reference to 'another use of words'. This appears to be the use for those 'other ends' noticed in Section 20 of the 'Introduction' to *The Principles*, and treated rather more extensively in the first draft of that 'Introduction'. The finding that there is this other use is here presented – most unpersuasively – as a deduction from the truth of the previous statement: 'It seems to follow, that there may be another use of words besides that of marking and suggesting distinct ideas, to wit, the influencing of our conduct and actions; which may be done either by forming rules for us to act by, or by raising certain passions, dispositions, and emotions in our minds.'

Nevertheless Berkeley makes it quite clear that he is not wanting to restrict his depreciation of the importance of ideas, and of the actual occurrence of ideas, to such a practical use, or uses, of language. On the contrary, the point of referring here particularly to this, or to these, is only and precisely to rally further support for the general campaign of depreciation. For in the following sentence Berkeley draws his present moral: 'A discourse, therefore, that directs how to act or excites to the doing or forbearance of an action may, it seems, be useful and significant, although the words whereof it is composed should not bring each a distinct idea to our minds.'

(d) After devoting a mere two sentences to this 'another use of words' Euphranor proceeds to his next contention, 'that those words which denote an active principle, soul, or spirit do not, in a strict and proper sense, stand for ideas'. In the second edition of *The Principles*, in 1734, he introduced into Sections 27, 89, and 142 passages suggesting that what we do have here – although we do not have ideas – should be called notions. In the second and third of these passages relations are added to a third category of which what we must have is not ideas but notions. What is new in the *Alciphron* is Berkeley's apparent willingness to extend indefinitely the list of significant words which do not, and perhaps cannot, stand for ideas.

Nor do these three sections – what is now Sections 5–7 – provide any basis for maintaining that this willingness is confined to words practically as opposed to theoretically employed. Certainly Euphranor does insist, in Section 5, that certain words for which 'neither you nor I can form distinct simple ideas' are practically indispensable: 'They direct us in the disposition and management of our affairs, and are of such necessary use, that we should not know how to do without them.' But then a little later, in Section 7, this practical indispensability is associated with theoretical speculations which discover the actual movements of the heavenly bodies: 'And if, by considering this doctrine of force, men arrive at the knowledge of many inventions in mechanics, and are taught to frame engines, by means of which things difficult and otherwise impossible may be performed; and if the same doctrine which is so beneficial here below serveth also as a key to discover the nature of the celestial motions – shall we deny that it is of use, either in practice or speculation, because we have no distinct idea of force?'

(e) Section 8 begins with Euphranor's question: 'Shall we not admit the same method of arguing, the same rules of logic, reason, and good sense, to obtain in things spiritual and things corporeal, in faith and science? And shall we not use the same candour, and make the same allowances, in examining the revelations of God and the inventions of men?' This granted, Euphranor spends the rest of the section arguing that the difficulties which beset the Christian doctrine of the Trinity are no worse than those afflicting any (Lockean) account of human personal identity. Sections 9, 10 and 11 defend other disputed doctrines similarly: Euphranor contends, that is to say, that the same tolerant and sympathetic treatment should be granted to these as

Alciphron and his friends are so willing to give to 'the little local difficulties' of science and mathematics.

These sections certainly justify Bennett's claim that 'Berkeley is replying . . . that the kind of intellectual respectability that mathematics can have is also available to the mysteries of religion'. But they provide no backing for Bennett's assertion that Berkeley here 'divorces meaningfulness from ideas only in respect of practical mathematics and practical uses of language'. For Berkeley never forgets, what he says in Section 11, that 'Science and faith agree in this, that they both imply an assent of the mind.' Certainly faith for him had always to be manifested in works. But neither he, nor any other bishop of his century, would have had any truck with a religion without propositions.

(f) Sections 12 and 13 are especially interesting, since they consist in an elaborate statement on the importance and the value of language. Bennett cites the closing words of the 'Introduction' to *The Principles*: 'Whoever therefore designs to read the following sheets, I entreat him that he would make my words the occasion of his own thinking, and endeavour to attain the same train of thoughts in reading that I had in writing them. By this means it will be easy for him to discover the truth or falsity of what I say. He will be out of all danger of being deceived by my words. And I do not see how he can be led into an error by considering his own naked, undisguised ideas.' Bennett comments fiercely: 'Compare that, as an example of emancipation from the associated-idea theory of meaning, with Locke's explanation of why nearly one-fifth of his *Essay* is about words.'[6]

Bennett then quotes from the *Essay* (III.ix.21). The similarity is indeed striking. But what is equally striking, and here more relevant, is the difference: between, on the one hand, these two passages from Locke's *Essay* and Berkeley's *Principles*; and, on the other hand, passages from these two sections of the *Alciphron* immediately preceding that presently under dispute.

> If we suppose rude mankind without the use of language, it may be presumed they would be ignorant of arithmetic . . . As arithmetic and algebra are sciences of great clearness, certainty, and extent, which are immediately conversant about signs, upon the skilful use and management whereof they entirely depend, so a little attention to them may possibly help us to judge of the progress of the

mind in other sciences . . . If I mistake not, all sciences, so far as they are universal and demonstrable by human reason, will be found conversant about signs as their immediate object, though these in their application are referred to things . . . I am inclined to think the doctrine of signs a point of great importance, and general extent, which, if duly considered, would cast no small light upon things, and afford a just and genuine solution of many difficulties.[7]

(g) Section 14, is, in effect, a summary of all that Euphranor has had to say in Sections 5–13. Section 15 is the last to bear upon the disputed question of the interpretation of Section 14. Its point is, once again, absolutely general: 'Be the science or subject what it will, whensoever men quit particulars for generalities, things concrete for abstractions, when they forsake practical views, and the useful purposes of knowledge, for barren speculation, . . . and labouring to attain precise ideas, which they suppose indiscriminately annexed to all terms, they will be sure to embarrass themselves with difficulties and disputes.' Berkeley mentions some 'which have sprung up in geometry'. He then proceeds, as before, to argue that, just as it would be wrong to repudiate geometry because of these, so it would be generally wrong to reject Christianity because of its notorious but parallel difficulties. Nevertheless, precisely because the parallelism is perfect, Berkeley does not require the intellectual degradation of either science or religion: 'There is no need to depart from the received rules of reasoning to justify the belief of Christians.'

So when Alciphron objects that 'According to this doctrine, all points may be alike maintained. There will be nothing absurd in Popery, not even transubstantiation', the future bishop in the Protestant Ascendancy puts into the mouth of Euphranor's good friend Crito a very sharp reply: 'Pardon me. This doctrine justifies no article of faith which is not contained in Scripture, or which is repugnant to human reason, which implies a contradiction, or which leads to idolatry or wickedness of any kind – all which is very different from our not having a distinct or abstract idea of a point.'

VII

The preceding survey has, I hope, abundantly vindicated the original two suggestions: that 'as accounts of Berkeley's full contribution to the theory of meaning Hume's two summaries are utterly insufficient'; and that in the *Alciphron* we find a 'revolutionary and historically premature insight'. But that, of course, is not to say that Berkeley himself saw how far he had moved; or that he himself appreciated how drastically the development of this insight might affect some of his own most cherished and distinctive philosophical moves. On the contrary: the claim that it was historically premature should suggest the very opposite; and it should also suggest that even Hume would not be ready to take the hint. As we have shown, he was not.

NOTES

1 Although the ensuing controversy, and the material discovered in Poland, has now established that the answer to Professor R. H. Popkin's general question 'Did Hume ever read Berkeley?' (*Journal of Philosophy*, 1959) must be 'Yes', it is still permissible to doubt whether Hume read all Berkeley. In particular it is possible, and even likely, that Hume – like many others since – gave at best only cursory attention to what he may have been inclined to dismiss as simply an exercise in Christian apologetics, adding nothing of philosophical interest to what Berkeley had published previously. Certainly the apologetic, not to say homiletic, is much more prominent in the *Alciphron* than in either the *Principles* or the *Three Dialogues*. Ernest Mossner as his most understanding biographer should enjoy savouring the thought of Hume reading some of Berkeley's sly sallies: for instance, the first paragraph of *Alciphron* VI(1), which begins: 'The following day being Sunday, our philosophers lay long in bed, while the rest of us went to church in the neighbouring town.'

2 *Enquiries*, XII.i, sect. 123. Here and in some other quotations later I have omitted some italics, and reduced some initial capitals to lower case.

3 This and the phrase quoted in the final sentence of the present paragraph come from my *Hume's Philosophy of Belief* (London: Routledge & Kegan Paul, 1961) pp. 261–2. But I have made similar claims elsewhere too: for instance, in a Critical Notice of Professor H. H. Price's *Belief* in *Mind*, 1970; as well as in *An Introduction to Western Philosophy* (London/New York: Thames & Hudson/Bobbs-Merrill, 1971).

4 *Locke, Berkeley, Hume: Central Themes* (Oxford: Clarendon, 1971) p. 54 (italics original).

5 Ibid., p. 55, (italics original).

6 Ibid., p. 56. I perhaps both may and should add that Bennett has
seen the typescript of the present chapter and is now persuaded that
my interpretation of Berkeley is substantially correct.
7 In his edition of Berkeley's *Works* (Oxford: Clarendon, 1901) A. C.
Fraser is moved to provide a note to this last sentence, referring to
'the doctrine of signs' in Locke's *Essay* IV.xxi.

BIBLIOGRAPHY

Anon., review of *Alciphron* in *Present State of the Republic of Letters* (London, 1732).

Bennett, J., 'Berkeley and God', *Philosophy* 40 (1965).

—— *Locke, Berkeley, Hume: Central Themes* (Oxford, 1971).

Benson, C., 'The Curious Case of Berkeley's *Alciphron* printed in 1755', *Long Room* 27–9 (1984).

Berkeley, G., *The Works of George Berkeley* (London, 1898) 3 vols, edited by G. Sampson.

—— *Berkeley's Complete Works* (Oxford, 1901) 4 vols, edited by A. C. Fraser.

—— *The Works of George Berkeley* (Edinburgh, 1948–57) 9 vols., edited by A. A. Luce and T. E. Jessop; vol. 3 comprises *Alciphron*, edited by Jessop.

—— *Works of Vision* (Indianapolis, 1963), edited by C. M. Turbayne.

—— *George Berkeley's Manuscript Introduction* (Oxford, 1987), edited by B. Belfrage.

Berman, D., 'Cognitive Theology and Emotive Mysteries in Berkeley's *Alciphron*', *Proceedings of the Royal Irish Academy* (1981).

—— 'Enlightenment and Counter-Enlightenment in Irish Philosophy', 'The Culmination and Causation of Irish Philosophy', *Archiv für Geschichte der Philosophie* 2 and 3 (1982).

—— 'The Jacobitism of Berkeley's *Passive Obedience*', *Journal of the History of Ideas* 48 (1986).

—— 'Deism, Immortality and the Art of Theological Lying', in *Deism, Masonry, and the Enlightenment* (Delaware, 1987), edited by J. A. Leo Lemay.

—— 'Deliberate Parapraxes', *International Review of Psychoanalysis* 15 (1988).

—— (ed.), *George Berkeley: Eighteenth-Century Responses* (New York, 1989) 2 vols.

—— *A History of Atheism in Britain: from Hobbes to Russell* (London, 1990).

—— and Berman, J., 'Berkeley's *Alciphron's* Vignettes', *The Book Collector* 31, 1 (1985).

Bolingbroke, *The Philosophical Works of . . . Henry St. John, Lord Bolingbroke* (London, 1754) 5 vols.

Browne, P., *A Letter in Answer to . . .* [Toland's] *Christianity not Mysterious* (Dublin, 1697).

[Browne, P.], *Things Divine and Supernatural Conceived by Analogy with Things Natural and Human* (London, 1733).

Burke, E., *Philosophical Enquiry into the Ideas of the Sublime and Beautiful* (London, 1757).

[Collins, A.], *An Essay concerning Reason* (London, 1707).

—— *A Vindication of the Divine Attributes* (London, 1710).

—— *Discourse of Free-thinking* (London, 1713).

—— *Philosophical Inquiry* (1717), in *Determinism and Freewill* (The Hague, 1976) edited by J. O'Higgins.

Flew, A., *Hume's Philosophy of Belief* (London, 1961).

—— 'Was Berkeley a Precursor of Wittgenstein', in W. B. Todd (ed.), *Hume and the Enlightenment* (Edinburgh, 1974).

Furlong, E. J., 'Berkeley on relations, spirits, and notions', *Hermathena* 106 (1968).

Gaskin, J. C. A., *Hume's Philosophy of Religion* (second edn, London, 1988).

Gaustad, E. A., *George Berkeley in America* (New Haven, 1979).

[Hervey, J.], *Some Remarks on the Minute Philosopher* (London, 1732).

Hickes, G. D., *Berkeley* (London, 1932).

[Hoadley, B.], 'A Vindication of Lord Shaftesbury's Writings and Character; against the Author of a Book, called Alciphron', *The London Journal* 676 June 10, 1732; 'The Vindication of Lord Shaftesbury's Writings Continued', *The London Journal* 677 June 17, 1732.

Hooker, M., 'Berkeley's Argument from Design', in *Berkeley: Critical and Interpretative Essays* (Minneapolis, 1982), edited by C. M. Turbayne.

Hume, D., *The Philosophical Works of David Hume* (London, 1875) 4 vols, edited by T. H. Green and T. H. Grose.

Hutcheson, F., *Inquiry into the Original of the Ideas of Beauty and Virtue* (fourth edn, London, 1738).

Jessop, T. E., *A Bibliography of George Berkeley* (revised edn, The Hague, 1973).

Johnson, S., *Elementa Philosophica* (Philadelphia, 1752).

Johnston, G., *The Development of Berkeley's Philosophy* (London, 1923).

Keynes, G., *A Bibliography of George Berkeley* (Oxford, 1976).

Kivy, P., *The Seventh Sense: A Study of Francis Hutcheson's Aesthetics* (New York, 1976).

Kline, A. D., 'Berkeley's Divine Language Argument', in E. Sosa (ed.), *Essays on the Philosophy of George Berkeley* (Dordrecht, 1987).

Luce, A. A., 'The Alleged Development of Berkeley's Philosophy', *Mind* 206 (1943).

—— *The Life of George Berkeley* (reprinted London, 1992), new Introduction by D. Berman.

[Mandeville, B.], *The Fable of the Bees: or, Private Vices, Publick Benefits* (London, 1728).

—— A Letter to Dion, Occasion'd by his Book call'd Alciphron (London, 1732).

March, W. W. S. 'Analogy, Aquinas and Bishop Berkeley', Theology 44 (1942).

Mill, J. S., 'Berkeley's Life and Writings', Fortnightly Review x (1871).

Molesworth, R., An Account of Denmark as it was in the year 1692 (1694, fifth edn, Glasgow, 1745).

Mossner, E., 'Anthony Collins', 'Deism', 'John Toland', in The Encyclopedia of Philosophy (New York, 1967) 8 vols, edited by P. Edwards.

O'Higgins, J., Anthony Collins: The Man and His Works (The Hague, 1970).

—— 'Browne and King, Collins and Berkeley: Agnosticism or Anthropomorphism', Journal of Theological Studies 27 (1976).

Olscamp, P., The Moral Philosophy of George Berkeley (The Hague, 1970).

Pittion, J.-P., Luce, A. A., Berman, D., 'A New Letter by Berkeley to Browne on Divine Analogy', Mind (1969).

Ramsay, I. T., 'Berkeley and the Possibility of an Empirical Metaphysics', in New Studies in Berkeley's Philosophy (New York, 1966), edited by W. Steinkraus.

Rand, B., Berkeley and Percival (Cambridge, 1914).

Shaftesbury, A., Characteristicks of Men, Manners, Opinions, Time (1711, third edn, 1723) 3 vols.

[Skelton, P.], Letter to the Authors of Divine Analogy and the Minute Philosophers (Dublin, 1733).

[Steele, R.] (ed.), The Tatler (Oxford, 1987) 2 vols, edited by D. F. Bond.

Stephen, L., English Thought in the Eighteenth Century (London, 1876).

Stewart, M. A., 'William Wishart, an Early Critic of Alciphron', Berkeley Newsletter 6 (1982/3).

Swift, J., The Correspondence of Jonathan Swift (Oxford, 1965), edited by H. Williams.

Synge, E., Gentleman's Religion . . . with An Appendix (sixth edn, Dublin, 1730).

—— Freethinking in Matters of Religion, Stated and Recommended (London, 1727).

Toland, J., Christianity not Mysterious (London, 1696).

—— Letters to Serena (London, 1704).

Trenchard, J. and Gordon, T., Cato's Letters: or, Essays on Liberty, Civil and Religious (fifth edn, London, 1748) 4 vols.

Turbayne, C. M., The Myth of Metaphor (New Haven, 1962).

—— 'The Origin of Berkeley's Paradoxes', in Steinkraus (ed.), New Studies in Berkeley's Philosophy (New York, 1966).

Twyman, S., David Hume, Dialogues Concerning Natural Religion (London, 1988).

Warnock, G., Berkeley (London, 1953).

Wechter, D., 'Burke's Theory concerning Words, Images and Emotion', PMLA 55 (1940).

Winnett, A. R., Peter Browne: Provost, Bishop, Metaphysician (London, 1974).

[Wishart, W.], *A Vindication of the Reverend D—— B——y from the scandalous imputation of being author of* . . . Alciphron (London, 1734).

Urmson, J. O., 'Berkeley on Beauty', in J. Foster and H. Robinson (eds), *Essays on Berkeley: A Tercentennial Celebration* (Oxford, 1985).

INDEX

231

science 122–3, 126, 129, 136, 138–40
self-deception ix
Seneca 77
Shaftesbury, Lord 4, 9, 11–12, 18, 65, 73–6, 79, 145, 175–7, 179f.; see also Cratylus
signs 8, 37, 92, 97, 99–100, 117, 130, 135; algebraic 140, 216
Skelton, P. 5
smells 8, 99, 191, 196–7
Socrates 49, 80, 82
soul 77–8, 126, 139, 143, 165, 186
Spinoza 105, 155–6, 176
Stephen, L. 5–6, 13; on Alciphron 177–8
Stoics 53–4, 72, 77, 152; on death 78
Suarez, F. 110
substance 9, 203; immaterial 88
superstition 26
Swift, J. 5
symbolism 138–9, 206
Synge, E. 13

tastes 8, 99, 196–7
Tindal, M. 12
Toland, J. 3, 12–13, 193, 207f.

Torricelli, E. 127
transubstantiation 141, 224
Trenchard, J. 13, 15n.43
triangle, idea of 122–4, 215
Trinity 129–30
truth 26, 29–31, 49–51, 65, 79–80, 85–6, 97, 150, 176; freethinkers' divinity 82; hurtful 82
Turbayne, C. M. 7

ugliness 72
unbelief, causes of 157–8
Urmson, J. O. 4; on Alciphron 179–84
utility 50, 66–71, 85, 176, 182

Virgil 69
virtue 56–7, 63, 135; abstracted 59, 63; beauty of 135, 169, 177
vision 92–103, 181, 193, 201f.
vulgar 30, 44, 75, 103, 105, 114, 117, 119, 122, 133–4, 148

Walpole, R. 4
will 143–4, 148–9
wisdom 102, 105, 108
Wishart, W. 4
Wittgenstein, L. 6–7, 214f.
worship 114–15